ABOUT THE AUTHOR

Dr. Andrew P. Johnson is Professor of Holistic Education and the Director of the Accelerated Teacher Licensure Program at Minnesota State University, Mankato. Here he specializes in educational psychology, holistic education, literacy instruction, and teacher professional development.

Before moving into higher education he worked for 9 years in the public schools as a second-grade teacher, wrestling coach, and gifted education coordinator. His most recent books include *Making Connections in Elementary and Middle School Social Studies* (Sage) and *Teaching Reading and Writing: A Guidebook for Tutoring and Remediating Students* (Rowman and Littlefield).

Dr. Johnson can be reached for comment at: andrew.johnson@mnsu.edu. For information related to workshops and professional development opportunities go to: www.OPDT-Johnson.com.

CONTENTS

CHAPTER SIX

METHODS OF COLLECTING DATA   66

CHAPTER ELEVEN

DISCUSSION: YOUR PLAN OF ACTION   161

CHAPTER TWELVE

WRITING AN ACTION RESEARCH REPORT   177

CHAPTER THIRTEEN
PRESENTING YOUR ACTION RESEARCH   198

PREFACE

The most important variable in determining the quality of our children's educational experience is the teacher standing in front of their classroom. As such, it is a wise investment to spend time and resources to help teachers become knowledgeable practitioners and to create the conditions whereby they are able to make informed, research-based decisions. Action research is one of the most practical, effective, and economically efficient methods to achieve this. This book takes you through all phases of the action research process. My hope is that it can be used as an agent of change as well as a vehicle for teacher empowerment.

NEW TO THIS EDITION

This book continues to evolve with each succeeding edition. I have made significant changes and additions here. As with the first three editions, I have tried to keep the text as short and as straightforward as possible. Too often in education, quantity and complexity are mistaken for rigor and effectiveness. I do not want to make this mistake.

The most significant change to this edition is the inclusion of my own personal website to enhance this product: www.AR-Johnson.com. Creating my own website enables me to create a multimodal, multidimensional learning experience that goes beyond the pages of this text. It also provides a platform for you to communicate directly with me via blog and e-mail. I will be constantly updating this so I would encourage you to check the site periodically. www.AR-Johnson.com is a public website that includes the following:

- Streaming video mini-lectures (three to eight minutes in duration), for each chapter to clarify and enhance content knowledge
- A blog for sharing ideas and asking questions
- Many examples of action research projects, literature reviews, action research proposals, and Master's theses
- Guidelines, additional information, and video tutorials related to academic writing
- A variety of downloadable forms, checklists, and data retrieval charts
- Instructor resources for teaching this as an online class
- Links to websites, articles, streaming videos, and other resources related to educational research

- Links to websites, articles, streaming videos, professional organizations, and other resources related to action research
- Links to professional development resources
- Expanded chapter content

Also New to This Edition

New additions and changes to this text include the following:

- New research questions for your action research projects are included at the end of each chapter. These will give you ideas for possible action research projects that you might conduct. Also, I have included tips to help you think of and formulate your own action research questions.
- Chapter 3 contains a short description of using action research as a strategy for instruction improvement by Dr. Carol Reed.
- Chapter 5 contains new information related to writing a literature review. Included here are step-by-step instructions that take you through all phases of action research including finding sources, note-taking, organization, drafting, using citations, and creating the reference page.
- Chapter 6 contains a variety of new data collection techniques including conducting e-mail interviews, conducting online surveys, and using online platforms. Chapter 6 also contains tips for designing and conducting surveys.
- Chapter 9: "Evaluating, Describing, and Proposing Research" is new to this edition. Included here are (a) a general overview related to the use and misuse of research in education, (b) a description of the principles and definition of scientifically based research, (c) specific guidelines for evaluation of quantitative and qualitative research, (d) a description of an annotated bibliography, and (e) a description of a research proposal. Two sample action research proposals are also included here.
- Chapter 10 contains revised tips for reporting quantitative and qualitative data (now organized into one chapter).
- Chapter 12 contains a significant amount of new information related to academic writing and *APA Publication Manual*, sixth edition. Included here is information related to grammar, elements of style, and guidelines for eliminating bias. Additional information related to academic writing along with streaming video tutorials are included on my website.
- Chapter 13 contains information related to presenting your action research. New information here includes tips for planning a presentation, general platform or presentation skills, guidelines for creating effective handouts and PowerPoint presentations, and tips for creating effective online streaming video presentations.
- Chapter 14 contains new information related to creating abstracts and full Master's theses.
- In this edition, all sample action research projects are found in the Appendix. Three new sample action research projects are included.

ACKNOWLEDGMENTS

I wish to thank those graduate students and teachers who have allowed me to use their fine work in this text: Dr. Carol Reed, Annie Oftedahl, Barb King, Ann Schmitz, Annette Tousignant, Darlene Cempa, Jessica Thomas, Karen Randle, Morgan Chylinski, Bethany Bickel, Shari Baker, Karie Ervans, Tina Williams, and Micki Archer. A special thank you goes to Kathryn Bell and Susan Stratton, who were central both in reviewing and revising this edition as well as in coordinating the new examples of student work found throughout the text and website. I wish also to thank managing editor Shannon Steed for her suggestions and work on this project, as well as editorial assistant Matthew Buchholz, and the reviewers for this edition: Kathryn Bell, Spring Arbor University; Kitty Hazler, Morehead State University—Prestonburg; and Susan Stratton, SUNY Cortland. Finally, I want to acknowledge all classroom teachers who have embraced the ideas in this text and put them to practical use. Your dedication to education and your determination to move the field of education forward does not show up on standardized tests results, yet it exists nonetheless, and it is truly inspiring.

CHAPTER ONE

SCIENCE, RESEARCH, AND TEACHING

This book describes how to conduct action research in an educational setting. This chapter contains a description of the nature of science, research, and teaching, all of which are complementary parts of the same pursuit of truth.

SCIENCE

Ask somebody what he or she associates with the term *science*. That person is likely to respond with something like biology, astronomy, physics, or chemistry. However, science is not solely a body of knowledge or a particular content area; rather, it includes the processes used to examine and organize the world around us (Johnson, 2000b). To engage in the process of science means to look, to seek to understand or know, to guess and test guesses, to create order from chaos, and to develop concepts. Science is "a way of thinking about and observing the universe that leads to a deep understanding of its workings" (Stanovich, 1992, p. 9).

Scientists are simply those who ask questions and find answers. In fact, we all use science in some way each day. Our questions might be as grand as, How did our universe begin? or as mundane as, Which line at the grocery store checkout is faster? or, I wonder what kind of response my new haircut will generate? Teachers are natural scientists. They engage in a form of science when they ask questions such as, How will this new teaching technique work? How are Sally's reading skills coming along? How can I help Billy learn long division?

Science and Pseudoscience

As consumers of scientific inquiry related to education, we must be aware of the differences between science and *pseudoscience*. Science uses perceived reality to determine beliefs. That is, data are collected to determine what is believed. Pseudoscience

Science

perceived reality ⟶ determines ⟶ belief

Pseudoscience

belief ⟶ determines ⟶ perceived reality

FIGURE 1.1   Science and Pseudoscience

uses beliefs to determine perceived reality. One starts with a strong belief, then looks for data to support that belief (see Figure 1.1). Pseudoscience is often used by companies, groups, or individuals to demonstrate that their product, method, or ideology is the most effective or best. Sadly, more education decisions today are made based on pseudoscience. Science provides an honest analysis of the situation and is much preferred to pseudoscience.

An example of pseudoscience is the type of "research" that is included with some of the phonics programs advertised on television, which are guaranteed to improve children's reading scores, usually with some snappy, new method. Before you believe these claims, however, consider this: More than a million teachers in our country and thousands of professors have been looking for effective ways to teach children to read for years. If some secret key or magic method were superior to all others, the mathematical odds alone dictate that a teacher would have found it by now and published many books and articles describing it.

A better example of science in education is the information published by the National Assessment of Educational Progress (NAEP), which is a part of the U.S. Department of Education. A representative sample of 30,000 students across the United States is selected at random for study (National Center for Educational Statistics, 1998). The kinds of tests, measures, and interviews given to this group are held constant across time and region. That is, a standardized math test given in 1970 in Georgia is similar in content, form, and length to one given in California in 2006 so that comparisons can be made. Thus, we are able to track the progress of U.S. students with some accuracy over time and place.

It is interesting to note that although many improvements are still needed for our schools, they are not in the miserable state of decay that some groups claim (Allington, 2006; McQuillan, 1998). When looking at basic skills, scores have remained constant or even risen slightly over the last 25 years (see Table 1.1). This is rather remarkable when one considers the influx of cultures and the many changes in our society, which have included an increase in drug use and violence. On the whole, U.S. teachers are doing a good job. However, NAEP shows that although basic skills have remained constant over the years, scores on tasks calling for higher-level thinking have dropped (Routmann, 1996). This contradicts the call for schools to get back to the basics, to have a standardization of process and product in education, and to engage in more testing. However, these are the kinds of remedies that are thrust on our children when pseudoscience is used to make important educational decisions.

TABLE 1.1   Average Scores on Standardized Test. 500 Points Possible

	SCIENCE		MATH				READING			
	1971	*1999*	*1973*	*1999*	*2004*	*2008*	*1970*	*1999*	*2004*	*2008*
age 9	225	229	219	232	241	243	208	212	219	220
age 13	255	256	266	276	281	281	255	259	254	260
age 17	305	295	304	308	307	306	285	288	286	286

RESEARCH

Scientific knowledge is a body of knowledge generated by research. *Research* is a way of seeing, a procedure used to view and re-view the world to understand it. Research is the systematic method used to collect data to answer questions. The systematic method used by the researcher is the lens through which the world is viewed. Different research methods or lenses provide different views of reality. A variety of scientific methods are used to study the unknown (Hodson, 1988; Stanovich, 1992); however, these methods tend to be put into two broad categories: quantitative and qualitative.

Quantitative Research

In *quantitative research*, sometimes called *experimental research*, the researcher takes an active role in setting up an observation or experiment to isolate a *variable*. A variable is the quality or condition about which the researcher wants to draw conclusions. The goal of experimental research is to figure out what the effect of a particular approach or treatment (variable) might be. To make an accurate prediction or to demonstrate a causal relationship, the researcher creates an environment that isolates a particular variable by controlling all the extraneous variables. Some important terms in understanding quantitative research follow.

1. The *independent variable* is the treatment or factor that the researcher manipulates to determine a particular effect. It is what is done or not done to a group of people, animals, plants, or things.
2. The *dependent variable* is the particular result or the effect of the treatment. An easy way to remember the distinction between these two variables is to think of the dependent variable as depending on the treatment or independent variable.
3. The *treatment group* or experimental group is the group of subjects, participants, or objects that are exposed to the particular treatment.
4. The *control group* is a group as similar as possible in all characteristics to the treatment group; however, this group is not exposed to the particular treatment for the purposes of comparison.

5. The *research question* is what the researcher hopes to find an answer for.
6. The *hypothesis* is a tentative statement that can be supported if the outcome of the experimentation is as expected. If a number of different tests continue to support that hypothesis, it may be elevated to the status of theory.
7. A *theory* is an interrelated set of concepts that is used to explain a body of data (Stanovich, 1992). Most hypotheses never make it to the level of theory because it takes a great deal of evidence to support a hypothesis before it can be viewed as valid. Hypotheses and theories are described further in the following sections.

To better understand this process, I have created a mock experiment. This mock experiment is purposely simplistic and exaggerated to demonstrate clearly the salient aspects of quantitative research.

The Coffee Study.   I wanted to find out whether drinking coffee (independent variable) would lead to higher student test scores on standardized achievement tests (dependent variable). To do this, I set up an experimental world in which two relatively similar groups of people had the same experience except for the independent variable. I randomly selected 200 college students and put them into two groups: Group A was the treatment group; Group B was the control group. Group A students were administered the treatment, which in this case was five cups of coffee each day. Group B students were not given coffee. The research question was, Does coffee improve students' performance on standardized tests? My hypothesis was, Drinking coffee improves students' ability to perform on standardized tests. The goal of this study was to prove or disprove my hypothesis.

A standardized test was given as a pretest measure to both groups to determine whether they were relatively equal at the beginning of the experiment. (If all the smart people happened to end up in the treatment group, this would confound the experiment and lead to a false conclusion.) For this experiment to be valid, I needed a sample size that was large enough to conclude that the results were not due to coincidence. The number depends on the research question, but in education, 30 is often seen as the minimum number of subjects needed in each group for a quantitative research study. Of course, more subjects are usually better than fewer subjects.

Next, I created a controlled environment in which everything about the two groups was exactly the same except for the independent variable (coffee). In this way, the independent variable (coffee) could be isolated, and I could say for certain that coffee did or did not affect the dependent variable (scores on standardized achievement tests). For this to happen, I put the subjects in a biosphere and gave each group controlled doses of study time, food, sleep, television, social interaction, and emotional stress.

In this exaggerated experiment you can begin to see one of the problems with controlled experimental research dealing with human subjects: Manipulating reality makes it nonreality. By controlling the environment, I created an unreal world. Data from this unreal world are then used to make conclusions about the real world. This is not to suggest, however, that empirical data from quantitative research studies are not valid, but rather that the research method used should be

TABLE 1.2   Results of Coffee on Achievement Test Scores

	PRETEST AVERAGE	POSTTEST AVERAGE	GAIN
Treatment Group A	78%	95%	17%
Control Group B	77%	78%	1%

determined by the research question. In this case, the research method is the best possible one to use in specifically answering my research question. However, if I wanted to understand why, when, or where college students drink coffee, I would need to use qualitative methods (discussed in the next section).

In this make-believe coffee experiment, I kept the two groups in their controlled environments long enough for the treatment effect to show up. In this case, it was 2 months. At the end of the treatment, I tested the two groups. These posttest scores were then compared to see whether one group's average was significantly higher than the other's. I also looked at the difference between pretest and posttest scores to see whether one group's gain score was significantly greater than the other's. Statistical procedures were then used to figure out whether the difference between the two groups was statistically significant, which means that the difference was larger than could reasonably be expected by chance or that it could not have happened by coincidence. Table 1.2 shows the results of this experiment.

The results show that the treatment group outperformed the control group by 17% on posttest measures. We will assume this difference is statistically significant. (I do not want to get into a description of statistical analysis here.) It appears that coffee does have a positive effect in students' ability to perform on standardized achievement tests. These results may transfer into other areas of academic performance. However, even in experimental research with the strictest controls, we can never claim absolute certainty. Maybe coffee has this effect only on college students. Perhaps the coffee effect is negated by a particular study method. Would coffee have the same effect on a group of elementary school students? Are there maximum and minimum levels after which there is no effect or a negative effect? Certainly, more research is needed in these areas.

Qualitative Research

As demonstrated, quantitative research uses numbers to reach a state of knowing. Controlled environments are created to isolate one particular aspect of reality. The questions are stated up front, and only data related to the research questions are observed and recorded. A cause-and-effect paradigm is used to make sense of the world.

Qualitative research, on the other hand, uses systematic observations to reach understanding. Researchers take the world as they find it instead of trying to manipulate conditions to isolate variables. The questions are more open ended and less defined, with plenty of room to collect a variety of data through collateral observations.

Also, qualitative researchers sometimes begin a study with only a focus or area of interest and allow the specific research question to form or begin to be defined with early observations. To demonstrate the differences between quantitative and qualitative research, I include another mock study. This mock study also is purposely simplistic to highlight the salient elements of qualitative research.

The Coffeehouse Study.   When I went to college in the 1970s, beer and bars were an integral part of the college culture, often the prime areas of socialization and interaction between genders. Many campuses even had a beer bar in their student union. Times have changed. The legal drinking age has gone up, awareness of the negative effects and dangerous situations created with the use of alcohol has increased, and most campuses today are alcohol free. This is something we could not have imagined in the 1970s.

On the campus of Minnesota State University, where I work, coffee and coffeehouses seem to have replaced beer and bars in the social milieu of the college culture. I wanted to see whether this was so. I was also interested in the nature of the interactions found in both types of environments.

Getting at my research questions meant going beyond numbers. I began my research spending a great deal of time observing the people and social interactions that took place in the coffeehouses and bars found near our campus. I did not try to control or manipulate the environment; rather, I observed individuals within their natural environment. After several observations, I developed a systematic method for collecting data that initially included taking detailed field notes and interviewing students on campus and in the bars and coffeehouses. (Data collection methods are described in detail in Chapter 6.) After my initial observations, certain behavior patterns began to emerge. I created a checklist listing these behaviors and put tally marks every time I saw them displayed. This checklist allowed me to quantify what I was seeing and provided me with a sense of the frequency, time, and gender related to each behavior.

In this study I became the lens through which this bit of reality was observed. My goal was to describe the quality of those things observed to help understand the nature of these places. What I found was that beer and bars were still an integral part of the social culture of this particular college campus. The types of interactions that occurred seemed similar in kind to what I remembered from the 1970s. The music was loud and affrontive, the atmosphere was highly sexual, conversation tended to be short and light, groups that came together tended to splinter and mix, and there were many instances of initial intergender interaction (III); that is, boy meets girl or girl meets boy. A sort of mating dance was going on here, complete with colorful plumage, strutting, dancing, and establishing territory. All that was missing was two bucks charging at each other and locking horns. But I am sure that had I stayed longer, I would have observed this in some form.

In the coffeehouses, the music tended to be quieter and more a part of the background. The general atmosphere seemed more subdued and cerebral without the sense of heightened sexuality. Also, conversation was on a much deeper level conceptually and of longer duration; groups seldom splintered off or mixed with other groups; and initial intergender interactions rarely occurred.

It appeared as if beer and bars were still an integral part of college social interactions; however, because the age of legal alcohol consumption is 21 in Minnesota, most students found in the bars were in their junior and senior years. In this study I was not able to find out much about the socialization of younger students, but this is perhaps worthy of consideration for future research. It appears as if coffee and coffeehouses have not replaced beer and bars in the college culture at Minnesota State University; rather, they have provided an additional outlet for a different kind of socialization.

Quantitative or Qualitative?

Is one type of research "better" than the other? No. Both are to be used to answer different kinds of questions. However, of these two categories of research, action research most often falls in the realm of qualitative research because action researchers study the world (their schools and classrooms) as they find them. And even though quantitative data may be collected, action researchers generally do not manipulate the environment to isolate variables. I often tell beginning action researchers to think of themselves as Jane Goodall studying a group of gorillas in the middle of the jungle.

TEACHING

Teachers and scientists are similar in many respects. Gallagher and Gallagher (1994) described seven essential activities of a scientist. Each of these, in various forms, is also an essential part of teaching.

What Scientists and Teachers Do

1. *Scientists develop content expertise.* The process of science is highly dependent on having a well-organized knowledge base (Armbruster, 1993; Gallagher & Gallagher, 1994; Hodson, 1988; Thelen, 1984). Knowledge helps the scientist structure and assimilate new information. Scientific inquiries are built on accepted theories and previous research. New data make sense only when they are grounded in what is familiar. Thus, methods of science involve generating relations between prior knowledge and new knowledge (Johnson, 2000b).

Effective teaching also requires knowledge related to subject matter, the learning process, and pedagogy. A sound knowledge base enables teachers to make thoughtful decisions about the teaching and learning process. Professional journals, workshops, conferences, and graduate courses are some traditional ways for teachers to expand their knowledge. Action research is one of the best ways to link theory to practice and expand teachers' knowledge base. This is described in more detail in Chapter 2.

2. *Scientists detect problems or ask questions.* As described earlier, scientists are continually asking questions about the universe and trying to solve problems (Stanovich, 1992). Teachers reflect on teaching experiences, looking for problems or ways in which to improve. They question and probe to see whether learning is occurring or whether students are grasping a particular skill or concept. The reflective teacher is continually asking, How is it going? How well and to what degree is learning taking place? What other strategies might I use? How is this new technique working?

3. *Scientists observe.* Scientists use observation in a variety of forms in collecting data. Kenneth Goodman (1986) tells us that effective teachers are kid watchers. They watch their students as they work with new skills and concepts and listen to them as they engage in small-group discussions to see how learning is taking place and what skills need to be taught. Observation and reflection are skills that are used naturally by teachers as they monitor students engaged in the act of learning (Erickson, 1986).

4. *Scientists organize and classify data.* Scientists use forms of categorization such as phylum, classes, and divisions to put order to the natural world. Using authentic assessment techniques, teachers often record their observations using anecdotal records. These data are then organized by looking for patterns and put into context so that they can be used to inform instruction or to evaluate and report students' progress.

5. *Scientists measure or collect data.* Teachers measure and collect data when they give any form of standardized tests or use other forms of authentic assessment and evaluation. They monitor assignments, record scores, make anecdotal records, give standardized tests, and create checklists, all to help them answer the question, How well is learning taking place with my students? Measurement takes place as teachers determine how far students have progressed. Portfolios are used to show growth over time.

6. *Scientists hypothesize or make predictions.* Hypothesizing occurs also when teachers say, "I think this technique or this new teaching idea might work in my class." It also occurs when teachers try to understand a particular student or learning problem.

7. *Scientists experiment.* Experimenting occurs when teachers try a new technique or methodology, or implement a new solution to a problem.

USING RESEARCH IN EDUCATION: THEORIES, HYPOTHESES, AND PARADIGMS, OH MY!

So why should educators be concerned about educational research? What relevance does it have to our everyday practice? We have all heard the common litany:

> "It's just a bunch of theory. You can make research say anything you want. Ivory tower researchers don't know what it's like in the trenches. It doesn't work that way in the real world."

Sigh.
Let me address some of these.

Theories and Hypotheses

Educational research is used to create the theories on which we design educational policies and practices. Theories help to organize relevant empirical facts (*empirical* means they can be observed or measured) to create a context for understanding phenomena. Sometimes people try to dismiss an idea or practice with which they do not agree by saying it is just a bunch of theory, meaning that the theoretical realm is somehow far removed from the practical realm, perhaps even having a different set of laws that govern it. But this would be a misunderstanding of what a theory is.

A *theory* is a way to explain a set of facts. Put another way, if reality were a dot-to-dot picture, a theory would be a way to connect a set of data dots (see Figure 1.2). However, varying theories connect different data dots in different ways, resulting in a wide variety of pictures and practices. Thus, varying theoretical perspectives, although based on a set of empirical data, can often advocate different practices or practical notions. An example is behavioral learning theory and cognitive learning theory, both of which are based on solid empirical evidence.

Theories are not meant to be eternal entities. They are designed to exist only as long as they continue to explain facts or connect the relevant data dots. When an abundance of new data are shown to conflict with established theories, the data are discounted or restructured. (You cannot put new wine in an old wineskin.) A list of common education theories is shown in Figure 1.3.

A theory is often confused with a *hypothesis*, which is an untested conjecture. A hypothesis is the first part of a study or experiment. Here the researcher says, "I think that _____," or, "What will happen to X when Y is present?" or, "I wonder about _____." This thinking is then put in the form of a research question or questions. In a formal quantitative experiment this becomes the basis of a null hypothesis, which is then either supported or rejected by data collected during the experiment. However, in qualitative or descriptive studies data are collected to answer or explore the question.

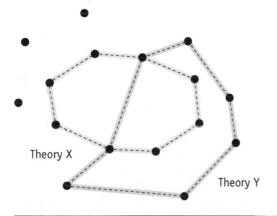

FIGURE 1.2   Connecting Data Dots to Create a Theory

- Theory of cognitive dissonance
- Constructivist theory
- Holistic learning theory
- Drive reduction theory
- Behavioral learning theory
- Information processing theory
- Levels of processing theory
- Multiple intelligence theory
- Triarchic theory of intelligence
- Social learning theory
- Situated learning theory

FIGURE 1.3   Common Education Theories

Finally, theories can often be used to justify a practice or procedure for which there may not be direct research-based evidence. For example, in one of my undergraduate classes students are taught how to use creative dramatics to enhance learning, not only in language arts but also in science and social studies classes. One day a student asked me if there was any research to show that using creative dramatics in a science classroom did indeed increase learning. Now I do not know if any studies have been conducted specifically to examine the effects of creative dramatics and learning in science. However, the levels of processing theory (Craik & Lockhart, 1972) states that when information is manipulated or processed at deeper levels, we are better able to understand, remember, and retrieve it for later use. Constructivist learning theory tells us that creativity, higher-order thinking, and social interaction all enhance learning (Sternberg & Williams, 2002). Holistic learning theory suggests that when students are able to make personal connections with what they are learning they learn more and learn more deeply (Kessler, 2000; Miller, 1996). Deeper levels of processing, creativity, higher-order thinking, social interaction, and personal connections are all components of creative dramatics. Therefore I can tell my students with a fair amount of confidence that creative dramatics can be used to enhance learning in science.

Paradigms

A *paradigm* is a shared worldview based on one or more theories. It includes a set of beliefs or assumptions that (a) establishes boundaries and principles within a particular field, (b) guides perception, and (c) describes a particular view of reality. Paradigms are useful in providing a form of cognitive scaffolding to guide understanding or new learning. However, if they become too rigid, they prevent more growth than they promote. That is, if we automatically discount all data or events that fall outside our particular paradigms, we become parochial in our thinking and locked into old ways of doing things. Progress and innovation become stymied.

An example of this paradigm-induced rigidity can be found in education in which a *positivistic paradigm* predominates. From this view, the only things that are valued are those that can be observed, weighed, or measured. Logic and knowledge reign, whereas emotion, intuition, creativity, and altered states of consciousness are ignored, demeaned, or dismissed. Yet these last four qualities have been instrumental in all the great human innovations and breakthroughs in science, the arts, the humanities, and other areas (Csikszentmihalyi, 1990; Harman & Rheingold, 1984). Thus it would seem logical that an education system that seeks to fully develop the potential of all its students in order to create a better society would address or cultivate these areas. Yet a paradigm gets in our way.

Better Decision Makers

The main point here is this: Educational research is a key factor in enabling school administrators, principals, teachers, and parents to make sound decisions (Marzano, 2003). Teachers and schools have a tremendous effect on student learning and achievement (Marzano, Pickering, & Pollock, 2001). This effect is more likely to be positive if the decisions related to policy, curriculum, and teaching practices are made based on what a body of research has determined to be best practice. Unfortunately, this is not always the case. Following are some general approaches that are often used to making educational decisions.

1. *Personal experience or anecdotal evidence.* Educational decisions are sometimes made on personal experience. You may have tried a strategy or approach or had a particular experience, and this becomes the basis of all future decisions. For example, "I tried cooperative learning once, and it didn't work." This is called anecdotal evidence, and although it is very powerful (because of the personal connection), it is not a sound approach to making decisions.

2. *One or two studies.* Here an educator starts out with a personal opinion or preconceived idea, then locates one or two studies to support this view. This also is not a sound approach to decision making because of the possibility of selecting studies that are limited, flawed, or biased. This is similar to pseudoscience described previously. Can you make research say anything you want? Not if you look at the broad spectrum of research. But it is likely that you can find one or two incomplete, poorly designed, or outlier studies to support a particular point of view. But, this is more likely to happen if a study has not been reviewed. Indeed, science is not science without the review of one's findings by a group of peers (Stanovich, 1992). For this reason, one should always be skeptical of "scientific studies" presented by companies or corporations that are intent on selling a product, political organizations, or any group that has an agenda.

3. *Famous person.* Sometimes decisions are made based on the statements of a well-known person. For example, William Bennett, the former secretary of education under the Reagan administration, received a bachelor of arts degree in philosophy from Williams College, a PhD in philosophy from the University of Texas, and a law degree from Harvard. With this background he was named secretary of education by Ronald Reagan in 1985. He has had much to say about education over the years, all of which should be taken with many grains of salt because they are statements based on philosophy and ideology, not on research-based theory.

His recommendations should not be considered research based or set in a solid theoretical context. Similarly, the statements of politicians, newspaper columnists, TV commentators, famous scientists, world leaders, or even action research textbook writers are all of interest as general statements but should not be used as the sole basis for making educational decisions. In all things you must say, "Show me the data."

4. *Tradition and folklore.* With the tradition and folklore approach, a decision is made or a particular practice is continued because "We've always done it this way." A case in point is the weekly spelling test that is given in most elementary schools every Friday. From Monday to Thursday students study a list of words in isolation (outside any meaningful context) that are selected by the textbook company. On Friday they are asked to recall the exact spelling of these words. This process is supposed to improve students' ability to spell; yet, there is no research evidence to show that doing this improves students' ability to spell under real-life conditions (Gentry, 1992), what Donald Graves calls "game conditions" (Graves, 1992). Although this idea seems to makes sense, there is no research to support this over other methods used for developing students' spelling. Why is it done? "Because we've always done it this way."

Likewise the common sayings that a teacher should not smile until Christmas or that student behavior problems can be solved by "getting tough" are both bits of folklore that are often repeated as truth. These are based on the assumption that an effective teacher has a stern demeanor and is able to control students. Control and manipulation are valued over relationship, shared goals, synergistic learning, community building, and cooperation. But if there were any research to suggest that simply being stern and getting tough actually worked, we would certainly be writing about these in our books and journal articles. We would also be teaching get-tough techniques to our students in all our teacher preparation courses. But they do not work. As behavioral learning theory describes, simply getting tough is not effective in changing behavior, whether one is dealing with mice in a Skinner box or humans beings in a second-grade classroom, because the mice or students simply learn to avoid the punishment or aversive conditioner, and when the punishment disappears, the behavior reappears.

5. *Magic bullets and flashy new packages.* Sometimes pedagogical decisions in schools and classrooms are made based on the claims of for-profit manufacturers of educational materials. Do not believe what is written on the outside of the package even if you see the word *research*. Again, research is not research without peer review. Even though commercial programs may claim to have the ultimate answer for teaching a particular skill or subject, there are no magic bullets (Allington, 2006). There is not one miraculous cure or single best method for teaching anything. Rather, there are many research-based strategies and pedagogical techniques, all of which should be intelligently adopted and adapted to meet the needs of particular teachers and learners in particular situations. What are these research-based strategies? The books listed in Figure 1.4 will give you a sense of some of them.

Best Practice: New Standards for Teaching and Learning in America's Schools (Zemelman, Daniels, & Hyde, 2006)

Classroom Instruction That Works: Research-Based Strategies for Increasing Student Achievement (Marzano et al., 2001)

What Really Matters for Struggling Readers: Designing Research-Based Programs (Allington, 2006).

What Works in Schools: Translating Research into Action (Marzano, 2003)

Effective Teaching Methods: Research-Based Practice (Borich, 2010)

How People Learn (National Research Council, 2000)

Learning and Teaching: Research-Based Methods (Kauchak & Eggen, 2006).

FIGURE 1.4   Books Describing Research-Based Teaching Practices

6. *The business model.* More often decisions related to education are made based on the "business model" (England, 2003; Berliner & Biddle, 1996). Despite the lack of any credible research, for-profit enterprises and the free market systems are seen as models to be used for educational reform. (When is the last time a third-grade classroom exploited workers from a Third World country?) These various business model reforms reflect a business paradigm put together by business-thinking people (certainly not educators). The untested hypothesis is that if there is competition, all the successful schools will grow and prosper, whereas all the underachieving schools will disappear someplace. The "reasoning" is that because this system seems to work well with shopping centers, fast-food restaurants, and convenience stores, it must work equally well with schools. Here competition is encouraged so that the successful will flourish, and the unsuccessful fade away. Although this paradigm may work in the business world, where profits are the bottom line, it does not transfer to education, where the bottom line is people. And, as the financial meltdown of 2008 demonstrated, the "business model" does not always work for business.

7. *Research-based theory and a synthesis of peer-reviewed studies.* This is the optimal decision-making approach, in which schools and teachers look at a body of research or make decisions that are solidly supported by research-based theory. This reinforces the need to have well-educated teachers, principals, and administrators with a substantial body of knowledge related to teaching and learning. Indeed, experts in any field have at their disposal a large body of knowledge to solve problems and make decisions (Sternberg & Williams, 2002). It is not possible to provide all the knowledge that teachers need in 2 years of an undergraduate teacher preparation program. That is why it is so important to have a plan for continued staff development activities for both teachers and administrators. Action research can be a part of this plan (see Chapter 15). Figure 1.5 contains Internet sources for teacher professional development.

PBS TeacherLine
www.pbs.org/teacherline/

Online Professional Development for Teachers
www.OPDT-Johnson.com

Annenberg Media
www.learner.org

Teacherfirst.com
www.teachersfirst.com

FIGURE 1.5   Online Professional Development for Teachers

SUMMARY

- Science is a body of knowledge generated by research.
- Science is the process of asking and answering questions.
- Research is the systematic method used to collect data to answer questions.
- Quantitative or experimental research manipulates the environment to isolate a variable so that a cause–effect relationship can be determined.
- Qualitative research looks at the environment as it is and uses systematic methods to understand things happening there.
- Action research is a form of qualitative research.
- Teachers and scientists engage in many of the same kinds of activities.
- Educational research is used to develop the theories that underly educational policies and practices.
- A theory is a way of explaining a set of facts.
- A hypothesis is an untested conjecture.
- Research-based theory can be used to justify practices or policies.
- A paradigm is a framework from which to view reality.
- Rigidly adhering to paradigms can stymie growth and lock us into old ways of seeing and doing.
- Educational research helps teachers and school administrators to make good decisions.

QUESTION AND ACTIVITIES

1. What is your favorite branch of scientific inquiry?
2. What scientific inquiry or research influences your teaching?
3. Describe an instance in which you think beliefs are used to determine reality.
4. Describe one thing you believe to be true about teaching and learning; then describe the facts related to this belief.
5. Describe 3 to 10 facts about the act of teaching and about learning how to become a teacher; then describe a belief related to teacher training.

6. Find a topic that interests you. It could be a topic related to education or another topic such as humor, sewing, motorcycles, or football. Using an Internet search engine or a database at a college library, enter your topic followed by the word *research*. Find and describe a piece of research related to your topic.

7. Pick one of the activities that scientists engage in as described by Gallagher and Gallagher (1994). Describe how this activity is manifested in your classroom or school.

8. Describe a practice in your classroom or school that seems to be based more on tradition than research.

9. Describe your plan for professional development.

10. Ask a question related to student achievement in the area of Civics, Geography, History, Mathematics, Reading, Science, or Writing. Use the NAEP website at www.nces.ed.gov/nationsreportcard to answer your question.

POSSIBLE RESEARCH QUESTIONS FOR ACTION RESEARCH PROJECTS

1. How do teachers view research in your school?

2. What education theories do teachers feel are important? What educational theories are used to guide practice?

3. What educational theories do principals and administrators feel are important? What educational theories are used to guide their decision making?

4. How do teachers and administrators differ in their perceptions of educational theories and practice?

5. What theoretical foundations seem to shape educational practices in your school or district?

6. How do the schools' standardized test scores in your class, school, or district compare with those of NAEP?

7. What do teachers believe are the most important characteristics of a good teacher? What do principals and administrators believe are the most important characteristics of a good teacher? How do these compare?

8. How has your school's population changed over the past 30 years?

9. How have your school's test scores changed over the past 30 years?

10. How has the focus on standardized tests changed your teaching practice? How has it changed the teaching practices in your school?

11. What types of decisions do you make during the course of the day?

12. Does all-day kindergarten have a lasting effect on student achievement? Do differences show up in fifth and sixth grades?

13. What are the types of professional development activities in which teachers engage in your school or district? What types of professional development activities do teachers think would be most beneficial? What are the topics that teachers would like addressed in professional development activities?

14. How closely do school policy and practices reflect the school mission statement and stated goals?

CHAPTER TWO

INTRODUCTION TO ACTION RESEARCH

Chapter 1 described research and the two major research categories. This chapter defines and describes action research and its various parts and examines the importance of action research in education.

RESEARCH IN ACTION

Action research can be defined as the process of studying a real school or classroom situation to understand and improve the quality of actions or instruction (Hensen, 1996; McTaggart, 1997; Schmuck, 1997). It is a systematic and orderly way for teachers to observe their practice or to explore a problem and a possible course of action (Dinkelman, 1997; McNiff, Lomax, & Whitehead, 1996). Action research is also a type of inquiry that is preplanned, is organized, and can be shared with others (Foshy, 1998; Tomlinson, 1995).

A Quick Overview of Action Research

The action research process involves five essential steps or parts. First, ask a question, identify a problem, or define an area of exploration. Determine what it is you want to study. Second, decide what data should be collected, how they should be collected, and how often. Third, collect and analyze data. Fourth, describe how your findings can be used and applied. You create your plan for action based on your findings. And finally, report or share your findings and plan for action with others.

Action research is a recursive process that does not always proceed in a linear fashion (Patterson & Shannon, 1993). You may find yourself repeating some of these steps several times or doing them in a different order (see Figure 2.1). Also, some action research projects incorporate a sixth step, which is to put the findings or the question in a theoretical context called the literature review. This and the other steps are described in detail in the chapters that follow.

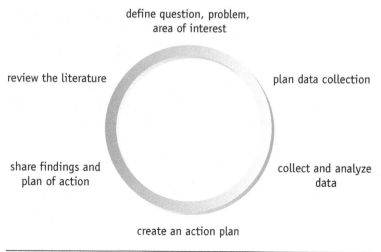

define question, problem,
area of interest

review the literature

plan data collection

share findings and
plan of action

collect and analyze
data

create an action plan

FIGURE 2.1   Steps of the Action Research Process

Descriptors of Action Research

The following 10 descriptors may help bring this type of research into clearer focus.

1. *Action research is systematic.* Although data can be collected, analyzed, and presented with a certain amount of freedom, you must create a systematic way of looking. Action research is not an "anything goes" type of methodology. Nor is it simply a matter of describing what you think about an issue, reporting about an interesting project or unit you have created, or explaining a pedagogical method that works well in your classroom. Action research is a planned, methodical observation related to one's teaching.

2. *You do not start with an answer.* An assumption underlying any research is that you do not know what you are going to find when you start; you are an unbiased observer. After all, if you had the answer, why would you be doing the research? Thus, even though you think Method X is the best way to teach reading, it is not appropriate to do a study describing why Method X is good and why Method Y is bad. Instead, you become an impartial observer (to the greatest degree possible) and study the effects of Method X as it is used in your classroom. The goal is to understand fully Method X and its effect (both positive and negative) on students' reading performance.

3. *An action research study does not have to be complicated or elaborate to be rigorous or effective.* Many beginning action researchers make the mistake of creating overly thick descriptions of every detail of their study in an attempt to be rigorous. This may often defeat the purpose. If too much material or too many details are included, you may miss what you are looking for, and the report will probably not be read or understood. Thus, what you do not include is often as important as what you do include in your observing and in your reporting. A well-organized, concisely described study is always preferable to a confusing, complicated study.

4. *You must plan your study adequately before you begin to collect data.* Having a plan and a schedule for collecting data before you start is what separates a systematic inquiry from an impressionistic view. However, plans and the type of data you collect can sometimes change as you get into your study.

5. *Action research projects vary in length.* The length of data collection in an action research study is determined by your question, the nature of your inquiry, the research environment, and the parameters of your data collection. For smaller action research projects, I suggest that my graduate students who are classroom teachers consider 2 weeks as a minimum length. For undergraduate students, there are some very interesting sorts of projects that can be done in 1 or 2 class periods. Major studies, such as a master's thesis or an article for an academic journal, generally have a duration of 2 months to a whole school year. Keep in mind that if your data collection period is too short, you run the risk of presenting an unrealistic view of that educational setting.

6. *Observations should be regular, but they do not necessarily have to be long.* The duration of observations might be anywhere from 1 minute to 1 hour or more. Many of your observations might be a quick note with the date and time recorded, whereas others might be longer and more formal. Although they do not have to be long, observations do have to be made on a consistent, preplanned schedule. Also, observations are only one form of data collection. Other data collection forms and methods are described in Chapter 6.

7. *Action research projects exist on a continuum from simple and informal to detailed and formal.* As stated, some interesting projects are short and simple. I suggest that beginning action researchers practice with these kinds of projects before tackling larger, more complicated ones. Action research can also be used for formal studies. Many of my graduate students who are teachers have done action research projects for their master's theses. A sample guideline for this purpose is described in Chapter 14. Because these projects directly related to what was happening in their classrooms, these teachers were able to link theory to practice in a meaningful way. Graduate students have been far more enthusiastic about investing themselves in these kinds of projects than in the kinds of secondary research often done as part of a master's thesis. And not surprisingly, action research projects always seem to be more interesting and enjoyable to read.

8. *Action research is sometimes grounded in theory.* Relating the questions, results, and conclusions to existing theory provides a context in which to understand your research. It also lets the reader know how your data relate to what others have said about the same topic. Most action researchers do a short review of the literature before they begin collecting data to provide a framework for the data collection. Others wait until the data are collected and then compare their conclusions to what others have written. Opinions about the place and extent of a literature review in action research vary. This topic is discussed further in Chapter 5.

9. *Action research is not a quantitative study.* In talking with beginning action researchers, this point seems to be the most common area of confusion. Thus, although I addressed this in the previous chapter, I want to mention it one more time here. Many beginning action researchers have to divest themselves of their previous notions about the nature of research. In an action research project, you are not trying to prove anything. You are not comparing one thing to another to determine the best possible thing. Also, there are no experimental or control groups, independent or dependent variables, or hypotheses to be supported. The goal is simply to understand. As an action researcher, you are creating a series of snapshots in various forms and in various places to help us understand exactly what is going on.

To illustrate this concept of understanding, consider the following example. One night in a graduate class, I asked a group of teachers to describe an event that happened that day. Alison Reynolds wrote of her interaction with a particular student that morning. Although she had described her teaching situation in early classes, it was not until I saw her snapshot of this student and the nature of their interactions that I began to understand some of the dynamics of her teaching situation. Her descriptions went far beyond the numbers and test scores in helping to comprehend the nature of teaching in an alternative high school and provided insight as to what an action research project might be. If she were to continue with this and make it an action project, she would create a systematic plan for describing a number of students and situations in her school. Out of this would grow a plan of action.

10. *The results of quantitative action research projects are limited.* Although quantitative methods can be used in action research, caution must be exercised in coming to generalized conclusions or in applying the results to larger populations. Such caution is necessary because of the small sample size of most action research projects and the many variables that are uncontrolled or unaccounted for.

For example, Mr. Miller did an action research project using quantitative methods to compare two approaches to reading instruction in his second-grade classroom. His statistical analysis found that the group using Method A scored significantly better than the group using Method B; however, Mr. Miller cannot reasonably conclude that Method A is the superior approach. The only conclusion he can reasonably make in this case is that Method A appears to be more effective than Method B. We do not know if the two groups were equal to begin with, and we do not know if the samples were representative. The action research was conducted in an uncontrolled environment, and there was nothing to address the bias and subjectivity of the researcher. To make a stronger conclusion, each of these issues would need to be addressed.

In another example, Ms. Reuter wanted to see whether her new approach to spelling instruction was effective in her fifth-grade classroom. Using quantitative methods, she found that when using her new approach, students showed a statistically significant gain in their ability to spell words over the period of 3 months.

However, like Mr. Miller she has to be careful in the kinds of conclusions she can reasonably make. In this case, we do not know how much of this gain was a result of general learning and maturity. That is, students naturally become better spellers as they write and are exposed to more print. Also, she cannot reasonably compare her class to another class because of the differences in teaching styles and approaches as well as many other unaccounted variables. At best, she might be able to say that her new approach appears to be effective in helping students learn new words.

THE IMPORTANCE OF ACTION RESEARCH

This section describes how action research can be used to fill the gap between theory and practice in education, empower teachers to become agents of change, and enhance the professional growth and development of teachers.

The Gap between Theory and Practice

Among other things, research is used to build theories that in turn help determine the best practices in education. These practices are then used to help teachers create effective learning experiences. However, sometimes a gap exists between researchers conducting and reporting their education research and teachers practicing in the field (Hensen, 1996; Patterson & Shannon, 1993; Tomlinson, 1995). That is, what goes on in public schools often does not reflect the wealth of research related to best practice in teaching and learning.

There are two possible reasons for this gap. First, it may be because research in education is sometimes written in a way that does not respect the demands of teachers' daily schedules in which time is a precious commodity. Research articles in academic journals can sometimes get overly descriptive, use jargon familiar to few readers, and focus on methodology and hypothetical notions that are not germane to the daily needs of teachers. This leads to the belief held by many teachers that education research is practically irrelevant (Barone, Berliner, Blanchard, Casanova, & McGown, 1996; Patterson & Shannon, 1993).

Second, the gap between research and practice might also be a result of the Moses Effect. The Moses Effect occurs when researchers hand down research edicts from on high with the expectation that teachers will be passive receivers of these edicts (see Figure 2.2). This creates a one-way flow of information that often does not value teachers' points of view, fails to reflect the complexities of teaching, or does not address the concrete problems and concerns that teachers face in their classrooms on a daily basis (Patterson & Shannon, 1993).

Action research is one solution to use in bridging this gap (Hensen, 1996; Knight, Wiseman, & Cooner, 2000). The Action Research Quadrant (Figure 2.3) illustrates the two-way flow of information in action research. Theories and research related to best practice are used to understand and observe what is happening in a classroom setting. At the same time, this data is used to understand or inform theories and research related to best practice.

FIGURE 2.2   The Moses Effect

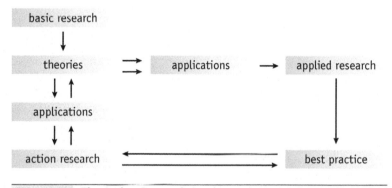

FIGURE 2.3   The Action Research Quadrant

Teacher Empowerment

Action research also facilitates teacher empowerment. Teachers are empowered when they are able to collect their own data to use in making decisions about their schools and classrooms (Book, 1996; Erickson, 1986; Hensen, 1996; Zeichner & Noffke, 2001). Empowered teachers are able to bring their talents, experiences, and creative ideas into the classroom. They can implement programs and strategies that best meet the needs of their students. Empowered teachers also are able to use the methodologies that complement their own particular philosophy and teaching style. When teachers are allowed to take risks and make changes related to teaching and learning, student achievement is enhanced (Marks & Louis, 1997; Sweetland & Hoy, 2002), and schools become more effective learning communities

(Detert, Louis, & Schroeder, 2001). The top-down approaches that are sometimes used to manage schools and solve classroom problems create an external locus of control that inhibits teacher empowerment and thereby lessens the effectiveness of schools (Book, 1996).

Teacher Inservice and Professional Growth

Action research can also be used to replace teacher inservices as a means of professional growth and development. Traditional teacher inservices are often ineffective (Barone et al., 1996). Here teachers are gathered, usually after a long day of teaching or on a busy workshop day, to listen to an expert describe an approach or methodology that often does not relate to their classroom situation or align with their teaching style. These traditional inservices generally do not give teachers sufficient time, activities, or content to increase their knowledge or affect their practice (Birman, Desimone, Porter, & Garet, 2000). To be effective, inservices need to be longer or extended over multiple sessions, contain active learning to allow teachers to manipulate the ideas and enhance their assimilation of the information, and align the concepts presented with the current curriculum, goals, or teaching concerns.

In regard to teachers' professional growth and development, Hensen (1996) described the following benefits of action research: It (a) helps teachers develop new knowledge directly related to their classrooms, (b) promotes reflective teaching and thinking, (c) expands teachers' pedagogical repertoire, (d) puts teachers in charge of their craft, (e) reinforces the link between practice and student achievement, (f) fosters an openness toward new ideas and learning new things, and (g) gives teachers ownership of effective practices. Thus, providing teachers time and incentive to engage in action research projects and giving them a platform to present their findings and engage in professional dialogue with peers enhances their professional growth and development, which in turn moves the field of education forward. Using action research as a form of teacher development also increases the sense of professionalism in education (Tomlinson, 1995), and it enables teachers to become agents of change (Hensen, 1996). Using action research for professional development is described further in Chapter 15.

SUMMARY

- Action research is the process of studying a real school problem or situation.
- The goal of action research is to improve one's teaching practice or to enhance the functioning of a school.
- Action research is a preplanned and systematic observation of one's teaching practice or teaching situation.
- The essential steps of action research are to (a) define a question or area of study, (b) decide on a method for collecting data, (c) collect and analyze data, (d) describe how those findings can be used and applied, and (e) share the findings and plan for action with others.

- A review of the relevant literature related to your topic or question might also be included in action research.
- Action research can be used to bridge the gap between education research and teaching practice.
- Teacher empowerment can be facilitated with action research.
- Action research can be used as a replacement for traditional inservices to enhance teachers' professional growth and development.

QUESTIONS AND ACTIVITIES

1. List or describe three to five things that interest you in your classroom or school.
2. What are some problems in your classroom or school that you would like to solve?
3. What are some aspects of your teaching that you would like to improve?
4. Describe some theory or bit of research that seems to have no direct link to your teaching situation.
5. Describe some theory or bit of research that seems to have a direct link to your teaching situation.
6. Describe a situation in which someone else has made a decision regarding your classroom practice. Would you have made the same decision?
7. Describe an instance when you would have made a different decision than what was made regarding your school or classroom. What reasons or evidence do you have to support your idea?
8. Think about the teacher inservices you have attended. What characteristics were effective? What characteristics were less effective?
9. What topic or topics would be of interest to you in a teacher inservice? Where might you go to get information on this topic?
10. Design a method that you think would be effective as a means for teacher growth and development.

POSSIBLE RESEARCH QUESTIONS FOR ACTION RESEARCH PROJECTS

1. What do teachers see as the use or uses of educational research?
2. What major decisions have been made by a school or a district in the last 2 years? What educational research or theoretical context was used to support these decisions?
3. What subjects or topics would teachers like to see addressed in a teacher workshop or inservice?
4. What do teachers think is the best method for introducing and implementing new teaching strategies?
5. What sorts of professional development activities are used by teachers in a particular school or district? How often and to what extent have they been used?

6. What sorts of professional development activities are used by principals and administrators in a particular school or district? How often and to what extent have they been used?

7. What does the research literature say is the difference between reading readiness and emergent literacy? Which is more effective? What approach is used in the kindergarten and first-grade classrooms in a particular school or district?

8. What does the research literature say about the best ways to meet the special needs of gifted learners in a general education classroom? How does this compare with what is currently being done in a particular school or district?

9. What does the research literature say about the best ways to meet the special needs of students with learning disabilities in a general education classroom? How does this compare with what is currently being done in a particular school or district?

10. What does the research literature say about the best ways to meet the special needs of students with emotional or behavioral disorders in a general education classroom? How does this compare with what is currently being done in a particular school or district?

11. What does the research literature say about the best ways to meet the special needs of students who are learning English as a second language in a general education classroom? How does this compare with what is currently being done in a particular school or district?

12. What does the research literature say about the best ways to develop students' ability to comprehend expository text? How does this compare with what is currently being done in a particular grade level, school, or district?

13. What types of decisions would the teachers in a particular school or district like to make? What types of decisions are being made by somebody other than teachers?

14. What changes would teachers like to make in a school or district to enhance learning?

15. What changes would students like to make in a school or classroom to enhance learning?

16. Who are the decision makers in your school or district? How do major decisions get made?

17. What impact do teachers have on curricular decisions and classroom practice?

CHAPTER THREE

USING ACTION RESEARCH FOR SOLVING PROBLEMS

Teachers are constantly challenged with a variety of problems for which they are required to develop solutions. Teachers who engage in action research projects become more flexible in their thinking, more receptive to new ideas, and thus better able to solve problems as they arise (Dinkelman, 1997). Problem solving consists of three elements: finding the problem, finding a solution, and testing the solution. This chapter examines the use of action research in problem solving.

FINDING THE PROBLEM

Problems cannot be solved unless they are first identified and defined. Identifying the problem occurs when the situation is observed and there is a recognition that things could be done better. Defining the problem involves seeking to understand the nature of the situation and discovering the possible causal factors. You look to see why things are as they are. For example, why are students not learning? Why are behavior problems occurring on the playground? Why does Suzanne have problems getting her work in on time? Why has Steven been acting the way he has? As stated in previous chapters, action research can be used to help see what is happening in a school or classroom or to identify and define problems.

The graphic organizer in Figure 3.1 can be used to help you define a problem. A problem is a difference between the present state and the desired state. To define a problem, start by describing the present state and desired state. Then list any and all objective facts in the first column. Next, list the possible consequences of the present state in the middle column. That is, what could happen or what is happening in regard to the present state? In the last column include any other information or facts you feel are important or relevant. State the problem as simply and succinctly as possible. Finally, restate the problem using different words.

Present state:

Desired state:

Objective Facts	Consequences	Relevant or Related Facts

The problem:

Restate the problem:

FIGURE 3.1   Problem Definer

FINDING SOLUTIONS

A variety of strategies can be used to find a solution. Two simple problem-solving strategies are described next: creative problem solving and means–end analysis (Johnson, 2010).

Creative Problem Solving

Creative problem solving (CPS) begins by defining the problem and generating ideas for solutions (Johnson, 2009). The key to successful implementation of this strategy is to produce as many ideas as you can. No evaluation of these initial ideas should be made because doing so would prevent the full range of possibilities from being explored. Sometimes when a new idea is put forth at a meeting or in a committee, individuals immediately respond by telling why that idea will not work. This only serves to preserve the status quo and prevent new and creative solutions from being considered. It is most effective to get all the ideas generated and listed, then to engage in an evaluative discussion to choose the one that seems best. Often two or three ideas can be combined for a solution. This would not be possible had you not first generated a number of ideas. The final steps are to refine, implement, and review and evaluate the solution. The CPS steps are listed in Figure 3.2.

Means–End Analysis

Means–end analysis (MEA) begins with a description of the desired outcome or end state. Where would you like to be? What outcome would you like to bring about? The next step is to define the goals necessary to bring about this end state. Goals are

1. Define the problem.
2. Generate as many solutions as possible.
3. Choose a solution that seems the best.
4. Elaborate and refine.
5. Implement the solution.
6. Review, evaluate, and refine as necessary.

FIGURE 3.2   Thinking Frame for CPS

the global objectives, traits, skills, behaviors, or specific conditions that make up your desired outcome. Goals are important in the eventual evaluation of your solution. That is, you can tell whether your solution is successful by ascertaining whether the goals are realized. Once the goals are described, the next step is to assess and describe the current situation. This is followed by an analysis of the means necessary to reach the end state. Finally, a plan is constructed to get from point A (current state) to point B (end state). As with CPS, solutions need to be reviewed, evaluated, and refined after implementation. You may recognize that this problem-solving strategy is similar to the process used in designing new curricula. The MEA steps are listed in Figure 3.3.

Problem-Solving Strategies in the Classroom

We cannot assume that students know how to solve problems effectively unless they first have been taught how to do so. The two problem-solving strategies just described can be taught to students in the form of thinking skills. This will improve their ability to solve problems and also enhance learning (Johnson, 2009). I recommend starting with CPS because this is usually easier for most students. You may want to simplify some of the steps for younger students.

You can teach problem-solving strategies in six steps. First, use the thinking frames in Figures 3.2 and 3.3 to create a poster to display in the classroom as a teaching aid. A thinking frame is a concrete representation of a particular cognitive process broken down into specific steps and used to support the thought process (Johnson, 2000b; Perkins, 1987). Second, identify the problem-solving strategy and describe each step. Third, model the problem-solving strategy by thinking out loud as you go through the steps to solve a problem. Fourth, use guided practice to solve a problem together. Fifth, create problems for students to solve by themselves or in small groups. And finally, embed problems into all aspects of the curriculum. For example, in reading or literature, use problems found in stories for students to

1. Describe the desired outcome.
2. Define the goals necessary to reach the end state.
3. Describe the current state.
4. Analyze the means necessary to get the desired outcome.
5. Construct and implement a plan.
6. Review, evaluate, and refine the plan.

FIGURE 3.3   Thinking Frame for MEA

solve. These can be interpersonal problems, problems that need the invention of a new product or process, or organizational problems. For social studies, science, and math, use problems that are found in history, society, or real life.

Testing the Solution

The final part of problem solving is to implement the solution and test it to see whether it works. Every new plan, program, or solution needs some adjusting during the implementation stage. Action research can be used as formative and summative evaluation. The next section is a description of how I used action research along with the three elements of problem solving to improve my teaching practice.

AN EXAMPLE OF ACTION RESEARCH AND PROBLEM SOLVING

I used to be the gifted education specialist for an elementary school in rural Wisconsin. In my first year in this position I conducted pullout sessions in which I met with small groups of students once a week. (This was several years ago. I would not recommend this as the most effective strategy today.) My students used to love the chance to learn more complex subjects, engage in high-level thinking, and have discussions and debates with like-minded peers. During my third year in the district, my job expanded, and I took over the gifted education duties in the middle and high schools. I was excited to resume weekly pullout sessions with a group of middle school students with whom I had not worked since my first year. However, at our first pullout session I found that my formerly eager and excited students were sullen and distant. They sat at the back of the room and rarely spoke or contributed, and when they did, it was with little enthusiasm.

Finding the Problem

A bit of problem finding and defining was needed. Had I tried to address this problem without first trying to understand the situation, I would have missed the whole point and probably made the situation worse. Instead, I gathered data by creating a systematic plan whereby I talked with students individually, talked with their teachers, and observed these students in a variety of classroom situations. I also went back and reread my textbooks on human development. What I discovered was that these young adolescents were reacting negatively to being singled out from their peers. They did not want to be apart from the group or be thought of as somehow different, which was a normal reaction for students at this developmental stage.

Finding a Solution

Having identified and defined the problem, the next step was to find a solution. I used MEA. The desired outcome was to create meaningful and enriching learning experiences whereby these students could reach their full potential. The goals were to engage these students in enriched content, teach high-level skills, and give them choices so that they could pursue topics of interest to them. The current state comprised three elements: (a) these students were engaged in a classroom curriculum that was far below their capabilities, (b) my pullout sessions were unrelated to their regular curriculum, and (c) a certain amount of social stress was being caused by separating these students from their peers.

It was clear that I had to create a structure that allowed these students to solve problems and create plans or products within their regular classroom experience. The gifted education literature describes a strategy called compacting and differentiation, in which students are able to test out of a unit to free up time to do other projects (Renzulli & Reis, 1997). The advantage of this approach is that it can be made available to all students and thus bypass the need for the formal identification of gifted students. It also reflects Howard Gardner's definition of intelligence, which is the ability to solve problems or create products that are valued in one or more cultural settings (1983).

To implement this plan, I worked with classroom teachers to design a structure that allowed students who had met a criterion pretest score to engage in inquiry projects, either individually or in small groups, that were related to the curriculum. Contracts were used to define specific goals, steps, and timelines to be met (see Figure 3.4). Instead of conducting weekly pullout sessions, I was in charge of a resource center where students would come to work on their independent projects. Among other things, I worked with students to teach them the skills necessary to complete their projects.

In looking at Figure 3.4, note that the inquiry projects contain the same elements as a teacher action research project. The research process I am describing in this book can be used and adapted to design inquiry activities for students at all grade levels.

Testing the Solution

Once this structure was in place (it took about 2 months to get it up and running), I designed a systematic plan for collecting data to evaluate the effectiveness of this program. I used student and teacher surveys, recorded field notes related to my work in the resource center, and analyzed students' projects. Essentially, I was using action research as a form of program evaluation. This collection and analysis of data helped me to revise and refine this program. Some of my findings included the following:

1. I worked with more students than just those who were formally identified.
2. Many students who were not formally identified as gifted created projects that were just as outstanding as those who were formally identified.
3. Students enjoyed having choice as well as challenge.
4. Teachers enjoyed having a gifted education strategy that augmented the regular curriculum.

Plan to Investigate

Investigator: _____

BEFORE THE INVESTIGATION

1. What is your question? What are you curious about? What do you want to investigate?

2. Important background knowledge? Use at least two sources to get information about your question. You may want to interview experts, read books or magazines, or use the Internet.

3. How will you collect data?

read ___	observe ___	checklist ___
weigh ___	measure ___	survey ___
interview ___	time ___	create and test ___
listen ___	count ___	other ___

4. When will you present your findings to the class?

AFTER THE INVESTIGATION

5. Organize your data. Look for groups or patterns, put data in order, or use tables or graphs.

6. What conclusions can you make, or what interesting ideas do you have based on your data?

7. How will you present your data and conclusions or ideas?

lab report ___	video ___	poster ___
photos ___	plan ___	visual art ___
graph ___	story ___	demonstration ___
brochure ___	speech ___	other ___

FIGURE 3.4   Contracts for Inquiry Projects

PROBLEM SOLVING AND INSTRUCTIONAL IMPROVEMENT

Following is a short article written by Dr. Carol Reed (used with permission). It describes some excellent examples that demonstrate how action research was used as a problem-solving strategy. It also provides an excellent overview of the action research process that will be described in the chapters that follow.

ACTION RESEARCH: A STRATEGY FOR INSTRUCTIONAL IMPROVEMENT
by Carol Reed, PhD

Action Research gives teachers the skills needed to work on problems specific to their classrooms and their schools. By using an actual research procedure, researching teachers can resolve their own teaching challenges. They learn how to ask a focusing question, define terms, collect relevant data, use an analysis process that rules out bias, and includes methods that yield validity and reliability. The findings become immediately applicable to their individual situations. For example:

Problem Behaviors

Jeremy's third-grade teacher watched him out of the corner of her eye. Though he sat quietly reading, she knew that he could, and often did, erupt into loud, emotional displays. On this particular day, the eruption came just after recess. Inexplicably, Jeremy jumped up, swept papers off his desk, and with a loud roar, tipped the desk over. The teacher managed to get him out of the classroom and into the safety of the nurse's office while his classmates patiently straightened his desk and gathered his scattered belongings. Still, in spite of their practiced efficiency, a half-hour passed before the teacher could get the class settled and working again.

Totally frustrated with the repeated loss of teaching time and the months it takes to complete Special Education referrals, the teacher decided to try what she learned in an Action Research class. She did a little Action Research project on Jeremy:

First, the question: In this case, it was simple. What upsets Jeremy?

Next, data collection: It was a little tougher to decide how to collect information that might respond to the question. It was tempting to think of the problem as originating in the home, on the playground, or within his psychological make-up. But true as that may have been, knowing it didn't do much for the classroom. Perplexed, the teacher decided to make brief notes about what happened immediately before each disruption.

Then, data analysis: Several disruptions later, the teacher spread the collected data, that is the notes, across her desk, reading them over and over, looking for patterns. Suddenly, she had it.

The findings: Jeremy erupted when she passed out papers asking students to work on new concepts.

The action plan: Gently confronting Jeremy with the "evidence," led to information that earlier "interrogations" had not revealed. Jeremy tearfully confessed that he always felt afraid he that could not do the new assignment. Together, they worked up a plan. When the teacher passed out work on new concepts, she promised to hand Jeremy a "fun" paper to work on. Jeremy agreed to practice patience. Thereafter, the teacher first got the rest of the class working well, then went to Jeremy's desk and helped him with the new concept until they both felt that he understood what to do. And it worked! The disruptions diminished significantly until, finally, the teacher withdrew her recommendation for a Special Education referral.

High School Dropouts

The same process works equally well in larger situations. For example: a middle school teacher, sitting in her staff lounge casually thumbing through a magazine, found an article citing research which alleged that high school dropouts make their decision to quit school during their middle school years. The teacher could not get the allegation out of her mind, repeatedly asking herself, "How does that happen?" "What do we do?" She, too, decided to implement an action research process.

First, the question: After considerable struggle and consultation, she chose: "What can this school do to make the transition from elementary to middle school 'user friendly'?"

Next, data collection: The teacher constructed a simple survey asking about various student experiences during students' transition time which she administered to her own sixth grade class. Startled by the students' response, the teacher enlisted the help of the school counselor. Together they surveyed two schoolwide randomly selected groups, one group consisting of "at-risk" students, the second of "average" students with the groups matched for gender and ethnic representation

Then data analysis: The teachers read through the surveys to find patterns in the responses and listed rubrics for the patterns (often called themes). Then they again read through the surveys to tally responses that fit under each pattern, a tally they could graph.

The findings: A significant number of students in both groups felt overwhelmed by the social challenge of being relatively anonymous in a large school setting.

The action plan: The teacher, the counselor, and the principal shared the information with the faculty who were, in turn, stunned. Student responses such as, "None of the teachers seem to know my name," and "No one speaks to me" tugged at their heart strings. The group not only faced up to the challenge by developing multiple plans that responded to revealed student information, they "commissioned" additional surveys that year and subsequent years to check their success in responding to the findings from the initial survey. Parents, impressed with the school's growing Action Research efforts, asked for the school's cooperation in surveying parents about the same issue. Eventually, other middle schools asked for information and adjusted their own transition plans accordingly.

Math Curriculum

The process works equally well for curriculum issues. For example, two teachers, working on separate projects in different time periods and at different levels, wanted to check the rumor that students who write down the thought process they use when they solve math problems actually do better in math. The elementary school teacher compared the length of time it took specific students to master specific skills when he taught in his standard manner, and then when he had students write out their thinking. The high school teacher compared three different classes grouped into underachiever, average, and advanced. The first year, he required only the underachievers to write. By the end of the year, that class had average test scores that exceeded those of the average group. The next year, he required all three levels to write and all three made greater than usual progress, but the underachievers still made the most progress. Both teachers wondered how much of the progress was due to their ability to "see" the glitches in their students' thinking, which allowed them to respond with appropriate pedagogy.

Spelling Program

In another school, a first year primary teacher, feeling confident about her spelling program and wanting to document its success, could barely pose a pedagogical question. She was already sure she had an effective way to teach spelling. What she did do was collect data: lists, and charts, and spelling profiles, as well as stories and sentence work. In January she administered a comprehensive test of the first semester's words. To her horror, most of the children failed it! Though temporarily undone, she resolutely pulled out her data and poured over it, finally determining that her program led students to use a broadened vocabulary in their sentences and their stories which was a good result, but she learned that she had more work to do on teaching for retention.

School-Wide Inquiry: Elementary School

Sometimes, some schools actually become centers of inquiry. In one instance a new elementary school principal, who looked so young that on his first day a teacher asked if he had come from the local high school to tutor, faced a staff of senior teachers. Respecting their experience and confidence, he began school improvement through gently administered Action Research projects. For example, one teacher coming into the lunch room after a frustrating morning sank into a chair saying, "Why does it take so long to get those children settled down after recess?" The principal, after a space of time and using his youthfulness to make his response credible, replied, "That is such a good question. Why does it take so long to get those children settled down after recess? How could we find out?"

The assembled group offered suggestions for collecting relevant information, that is, good data sources. They analyzed the information at the next teachers' meeting and set up an action plan based on their findings. Changed recess procedures solved the problem. By the end of the second year, at any given time, at least half the teachers worked on research projects with questions ranging from, "Why don't our children make better scores on those reading tests?" to "How can we get them to eat their lunches?" As a side result, no one missed teachers' meetings, or even came late. Relevant stuff was happening there!

School-Wide Inquiry: High School

A local high school became a center of inquiry over a three-year period by sending a number of teacher–leaders through Action Research coursework with each working on separate projects. In the words of one (whose initial project could barely be called Action Research), "You know, I'm beginning to see the long-term effect of this. It isn't just what we learn from our projects. It's an attitude about teaching. When we have a problem in this school, we don't just sit around and complain about it anymore. We face up to it. We ask the question. We collect information. We solve our problem. In a way, we've taken control of our professional lives."

Action Research as Problem Solving

In each of the descriptions above, teachers identified the problem, teachers chose the question, collected and analyzed the data, and teachers developed action plans based on findings. One huge gap in the evaluations developing around the current drive for accountability is that it often does not allow for a process that teachers themselves can use to solve their own problems, to evaluate the effect of their own teaching practices. That's what Action Research, in its current reincarnation, is intended to do. And, that is how it can be most helpful.

Source: New Horizons for Learning
www.newhorizons.org/strategies/action_research/front_action.htm#intro.

SUMMARY

- Solving problems is an inherent part of teaching.
- Problem solving consists of three parts: finding the problem, finding a solution, and testing the solution.
- Creative problem solving and means–end analysis are two strategies that can be used to solve problems.
- Problem-solving strategies can be taught to students to improve their ability to solve problems.
- Problem solving can be embedded within a curriculum to enhance learning and reinforce problem-solving strategies.
- Action research can be used to identify and define problems and to evaluate solutions.

QUESTIONS AND ACTIVITIES

1. Find a picture book or a chapter in a trade book that you might use with students. Generate a list of problems associated with each.
2. List 5 to 10 real-life problems related to science or society. Describe where and how these might be integrated into a curriculum.
3. Find a problem related to your daily life in some way. This could be an interpersonal problem or a problem related to school, work, or some product or process. Use CPS to generate ideas and find a solution.
4. Find a problem specifically related to education. Use MEA to design a plan.
5. Find a problem in your classroom or personal life situation and then define it. Why is it occurring?
6. Find a solution to a problem occurring in your classroom or personal life. How might you evaluate that solution?

POSSIBLE RESEARCH QUESTIONS FOR ACTION RESEARCH PROJECTS

1. What do teachers see as the major problems in their classrooms, school, or district?
2. What do students see as the major problems in their classrooms or school?
3. What do principals and administrators see as the major problems in their school or district?
4. What do parents see as the major problems in their school or district?
5. What interpersonal or social problems do students at a particular age or grade level encounter?
6. What kinds of ideas do students have for a specific interpersonal or social problem?
7. Identify a problem in your classroom or an area of teaching that you would like to improve. Use one of the problem-solving strategies to address this problem. As your action research, do a summative evaluation.

8. What makes students at a particular age or grade level happy?
9. What types of questions are most often asked by you during a classroom discussion?
10. What topics or kinds of things would students at a particular age or grade level like to learn about? What would the experience be like if you could incorporate this into a curriculum?
11. Is your spelling (math, reading, science, etc.) curriculum effective? Are students learning?

CHAPTER FOUR

THE BEGINNING

"But how do I start for Emerald City?" Dorothy asked. Glinda replied, "It's always best to start at the beginning. And all you do is follow the Yellow Brick Road."
—The Wizard of Oz, 1939

AN OVERVIEW OF THE ACTION RESEARCH PROCESS

I want to reiterate an important point once again: Action research does not mean that you have to prove something. It is not an experiment (although it could be). It is often conducted simply to find out what's going on. The goal is to understand, evaluate, problem-solve, or even to find new ideas and see how they work. Chapter 2 described five essential parts of action research. In this chapter, these five parts are broken down further into 10 steps. You will notice that these are similar to those described in the previous chapter. These steps are meant to be a guideline to be adapted to your particular research topic or situation. Also, as stated previously, there is no universal order to these steps (they are descriptive not prescriptive). You might find yourself skipping steps, rearranging their order, or repeating some steps.

Action Research Steps

1. *Identify a problem or research topic.* The first step is to decide what to study. What are you curious about? Ask a question, identify a problem, or define an area of interest for exploration. Find something that intrigues you, something you would really like to examine in depth.

2. *Set the problem or research topic in a theoretical context.* This means doing a review of the literature (described in detail in the next chapter). Look in professional journals, books, and Web sources to see what others have found out or have to say about your research topic. Relating your research topic to current theories gives you more credibility and provides a theoretical context for your findings. It also enables you to link theory and practice by connecting what you find in the literature to what is happening in your classroom. You might take one of three approaches in doing a literature review. The first approach is to do the review of the literature before you begin collecting data. Besides setting your study in a theoretical context, the literature review might also be used to help formulate your question, refine a pedagogical method to be studied, or give you ideas for collecting data. The second approach is to review the literature as you report the data and make your conclusions. The literature is related to each of your concluding points. The third approach is not to do a review of the literature at all. Many short action research projects do not include this element. As you can see, there are many ways to organize your action research project. The onus is on you, however, to create a credible and coherent report. Linking your study to theories and previous research is one way to do this.

3. *Make a plan for data collection.* In traditional research this is known as methodology. What data are you going to study? How are you going to collect the data? How often will you collect data? Action research is not impressionistic, nor is it a brochure supporting a particular teaching methodology. Rather, action research is a systematic observation; therefore, data collection must be focused, and the elements of data collection must be determined and described before the research begins. Several data collection strategies are described in Chapter 6.

4. *Begin to collect and analyze data.* After you have identified at least two kinds of data, you begin the data collection process. As you collect your data, analyze them by looking for themes, categories, or patterns that emerge. This analysis will influence further data collection by helping you know what to look for.

5. *If necessary, allow the question or problem to change as you collect data.* Action research is a dynamic, ever-changing process. As a human you cannot help but be influenced by the data you collect. It is common, therefore, to change a particular teaching strategy, the sources of data, or even the focus of the study as you are collecting data. This is acceptable as long as you let the reader know what you did and why you did it when you are writing your report. That is, your action research report, article, or master's thesis should take the reader along with you in all phases of your action research.

6. *Analyze and organize the data.* Hopefully you have been analyzing and organizing the data as you have been collecting them; thus, this should be the final step of an ongoing process. In analyzing your data, you need to establish how many total things were recorded, how many categories or kinds of things there are, and how many things are in each category. This is a quick view of analytic induction, which is described in Chapter 7.

7. *Report the data.* Present the facts or findings. This presentation includes an overview with detailed descriptions and illustrative samples of important events, activities, and responses. Also reported are the number and types of themes, categories, or patterns present in the data. In this section of your report you take the role of a journalist or anthropologist by describing what you saw and providing examples that demonstrate your perceptions.

8. *Make your conclusions and recommendations.* The next step is to interpret the data or tell the reader what they mean. Based on the data, what can you conclude? What do you recommend based on your conclusions? You then answer your research question, provide answers for a problem, or make suggestions based on your new understanding. Also, as stated in step 2, some action researchers do a review of the literature at this point to set their conclusions in a theoretical context.

9. *Create a plan of action.* This is when you put the action in action research. Based on your conclusions and recommendations, what will you do? You create a plan of action. And as you implement your plan of action, you assess what is happening or how effective it is; thus, the action research cycle continues.

10. *Put your plan into action and evaluate.* Does it work? What needs to be changed or tweaked? Few plans work perfectly. Evaluating your plan could become the basis of another action research project, and thus, the circle of action research life continues.

FINDING YOUR RESEARCH TOPIC

To begin, you must first determine an area to research. Three common research possibilities are (a) study or evaluate a teaching strategy, (b) identify and investigate a problem, or (c) examine an area of interest.

A Teaching Strategy

Would you like to try a new teaching strategy or technique? Maybe you want to see how a writing workshop works. Perhaps you are interested in finding out what happens if you let students choose their own writing topics. What new method or teaching idea might you be willing to experiment with in your classroom?

Chris Reed, a primary grade teacher, was intrigued by the idea of using an embedded approach to spelling. Instead of the prescribed list of spelling words and traditional approaches to spelling instruction, she used words found in students' literature and science units and created her own activities. Some weeks she also experimented with allowing students to choose their own words to study. She wanted to see whether this approach was effective in improving students' ability to spell under real writing conditions. As she started her action research project, she also became interested in seeing whether this approach was more enjoyable for her students, what effects it might have on students' writing, what kind of words students chose to study, and how those words related to the lives of students.

Mary Kaymeyer, a fifth-grade teacher, had always loved teaching her poetry unit in language arts, but because of a crowded curriculum, she felt she never had enough time to really enjoy and explore this form as much as she would like. She decided to try embedding poetry across her fifth-grade curriculum. Mary redesigned her curriculum so that poetry was included in social studies, math, science, health, and reading as well as in language arts classes. Poetry was used to reinforce important concepts and to create alternatives to tests and written reports in helping students organize and demonstrate their knowledge. After her first year of using this approach, she decided to use action research to see how it was going and to provide support for either continuing or abandoning this idea.

Identify a Problem

Problems can be turned into action research projects. Is there a subject or an area in your teaching that does not flow as well as others? Is there a particular problem in your school or classroom that is disrupting the learning process? Action research is a tool that can be used to systematically study a problem area. It can help to understand what is happening and the possible causes of the problem. It can also be used to explore various solutions. In addition, a review of the literature will help you connect the literature to the problem and to find solutions that others may have tried. The prompts in Figure 4.1 can be used to identify possible problems for your action research project.

Al Norton, a high school social studies teacher, noticed that the students in his senior-level classes seemed to be bored and disinterested. They appeared to be going through the motions on weekly assignments and often were talking or zoning out during class. He conducted a series of short written surveys and class discussions to find out what students were interested in, what they wanted to learn, how they best liked to learn, and what was useful in helping them understand new ideas. This allowed Al to connect his social studies curriculum to issues that were

The following prompts might be of help in finding problems for action research projects:

- My class would be better if . . .
- This is a problem on the playground . . .
- This is a problem in the cafeteria . . .
- This is a problem in my classroom . . .
- Our school would be better if . . .
- Learning would improve if . . .
- Classroom management would improve if . . .
- I would like . . .
- I would like to improve . . .
- I wish that I could . . .
- I am interested in finding an answer to . . .
- If only . . .
- I would like to increase . . .
- I would like to decrease . . .
- I am looking for a better way to . . .
- I would like to help students . . .
- I would like to make _____ better.
- I wish that I did _____ better.

FIGURE 4.1   Problem Prompts for Action Research Projects

relevant to students. A review of the literature gave him ideas for using different teaching strategies and activities. Al also shared his findings with his students and, in so doing, modeled a method of inquiry used by social scientists.

Examine an Area of Interest

Are you interested in a particular topic? Are you curious about something? Action research can be used to explore your interests. For example, Jim Soderholm, a middle school English teacher, has always been interested in comedy and humor. He wanted to discover what middle school students found funny and how they used humor in their socialization process. He began his study by recording instances of students' humor that he observed in classes, in the halls, or in other situations. From this, he created a form that allowed him quickly to note the instance of humor, the name and gender of the humorist, the recipient of the humor, and the type of humor (see Figure 4.2).

This project improved Jim's teaching in three ways. First, it helped him further his understanding of his students and the nature of their social interactions and emotional status. Second, he found humor to be a hot topic for these middle school students. This led him to incorporate humor into his English curriculum by teaching students to write and perform their own stand-up routines and comedy sketches. Third, Jim shared the findings of his action research with his students. They were fascinated by what he discovered and the process he used. This led to his teaching students how to do their own inquiry projects. Jim was able to use their accompanying reports as vehicles for teaching technical writing skills, oral speaking, and presentation techniques.

Date: Time: Place/setting:

Name of humorist: Gender:

Humor recipient:

Type of humor:

Key for humor recipient:
1 = student to student; 2 = student to teacher; 3 = student to anybody else

Key for type of humor:
P = physical; SC = sarcastic; A = absurd or silly; W = word play; S = sexual

FIGURE 4.2   Form for Recording Students' Humor

STILL HAVING TROUBLE STARTING?

It may be possible that you are still having trouble getting started—not to panic. The key is to first find something of interest for your topic and then create a question related to this topic. The question helps to narrow and define your action research project. Following are some additional ideas that might help you get started.

1. *Brainstorm and list.* Draw a line down the middle of a blank sheet of paper. On the left side begin listing topics of interest. Do not think about or evaluate your ideas yet as this will only stymie the flow. Then begin conversing with other faculty, asking what they are interested in or would like to know more about in regard to their classroom or teaching and learning. You will see that as the ideas appear, they lead you to other ideas. When you have exhausted your possible topics, on the right side of your paper, list specific questions for each topic. Each topic can have one or many questions related to it. For example, Mr. Fife, a sixth-grade teacher, knew that he wanted to spend some time looking at his science class (Figure 4.3). He was never satisfied with the way he was teaching it. He hoped his action research project might give him some ideas.

Possible Topics	Possible Action Research Questions
Science	**1.** What's going on in my science class?
	2. What things make learning interesting for my students in science?
	3. What best practice ideas might I incorporate into my science class? How will these work?
	4. What are some new strategies or teaching ideas that I might use in my science class to make it more interesting? How will these work?
	5. What topics are of interest to my students?
	6. How might I go about incorporating current events into my science class? How will this work?
	7. How do the school mission statement, goals, and philosophy apply to my science class? What elements are reflected? How?
	8. What topics are generally covered in a science class?
	9. What interesting projects or ideas are other teachers using in their science classes?
	10. Am I helping students make personal connections with the content? If not, what happens if I do?
	11. How do students perceive science?
	12. How does my science curriculum compare to thematic standards as proposed by the National Science Teachers Association (NSTA)?
	13. What important skills and concepts should students learn in my science class?

FIGURE 4.3 Possible Questions for a Science Action Research Project

For his action research project Mr. Fife simply wanted to find some ways to improve his science class. His research question was, How can I make my science class better (enhance learning, increase interest and motivation, and make it more active and student centered)? For his action project, Mr. Fife audiotaped some of his science classes to get a sense of what was happening. He used field notes to jot down what he noticed as he listened. He also reviewed his science lesson plans. Next he used surveys and interviews to find interesting or creative strategies that the teachers in his school and district were using. He was looking for ideas here that he could adopt and adapt. Finally, he did a quick review of the literature to look for new teaching strategies. He examined his data (field notes, surveys and interviews, notes from his review of the literature) and looked for groups or patterns. From this he created his action plan for improving his science class.

This led to a second, follow-up action research project, which was to evaluate his new approach. His research question here was, How is my new approach to science working? For this he used student surveys, analyzed audiotapes, and had a colleague come in and observe several of his classes during a 2-week period.

2. *Evaluate programs, policies, pedagogy, or plans.* Evaluation examines the effectiveness of an endeavor. Every program, policy, pedagogical strategy, and plan should have some sort of formal as well as informal evaluation. You want to see if the plan is working. To do this, first identify its original purpose. Is that purpose being served? Next examine the criteria. What would it look like if the program, plan, teaching strategy, or policy were successful? Then compare the current program, plan, or policy to the criteria.

Teachers at Greenwood Elementary School wanted to improve students' writing. After reviewing the literature they found two things that might improve students' writing: (a) teaching writing as a process and (b) allowing students to choose their writing topics. They developed a plan that included these two elements along with monthly teacher inservices and updates. After the first year, Ms. Furley, the principal, decided to evaluate the new plan.

The purpose of the new plan originally had been to improve students writing ability by using a process approach to writing instruction and allowing choice of writing topics. Her evaluation consisted of three parts. The first part was designed to find out whether writing processes were being taught (see Figure 4.4) and to see whether students were indeed being allowed to choose their own writing topics. She did this by surveying students and teachers and by making observations. For the second part Ms. Furley looked at students' writing. Greenwood Elementary had been doing a holistic writing test every year in which students were given a prompt and a piece of scratch paper for prewriting and thinking. Students were then asked to compose a writing sample within a 50-minute time period. Writing samples were then sent off to be rated by the testing company. Although it is not a valid indicator of students' ability to write by itself, Ms. Furley also looked at the language arts/writing portion of yearly achievement tests to get a sense of how students were scoring in regard to grammar and punctuation. For the third part of her evaluation, she wanted to know students' perceptions of the process approach to writing. Did they see it as helpful? What parts were seen as helpful? Did they

1. Prewriting strategies: lists, brainstorming, conversations, semantic webs
2. Drafting: using the first draft to capture ideas without regard to quality (allowing the first draft to look truly terrible)
3. Multiple revisions with feedback from others
4. Edit for grammar, spelling, and punctuation only after revision process is complete
5. Publish: to get a sense of audience, create books and collections of writing, public posters, author's chair, radio drama, and other methods to get students reading and listening to each other's work

The mechanics of writing (grammar, spelling, and punctuation) are taught in short mini-lessons using the context of students' own writing.

FIGURE 4.4   Five-Step Writing Process

enjoy writing? Ms. Furley used a Likert scale (see Chapter 6) in which students were asked to rate various statements related to writing and the writing process. She planned to continue this type of evaluation every year. To do this, she kept her measures and evaluation processes simple. Remember, rigor is different from complexity.

3. *Examine perceptions and attitudes.* Would you like to know what somebody thinks about something? You might examine the perceptions or attitudes of students, teachers, or parents on a variety of issues: How do students perceive something? What do they find valuable? What helps them learn? What makes learning more difficult? What are their preferences? What kinds of books would they like to read? How do they like to learn? How do they like to demonstrate their learning? What do they think about current events? How much time do they spend reading each day? What types of things do they do at home? How much time do they spend on homework each day? What do parents think about the homework policy? What do parents know about whole-language approaches? What do parents value?

Note again that action research projects do not have to be long, complicated, or filled with many subjects to provide useful information (although they could be). Becky Yuzna of Crystal, Minnesota, conducted the action research survey in Figure 4.5 with only the 15 students from a reading class. Her goal was to get some ideas about how to make the class more interesting and student centered, while enhancing students' ability to read.

4. *Check for learning.* Are students learning in your classroom? How do you know? What are they learning? What are some ways, other than using scores on standardized tests, that you could demonstrate what students learn? What types of measures might you use? What products or performances would indicate learning? What kinds of checklists or other data sources might be used (see Chapter 6)? What big lessons are students taking from your classroom?

5. *Make a case for your effectiveness as a teacher.* What evidence can you collect to demonstrate that you are an effective teacher? Can you collect lesson plans that demonstrate your effective use of one or more new teaching strategies? Can you

I surveyed 15 sixth- and seventh-grade students using open-ended questions to get information about their attitudes toward and interests in reading. In this survey, students were asked to finish nine open-ended sentences.

1. When I have to read . . .
2. I like to read when . . .
3. I read more if . . .
4. Reading is . . .
5. I cannot read . . .
6. My favorite type of reading material is . . .
7. School is . . .
8. When I read new words . . .
9. In reading class I wish we would do more . . .

Their attitudes varied quite a bit. Some students indicated that they like to read, others that they read only when they have to, and still others indicated that they do not like to read at all. When asked to name their favorite type of reading material, 10 students answered with a specific genre such as comedy, mysteries, comics, sports, scary stories, and "anything that's not fantasy." Many students also said that they liked reading alone or in a quiet place.

Given this information, it seems apparent that students like reading more when they are reading something they like or are interested in. A course of action I will take is to allow students to have input on the reading selections they will be accountable for. They can make choices about the type of material or the topic they read for reading class. I will probably need to establish some parameters on this. I will also make sure there is quiet time and space available during the day to read. I feel that if students are given the opportunity to get hooked on a book during school, they will be much more likely to take it home and enjoy it merely for the sake of reading and not because they had to.

Another interesting response was that several students wanted to do more "fun things" in reading class. Others indicated that they would like to draw or do activities. Given this information, I will try to do more fun activities designed to engage kids in reading. Drawing can easily be incorporated into reading class. Students can draw characters, book covers, maps, etc. I also think I will incorporate book talks for those kids who like to get up in front of people. Students like to share things that they are interested in. Fun is often underrated in an academic setting. It is much easier to engage students in the learning process when they enjoy it. I understand that there are times for traditional academics; however, getting kids to enjoy reading and learning makes traditional academic subjects much more meaningful and interesting.

FIGURE 4.5   Reading Survey Conducted by Becky Yuzna of Crystal, Minnesota

provide a list of books and articles that you have read to demonstrate your continued growth? Have you written articles or designed units, curriculum, or other programs and policy? Can you show that you are engaged in teaching as an intellectual endeavor? Can you provide evidence of your continued involvement with and service to the school, students, families, or community?

6. *Evaluate practice as compared to the school mission statement.* Although I suspect many mission statements are ignored and unused, a school's mission statement should be the starting point from which effective schools or school districts begin

all endeavors. It is like the objective on a lesson plan that sets the purpose and course for everything a school does. Like a lesson plan objective, all activities and endeavors thereafter should support the mission statement. Many action research projects can be based on one or more of the elements in a school's mission statements (see Figures 4.6 and 4.7).

Ask yourself whether this element of the mission statement is occurring. If so, to what extent does it occur? These projects can be undertaken for schoolwide improvement, but also at the classroom level.

7. *Observe students.* If you are still having trouble wondering where to begin, simply start observing students. During free time when students are working independently or on the playground, become an anthropologist and begin recording what you see. Using a form for field notes similar to that in Figure 4.8, record your observations on the left and interesting insights or questions on the right. Start these sorts of observations with no intent in mind. Research questions will arise out of your observations. That is, you will find something you would like to know more about or explore in depth as you begin to observe.

Bass Lake High School Mission

The mission of Bass Lake High School's faculty, staff, students, parents, and community is to provide a safe learning environment that enables all students to develop their full potential through a variety of rich educational experiences.

The Belief Statements of Bass Lake High School

A Caring Environment
- Learning is enhanced by a community of learners that supports the growth, exploration, and self-actualization.
- An emotionally and physically safe environment promotes student learning.
- A student's education is enhanced by positive relationships, extracurricular activities, and a system of intellectual and emotional support.

Focus on Learning
- Students' intellectual growth should be the primary focus of all decisions impacting the work of the school.
- Students learn in different ways and should be provided with a variety of instructional approaches, including the use of technology, to support their learning.
- Students need to be given the opportunity to participate in extracurricular activities to fully develop all skills and potential.

Commitment to Quality
- The commitment to continuous growth and evolution is imperative if our school is to enable students to reach their full potential and enhance local and global communities.
- Students need to define personal goals and demonstrate their ability to work toward and achieve their goals.
- Student learning will be demonstrated using a wide variety of methods and criteria, including authentic assessment, student products and performance, performance-based standards, and standardized tests.

FIGURE 4.6   Mission Statement for Bass Lake High School

Mission Statement for Elmwood Elementary School

Our mission is to create a community of independent, lifelong learners equipped to

- Think critically, creatively, and compassionately
- Make decisions that nurture the self, society, and the environment
- Make effective use of their multiple intelligences
- Interact with others cooperatively
- Read, write, and use mathematics
- Effectively use the various forms of inquiry for personal and intellectual growth

To actualize this mission, Elmwood uses a constructivist, experiential approach to teaching and learning. We believe that children must become independent thinkers and learners. Further, we believe the most effective way to achieve this is to offer them a number of experiences to solve meaningful problems with connections to theory. Constructivism or experiential teaching provides children with the opportunity to connect new learning to prior experiences to create new understandings of the world in which they live. The experiential approach to teaching and learning offers students opportunities to apply the various disciplines in meaningful ways or learning with connectedness.

Elmwood's foundation supports these principles:

- Children are our most precious resource.
- We devote the necessary energy and resources to actualize our "ideal" elementary school.
- We remain committed to performance-based learning, in which learning has an experiential connection and makes sense to the learner.
- We continue to deliver an educational program in which students are encouraged to be closely observant—in which they exhibit skeptical and open minds.
- We ensure that all our children master the essential elements for continued learning.

FIGURE 4.7   Mission Statement for Elmwood Elementary School

Objective Observations	Thoughts, Analysis, Questions

FIGURE 4.8   Form for Field Notes

SUMMARY

- The five parts of action research described in Chapter 3 can be broken down further into 10 steps: (a) identify a problem or research topic, (b) set the problem or research topic in a theoretical context, (c) make a plan for data collection, (d) begin to collect and analyze data, (e) allow the question or problem to change as you collect data, (f) analyze and organize the data, (g) report the data, (h) make your conclusions and recommendations, (i) create a plan of action, and (j) put your plan into action and evaluate.
- The order and nature of these 10 steps should be adapted to suit the demands of one's research topic and teaching situation.
- Finding a topic or an area of interest is one of the beginning steps of an action research project.
- Three research possibilities are to examine a teaching method, a problem, or an area of interest.
- In starting an action research project you must first find a topic and then create a question related to this topic.
- Additional ideas for getting started include the following: (a) brainstorm and list; (b) evaluate programs, policies, pedagogy, or plans; (c) examine perceptions and attitudes; (d) check for learning; (e) make a case for your effectiveness as a teacher; (f) evaluate practice as it compares to the school mission statement; and (g) observe students.

QUESTIONS AND ACTIVITIES

1. Describe the new teaching methods or ideas you would like to try.
2. Generate a list of problems or areas that might be improved in your school or classroom.
3. Describe your interests related to teaching, learning, or human interaction.
4. Find your school's mission statement. Which elements might become the basis for an action research project?
5. Find four colleagues or classmates. Brainstorm and list a minimum of 15 possible action research projects.
6. Using the form for field notes in Figure 4.8, observe a group of students interacting on the playground or during a class. Look for two or three possible research questions.
7. Give the reading survey in Figure 4.5 to your students. Are your results similar to Becky Yunza's? What was interesting or surprising in what you found?
8. What things might you include to make a case for your effectiveness as a teacher?

POSSIBLE RESEARCH QUESTIONS FOR ACTION RESEARCH PROJECTS

1. Are students in your class learning? How are students doing in your math class? How are students doing in your science class? What things are they learning? What skills have they mastered? How does their mastery of skills compare to those skills identified by a national organization in a particular field?

2. What things help students learn? What things get in the way of students' learning?

3. Do students have and use study skills? What skills do they use? What comprehension skills do students use to read expository text? What do students do to prepare for a test?

4. Find one or more elements of your school's mission statement that you feel need examination. How does this element compare to practice in your classroom? How does it compare to practice in the school? Use any discrepancies to make a case for change.

5. What do students like to read? What types of books or genre does your class prefer? How do they prefer to read?

6. What would your students like to write about? What would make a writing or language arts class more interesting? How would they like to write?

7. What type of social interactions do you see occurring on the playground? What kinds of games do students play? Are there any rules? What characteristics of students do you see in a playground setting that you do not see in the classroom?

8. What subjects or things are students interested in? What questions do they have? What would they like to know more about? How might these be incorporated into one of your curriculum areas?

9. Who are students' heroes? Who do they look up to? What characteristics do these heroes share? How might you use these characteristics to teach about values or citizenship education? How might students identify these characteristics within themselves?

10. Based on your observation of students and their conversations, what social skills would be of value to teach? According to a review of literature, how should these be taught?

CHAPTER FIVE

REVIEWING THE LITERATURE

This chapter contains a brief description of a literature review and how it might be used in an action research project.

REVIEWING THE LITERATURE

A literature review is an examination of journal articles, ERIC documents, books, and other sources related to your action research topic. The purpose of the review is to set your topic in a theoretical context and to make connections between research, theory, and your classroom practice. A literature review also helps tie your action research project to what others have said and done before you. That is, you do not have to reinvent the wheel; instead, you can use the insights of others to make your research more efficient and effective. A review of the literature may also provide you with examples of classroom applications, research questions, data collection methods, or data analysis techniques, all of which can be adopted and adapted for your own particular action research project.

Finally, a thorough review of the literature enables you to become an expert in the area you are studying and to become a more knowledgeable teaching practitioner. This will guide you in all phases of your action research and enhance your ability to teach.

SOURCES FOR THE LITERATURE REVIEW

This section describes the kinds and number of sources that might be used in a review of the literature for an action research project.

Academic Journals

Academic journals are usually the best source for literature reviews. They contain articles written by specialists in the field (usually college professors) who describe their research, secondary research, novel applications of existing theories, or interesting new ideas set in a theoretical context. Hundreds of different academic journals are published in all areas, from medicine to psychology, cosmetology, farming, and education.

An academic journal is not the same as a magazine. Magazines are designed to attract a wide audience and generate profit. They are usually written by a staff of writers or reporters who often have little expertise in the subjects about which they are reporting. To report accurately about a subject on which you have little knowledge is difficult; thus, accuracy is often compromised. Also, magazines depend on advertising revenue, which does in some way affect what is published.

Academic journals, on the other hand, are designed to inform the field. Journal articles are written by scientists, researchers, and other academicians who send in their work to be considered for publication. Each article is then peer-reviewed, which means it is critiqued by a jury of three to six experts in the field to check for accuracy and validity. Each reviewer makes a recommendation about whether to accept the article for publication. Often many revisions are made before an article is finally accepted for publication. Also, most academic journals contain little or no advertising, and authors are required to cite and list all their sources.

Books

Books are fairly credible sources. Keep in mind, however, that just because information is printed in a book does not mean it is true. Authors who cite their sources and books that are published by major publishing houses are generally those that can be trusted to provide credible information. When using books, learn to skim and read only the chapters or parts that pertain to your research topic.

The Internet

The Internet is a good place to find a great deal of information quickly; however, this information is not always credible. Whereas journal articles are peer-reviewed before being published, the only criteria for putting information on the Internet is that one has a website and the technical knowledge to post it. Therefore, the Internet should always be used with caution because the information is not always credible.

Thus said, you can find some peer-reviewed articles and reports on the Internet that may be appropriate for use in a literature review. These are described next.

The U.S. Department of Education.   The U.S. Department of Education maintains a homepage that can be accessed directly at www.ed.gov. Here there are links to the National Center for Education Research, the National Center for Education Evaluation and Regional Assistance, the National Center for Special Education Research, the What Works Clearinghouse, Evaluations Reports, and the Education Resources Information Center (ERIC).

You can find some good basic information at all of these sites, but materials should always be approached with a healthy degree of scepticism because much of it is created without peer review. It is common to find reports such as those produced by the National Reading Panel that are put together by a panel of experts who were chosen to reflect a predetermined political or philosophic bent (Allington, 2002; Coles, 2003). As well, I have found that the "experts" chosen to write these reports are not always experts in the field in which they are writing.

ERIC.   The two U.S. Department of Education websites that are most promising are ERIC (Educational Resources Information Center) and Ed Pubs. ERIC (www.eric.ed.gov) is designed specifically for educators. This site contains thousands of journal articles, research reports, curricula, conference papers, and teaching guides.

ED Pubs.   Ed Pubs (www.edpubs.gov) offers a variety of publications free of charge. There are research articles, reports, reference material, statistical information, monographs, and books related to a variety of educational topics. Many of these can be downloaded directly as PDF files. Again, one must discriminate when selecting documents from these two sites. Because many lack peer review they vary widely in their validity and credibility.

PsychINFO.   The American Psychological Association maintains a database at www.apa.org/pubs/databases. You can find a variety of sources including journal articles, abstracts, monographs, and books. Some of these are free, and others must be purchased. This is a very good source to use for finding research and peer-reviewed articles; however, as the name suggests, the focus is on the psychological aspect of topics.

Professional Organizations.   National or international professional organizations are good sources for finding peer-reviewed articles, research reports, and books. Figure 5.1 contains a list of major professional organizations in a variety of areas.

How Many Sources?

Exactly how many sources or pieces of literature do you need for your literature review? This is a question most often posed by my graduate students. Again, this is dictated solely by your research topic, the purpose of your research, and the type of research you are conducting. A master's thesis generally calls for 25 or more sources and a doctoral dissertation for 50 or more sources. Smaller action research projects designed to be published in an academic journal, presented at a conference, shared with your peers, or conducted to fulfill a graduate course requirement might use from 4 to 15 sources. Moreover, many action research projects conducted for professional development or used for evaluative or problem-solving purposes do not include a review of the literature and so do not use any sources. (Note: The numbers used here are meant only to give you some sense of the depth and breadth of your literature review. There are certainly many other views on this topic.)

International Reading Association: www.reading.org

National Council of Teachers of English: www.ncte.org

National Council for the Social Studies: www.ncss.org

National Council of Teachers of Mathematics: www.nctm.org

National Science Teachers Association: www.nsta.org

National Association for the Education of Young Children: www.naeyc.org

Association for Childhood Education International: www.acei.org

Council for Exceptional Children: www.cec.sped.org

National Association for Gifted Children: www.nagc.org

American Alliance for Health, Physical Education, Recreation, and Dance: www.aahperd.org

American School Counselor Association: www.schoolcounselor.org

National Association for Music Education: www.menc.org

National Association for Multicultural Education: www.name.org

International Society for Technology in Education: www.iste.org

FIGURE 5.1   Professional Organizations in Education

STEPS FOR A LITERATURE REVIEW

People often have trouble writing literature reviews initially because they do not know or understand the process. I have broken the process into specific steps. These steps are meant to be descriptive not prescriptive. That is, they describe a process that can be used to guide you at the outset. They do not prescribe a process that must be followed exactly. Please, adopt and adapt they steps as you find necessary.

Step 1: Find a good college library or journal database.   Public libraries usually do not have the academic journals and books needed to complete a literature review. Most college libraries do have a wide variety of academic journals as well as recent books published in the area of education. As indicated earlier, it is possible to find peer-reviewed academic journals on the Internet. Many sites require a subscription fee of some sort; however, if you are a great distance from a collage library, this will be far less than the time and expense required for travel. Also, most universities now provide off-campus access to journal databases to students who are currently enrolled.

Step 2: Locate possible sources.   The library will have some sort of database system in which all its journal articles and books are entered by subject, author, and key words. It sometimes takes a little detective work using a variety of different key word terms to find exactly what you are looking for. When you enter your topic in the search engine, the database provides you with one or more entries that look something like this:

> Johnson, A. (1998). What exactly are comprehension skills and how do I teach them? *Reading, 32*(2), 22–26.

This entry tells you the author (Johnson, A.), the year the article was published (1998), the title of the article ("What Exactly Are Comprehension Skills and How Do I Teach Them?"), the name of the journal (*Reading*), the volume (*32*), the journal number within that volume (2), and the page numbers on which it can be found (pages 22–26).

If you are in a library you will have to physically find the journal article. Most libraries organize their journals and magazines alphabetically by journal title. Once you locate the journal, the year and volume number should be listed on the front cover. When journals are 2 years old or older, libraries usually take all the journals from a particular year or volume and bind them in book form. This makes the journals easier to find and helps them last longer.

For example, to find the article listed earlier, go to the R section of the journals and magazines until you find the journal *Reading*. Then look for volume number *32* (several *Reading* journals will be listed as volume *32*), and find the second journal (number 2) published within that volume. The article will be found on page 22 of that journal.

Sometimes, journals are organized by Library of Congress number. On the computer screen the number will look something like this:

LB 1101. R2

Go to the journals found in the L section (these will all be journals of similar topics). Then move down until you find the LB section, then the 1101s, and finally, 1101.R2. In another database, all the books contained at that library are categorized and described. To locate relevant books, enter the title, author, or subject. Books may be organized either by Library of Congress numbers or the Dewey decimal number. In all cases, if you are lost or confused (a common experience), find a librarian. They are usually glad to help. I recommend using journal articles instead of books for the majority of your sources because they are more current and more focused, and they allow you to get a great amount of information from a variety of sources in a short amount of time.

If you are conducting your search from the Internet using one of the sources described, again you must plug in your topic search terms. Your initial search terms may not always get you exactly what you are looking for; thus, you will need to experiment with a variety of related terms. As an example, here are a variety of search terms I used when looking for articles on teaching context clues:

> **Search terms:** research-context-clues, context-clues, context-clues-activities, context-clues-teaching, context-clues-reading, context-clues-lessons, research-cloze, cloze, cloze-activities, cloze-teaching, cloze-reading-context clues

If you are looking specifically for research articles related to your topic, include the word *research* in your search terms.

Step 3: Peruse your sources.   After you get a pile of books or journals, take a few minutes to see whether your sources provide information related to your question. For books, look at the table of contents and the index and skim a few chapters. For journal articles, read the abstract and scan the headings, subheadings, and final paragraph. A few minutes here saves you much time later on. It also prevents you from having to carry around a pile of books and journals.

If you are conducting your search from the Internet or a database, first read the abstract found at the beginning of the article and then quickly scan the first and last sections. Look to see if the information found here is directly related to your research question before you print out a copy. I recommend printing off hard copies instead of trying to read and take notes from an online version saved on your computer as it is much easier to take notes. But people will differ in their preference here.

Step 4: Read and take careful notes.   It is common to spend a great deal of time during the beginning stages of a literature review reading articles and taking notes. Although this may seem time consuming initially, it makes the writing process much more efficient and effective in the long term. It has been my experience that shortcuts here result in more time and frustration during the later stages and produces a writing product that is of lesser quality.

When taking notes, first record the full reference citation at the top of the page. Having the citation here saves you the task of looking up the articles again when creating the reference page. Next, record your notes using only one side of the page. This allows you to spread all your notes out in front of you when you begin to write your first draft. Record only the information that is directly related to your research question.

To illustrate this process, I have included some of the notes that I used in writing an article related to quality teacher education programs and field experiences (Johnson, 2010). This literature review was used to guide the development of our department's special education teacher preparation program here at Minnesota State University, Mankato. Which brings up a very important point: The development of any new program, plan, or policy for a school should always begin with a question and a review of the literature. This ensures that what you do is research-based, evidence-based, or set in a strong theoretical context and not based simply on "*I-think-isms.*"

In taking notes, I recorded only the information that was needed to support the question: *What are the characteristics of effective field experiences in a teacher education program?* These notes were written using short, abbreviated sentences. The goal during note taking is not to create grammatically correct writing; rather, it is to restate and remember the author's ideas in a way that makes them readily accessible to you. Following is a sample of some of the notes.

Notes for Article: Field Experiences

Guyton, E. & McIntyre, D. J. (1990). Student teaching and school experiences (pp. 514–534). In W. R. Houston, M. Haberman, & J. Sikula (Eds.). *Handbook of research on teacher education*. New York, NY: Macmillan.

1. Experiences (field experiences) in classroom must correspond to goals of program and campus classroom.

    a. congruence—on-campus courses and field experiences (CF).

2. Field experiences = improves teacher performance and academic achievement.

3. Need link field experience & course work to goals of program (PG, CC).

Zeichner, K. (2008). Introduction: settings for teacher education. In M. Chochran-Smith, S. Feiman-Nemser, D. McIntyre, & K. Demers (Eds.). *Handbook of research on teacher education*. New York, NY: Routledge (pp. 263–268).

1. Clinical components must be connected to course components (CC).

2. Good field experiences = reflect program goals and are interwoven with coursework (CF).

3. Good programs integrate instruction of students into practice.

    a. case studies, teacher research, performance assessment, portfolio assessment.

    b. connect learning to teaching practice.

McIntyre, D. J., Byrd, D. M., and Foxx, S. M. (1996). Field and laboratory experiences (171–193). In J. Silua, T. Buttery, and E. Guton (Eds.), *Handbook of research on teacher education* (2nd ed.). New York, NY: Macmillan.

1. Increased field experience doesn't correlate to improved teacher growth.

2. Coop teachers, should be aware program goals (PG).

3. Need coherent program, program goals, curriculum goals.

4. Quality control—problem with early field experiences.

    a. do not reinforce course content (CC)

5. Early field, often lack a common goal.

    a. no coherence, course instruction and cooperative teacher (CC)

Cochran-Smith, M. & Zeichner, K. (2005). Eds. AERA. *Studying teacher education: The report of the AERA panel on research & teacher education*. Washington, D.C.: LEA (pp. 1–36).

1. Conflict goals and expectations—university instructors and cooperative teachers.

    a. less growth for students (CF)

2. Classroom teacher congruent with teaching practices advocated by faculty (CC).

   a. more growth for students.

Grossman, P. (2005). Research on pedagogical approach to teacher education. In M. Cochran-Smith & K. Zeichner (Eds.). AERA. *Studying teacher education: The report of the AERA panel on research & teacher education.* Washington, D.C.: LEA (pp. 477–548).

Study of Distinctive and Exemplary Elementary Ed Programs

1. Goal of programs—clear and explicit.

   a. goals—themes—course work and field experiences (PG).

2. Balance of general knowledge and pedagogical knowledge.

3. Strong articulation between campus-based and school-based program (CF).

4. Programs connected to research and development in teacher education.

Darling-Hammond, L. (2006). *Powerful teacher education: Lessons from exemplary programs.* San Francisco, CA: Jossey-Bass

Clinical Experiences

1. Need communication between school and university professors.

   a. expectations for clinical clearly described (CF).

2. Extended clinical experiences—carefully developed—support ideas, practice, concepts from coursework (CC).

3. School and university are linked by strong relationship—common knowledge, shared beliefs (CF).

Step 5: Organize notes and look for emerging themes.   Once you have your notes, the next step is to look for emerging themes. Spread your notes out on a table so you can see them all. When I did this with the preceding notes, the following themes began to emerge: (a) congruence or similarities between campus experience and the field experience, (b) the field experience should be linked to program goals, and (c) the field experience should be linked to campus courses. I used the following abbreviations to mark these emerging themes in the notes:

CF = congruence between campus experience and field experience
PG = field experience linked to program goals
CC = field linked to course components

Step 6: Express emerging themes with declarative sentences.   At this step the emerging themes must be captured, simplified, and expressed with specific ideas or declarative statements. As the declarative statements were formed, I used a code to remember where I got each idea so that I would be able to cite it later. For example, GM-90 is a code for Guyton & McIntyre (1990). Z-08 is a code for Zeichner (2008).

1. There should be congruence between campus and field experiences (CS-05, G-05, GM-90).

2. Field experiences should reflect or be linked to the goals of the teacher preparation programs (DH-06, GM-90).

3. Knowledge and skills in college courses should be linked to what happens in field experiences (CS-05, DH-06, D-04, MBF-96, Z-08).

As each idea from my notes was used to support a specific idea, I used a high-lighter marker to cross it off. Some people use different colored markers to keep track of the different ideas.

Step 7: Create an extremely rough first draft.   Once I had all my initial ideas I was then ready to begin constructing an extremely rough first draft. Because you will be moving many of your ideas around and throwing away much of what you write during the revising stage, it makes little sense to polish. There will be time enough for this during the final revising stages of your literature review. Following is an example of a rough draft paragraph that was created for this article:

> In a teacher preparation program there should be congruence between the campus experience and the field experience (Cochran-Smith & Zeichner, 2005; Grossman, 2005; Guyton & McIntyre, 1990). That is, there are similarities between what happens on campus and what happens in the schools. To this end, field experiences should be linked to program goals (Darling-Hammond, 2006; Guyton & McIntyre, 1990) and to course components (Cochran-Smith, Zeichner, 2005; Darling-Hammond, 2006; McIntyre, Byrd, & Foxx, 1996; Zeichner, 2008). In this way the field experience can be used to extend, enhance, and reinforce skills and concepts taught in methods course work.

Step 8: Start the revision process.   The preceding paragraph is an extremely rough first draft. I quickly slapped it together and moved on knowing that I would be coming back to shape it later. In this case, I eventually added some things and took others out based on what came before and after. The revision process should take up the majority of your time. Here you move parts around and take things away to create a document that is easy to comprehend and flows easily off the page. A useful analogy is that the first draft is like a potter throwing a blob of clay on the wheel. The revision process is where the potter shapes the clay into a specific shape. (Note: It is always helpful to get other people to read your work and provide feedback toward the end of the revision process.)

Step 9: Edit.   After you have spent a great deal time in revision, you can then look to edit your writing (see Chapter 14).

CITATIONS

The use of citations within your literature review supports your ideas and sets them in a theoretical context. As well, citations (a) lend credibility to your writing, (b) acknowledge the authors, and (c) enable the reader to find your supporting documents. This section describes how to cite various types of material in the body of your work according to the sixth edition of the American Psychological Association's *Publication Manual* (APA).

One Author—One Article or Book.   If you are citing a study or an article written by one author, the author's name appears within parentheses, followed by a comma and the year of publication. Any punctuation used for the sentences appears outside the parentheses:

> A recent study found that those teachers who used Johnson's action research book earned significantly higher salaries than those who used other books for their action research projects (Majkowski, 2010).

More than One Author—One Article or Book.   If the article has more than one author, use a comma to separate the authors and the "&" symbol instead of the word *and* inside the parentheses.

> Those people who read Johnson's action research book were significantly healthier than those who did not (Favre, Rogers, & Starr, 2010).

More than One Article or Book.   If many articles describe the same idea or reach a similar conclusion, you will need to cite more than one article or study. Within the parenthesis, the authors are put in alphabetical order. A semicolon is used to separate them.

> A statistically significant number of dentists have found that Johnson's action research book resulted in fewer cavities (Hadl, 2010; Starr, Bratkowski, & Hunter, 2007; Wright, Dickey, & Whitehurst, 2009).

THE REFERENCE PAGE

Any source used in your literature review must be referenced fully on the reference page. This informs readers as to what sources were used and allows them to locate these sources if necessary. Reference citations are listed in alphabetical order by the author's last name. You may not put any citations on the reference page that do not appear in the body of your text. Hanging citations are used on the reference page. That means you begin flush left (to the margin). The next line of the citation and all that follows are indented five spaces. This section describes the basics of full reference citations.

Journals

Journal Articles with One Author.   A reference citation for a journal article contains the following: (a) the author's last name, a comma, initials, comma, and a period; (b) year the article was published in parentheses followed by a period; (c) the name of the journal article capitalizing only the first letter of the first word and the first letter of the word that appears directly after a colon, followed by a period; (d) the name of the journal, capital letters on the first letter of the major words, italicized, followed by a comma; (e) the volume number with a continued italics, followed by a comma; and (f) the pages on which the article is found followed by a period.

Author, P. (2001). Name of the article. *Name of the Journal, 32*, 34–41.

Marx, G., (2010). Action research in elementary schools. *Journal of Education, 3*, 123–129.

Journal Articles with a Colon in the Title.   The first word in the title of a journal article that follows the colon is capitalized. There are no extra spaces between citations.

Hardy, O. (2010). The referenced page: Indenting is important. *The Journal of Writing, 34*, 87–90.

Journal Articles with More than One Author.   Articles with more than one author are the same as above except that the authors' names and initials are separated with a comma.

Laurel, S., Abbott, B., & Costello, L. (1998). The importance of reference citations. *The Brighton Journal of Writing, 57*, 122–131.

Books

Books with One Author.   A reference citation from a book is similar to that of a journal article. It contains the following: (a) the author's last name, a comma, initials, comma, and a period; (b) year the book was published in parentheses followed by a period; (c) the name of the book italicized, capitalizing only the first letter, followed by a period; (d) the place in which it was published; and (e) the publisher.

Author, P. (2010). *Name of the book.* City, State: Publisher.

Johnson, A. (2002). *A short guide to action research.* Boston, MA: Allyn and Bacon.

Books with a Colon in the Title.   Just as with a journal article, the first letter of the first word directly following a full colon in the title is capitalized.

Keaton, B. (2009). *Academic writing: A key to professional success.* Minneapolis, MN: Elitist Press International.

Books with Many Authors.   Just as with journal articles, include a comma between the authors and use the symbol "&" instead of the word *and*.

Arbuckle, F., Lewis, J., & Chaplin, C. (2010). *How to write.* New York, NY: Ellen & Beacon Publishing.

Books of a Later Edition.   A book published in 2011 may be the third or fourth edition of one written earlier. This tells the reader that the book was so popular that it was updated and later editions were printed. Here, (4th ed.) is in parentheses, and "ed" is in lowercase with a period after it. A period also follows the last paren.

> Johnson, A. (2011). *A short guide to action research* (4th ed.). Boston, MA: Pearson Education Inc.

An Edited Book.   This means that one or more people have edited the writings of several different authors and put them in a book. This is identified by including (Ed.) for one editor or (Eds.) for more than one editor. "Ed." starts with a capital letter so that the reader is able to quickly make the distinction between edition and editor. In the first citation that follows, we can assume that editor Rickles has put together a book where several different action researchers are describing their craft. In the second citation, editors Burns and Benny have put together a selection of writers who describe the importance of Andy Johnson on action research in the 21st century.

> Rickles, D. (Ed.). (2009). *Handbook of action research.* New York, NY: Hollywood Publishing.
> Burns, G., & Benny, J. (Eds.). (2009). *The impact of Andy Johnson on action research in the 21st century.* New York, NY: Hollywood Publishing.

A Chapter in an Edited Book with One Editor.   To cite the work of one author in a chapter in an edited book, the following information is listed in this order: (a) the author of the chapter, (b) the year published, (c) the title of the chapter, (d) the editor or editors (initials before the last name), (e) "Ed." in parentheses followed by a comma, (f) the book title, which is italicized, (g) the page number or numbers in which the article is found in parentheses with a period at the end, and (h) the publishing information.

> Curtain, J. (2009). The importance of accurate data collection. In D. Rickles (Ed.), *Handbook of action research* (pp. 57–84). New York, NY: Hollywood Publishing.

A Chapter in an Edited Book with More than One Editor.   The only difference between this citation and the previous one is that you would include "Eds." instead of "Ed."

> Hope, B. (2010). The important of academic writing. In. J. Seinfeld & R. Williams (Eds.), *Academic writing in the 21st century* (pp. 102–149). New York, NY: Hollywood Publishing.

A SAMPLE LITERATURE REVIEW

A literature review varies with regard to its form and placement in your action research report. Following are two examples of literature reviews: one inserted at the beginning of an action research report (typical) and one at the end (less typical).

Literature Review at the Beginning

I was interested in designing a new method to be used in identifying students for inclusion in gifted education programs in elementary schools. What follows is a sample of part of the literature review that was included at the beginning of my action research report. This review gave me some ideas to use in designing my new identification method; it also lent credibility to my eventual design by putting it in a theoretical context. Nine sources are used here.

IDENTIFYING STUDENTS FOR GIFTED EDUCATION PROGRAMS

The methods many schools use to identify students for gifted education services are not based on what is known about intelligence and creativity.

Intelligence

Howard Gardner (1995) defines intelligence as the ability to solve problems and create products that are valued within a cultural setting. Robert Sternberg (1996) describes it as knowing when and how to use analytic, creative, and practical abilities to reach a goal. Few in the fields of psychology and gifted education would define intelligence solely in terms of scores on standardized measures; yet IQ and achievement test scores are the predominant criteria for entrance into gifted education programs (Aamidor & Spicker, 1995; De Lieon, Argus-Calvo, & Medina, 1997; Hunsaker, Abeel, & Callahan, 1991; Richert, 1997). Identifying prospective students based solely on standardized quantitative measures does not reflect the latest theories related to intelligence, creativity, and productivity, yet schools continue to use such measures because their use is clean, efficient, and quantifiable. These methods are outdated and should not be used as the exclusive means for identification or acceptance into gifted education programs.

Creativity

Creativity is a cognitive process that leads to new or improved products, performances, or paradigms. It is a quality of thought that allows an individual to generate many ideas, invent new ideas, or recombine existing ideas in a novel fashion (Gallagher & Gallagher, 1994). Creativity is the ability to go beyond the given to generate novel and interesting ideas (Sternberg, 1996) or to produce something apart from the ordinary: something remarkable and something new (Feldman, Csikszentmihalyi, & Gardner, 1994). This is an important trait for achievement in all fields; however, the creative process is a trait that does not easily lend itself to measurement. Although standardized creativity tests may be useful in identifying students with creative capabilities such as the ability to generate many ideas or many different kinds of ideas, such measures cannot predict an individual's eventual creative achievement (Davis, 1997). The best predictor of future achievement, especially creative achievement, is past achievement (Davis, 1997; Sternberg, 1996). Therefore, it is reasonable to suggest that past performance be included in identification processes.

References

Aamidor, S., & Spicker, H. H. (1995). Promise for the future gifted education in rural communities. *Rural Special Education Quarterly, 14*(2), 39–46.

Davis, G. A. (1997). Identifying creative students and measuring creativity. In N. Colangelo & G. A. Davis (Eds.), *Handbook of gifted education* (pp. 269–281). Needham Heights, MA: Viacom.

De Lieon, J., Argus-Calvo, B., & Medina, C. (1997). A model project of identifying rural gifted and talented students in the visual arts. *Rural Special Education Quarterly, 16*(4), 16-23.

Feldman, D. H., Csikzentmihalyi, M., & Gardner, H. (1994). *Changing the world: A framework for the study of creativity*. Westport, CT: Praeger Publishing.

Gallagher, J. J., & Gallagher, S. A. (1994). *Teaching the gifted child* (4th ed.). Needham Heights, MA: Allyn and Bacon.

Gardner, H. (1995). Reflections on multiple intelligences: Myths and messages. *Phi Delta Kappan, 77*, 206–209.

Hunsaker, S. L., Abeel, L. B., & Callahan, C. M. (1991). *Instrument use in the identification of gifted and talented children*. Paper presented at the meeting of the Jacob Javits Gifted and Talented Education Program Grant Recipients, Washington, DC. (ERIC Document Reproduction Service No. Ed 334 732.)

Richert, E. S. (1997). Excellence with equity in identification and programming. In N. Colangelo & G. A. Davis (Eds.), *Handbook of gifted education* (2nd ed.; pp. 75–88). Needham Heights, MA: Allyn and Bacon.

Sternberg, R. (1996). *Successful intelligence: How practical and creative intelligence determine success in life*. New York, NY: Plume.

A Literature Review at the End

I could also wait until my data are collected and then compare my findings or recommendations to what others have written. The sample literature review that follows uses the same topic as the previous review—identification methods in a gifted education program; however, this literature review appears at the end of the action research report.

Recommendations

In reviewing my data, three recommendations are made for identifying students for our gifted education program.

1. **Make methods of identification consistent with your school's definition of giftedness.** A common definition of giftedness must precede any discussions related to methods of identification so that we are clear about what exactly we are trying to identify. Our district uses the U.S. Department of Education's (1993) definition in which a variety of talents is described, including the visual and performing arts, creativity, specific academic areas, leadership, as well as intelligence. If we are not going to address all these areas with equal emphasis, we need to revise our definition.

2. **Use the threshold model to identify gifted students.** The threshold model describes a more inclusive method of defining and identifying gifted students (Davis, 1997; Piirto, 1994). Instead of using high criterion scores on intelligence tests for inclusion into gifted education programs (140 or above), students break a lower threshold (score of 115 to 120), as well as meeting other types of criteria. This allows for a conception of giftedness that includes a variety of talents. The threshold model also complements Renzulli and Reis's (1997) schoolwide enrichment model. Anywhere from 10% to 20% of the population are eligible to go to an enrichment center for special instruction.

3. **Use products and performances as one type of identifying criterion.** Identification for any type of special programming requires more than one type of measure or multiple criteria (Davis & Rimm, 1998; Richert, 1997). Students, teachers, or parents are allowed to make a case for inclusion by gathering a variety of evidence to support the need for special programming opportunities.

References

Davis, G. A. (1997). Identifying creative students and measuring creativity. In N. Colangelo & G. A. Davis (Eds.), *Handbook of gifted education* (pp. 269–281). Needham Heights, MA: Viacom.

Davis, G. A., & Rimm, S. B. (1998) *Education of the gifted and talented* (4th ed.). Needham Heights, MA: Allyn and Bacon.

Piirto, J. (1994). Talented children and adults: Their development and education. New York, NY: Macmillan.

Renzulli, J. S., & Reis, S. M. (1997). The Schoolwide Enrichment Model: new directions for developing high-end learning. In N. Colangelo & G. A. Davis (Eds.), *Handbook of gifted education* (2nd ed.; pp. 136–154). Needham Heights, MA: Allyn and Bacon.

Richert, E. S. (1997). Excellence with equity in identification and programming. In N. Colangelo & G. A. Davis (Eds.), *Handbook of gifted education* (2nd ed.; pp. 75–88). Needham Heights, MA: Allyn and Bacon.

United States Department of Education. (1993). *National excellence: A case
for developing America's talent.* Retrieved from http://www.ed.gove/
pubs/DevTalent/part3.htrr

You can see other examples of literature reviews, including complete master's theses, at my website: www.AR-Johnson.com.

SUMMARY

- A review of the literature contains an examination and description of journal articles, Internet information, books, and other sources related to a particular topic.
- The literature review sets your topic in a theoretical context.
- A review of the literature enables you to connect education theory directly to your classroom practice.
- The number of sources used in a literature review is determined by your research topic and the type of research you are conducting.
- Some action research projects do not require a literature review.
- A review of the literature can be included at the beginning or the end of the action research report.
- The steps in creating a literature review are to (a) find a good college library, (b) locate possible sources, (c) peruse your sources, (d) read and take careful notes, (e) organize notes and look for emerging themes, (f) express emerging themes with declarative sentences, (g) create an extremely rough draft, (h) start the revision process, and (i) edit.
- Any book or article that you cite in your text must be listed on your reference page at the end of your report.
- Literature reviews can vary in their form and placement within an action research report.

QUESTIONS AND ACTIVITIES

1. Find a topic you are interested in as a possible action research project. Find one journal article that contains a review of relevant literature at the beginning. What do you notice about the style of writing?
2. Using a topic that interests you, find and list one of each kind of the following sources: journal article, Internet website, book, and a professional organization.
3. Find an example of an article in an academic journal that has a well-written literature review. Describe at least three things the author does well.
4. Use ERIC to find articles related to an area of interest.

5. Find an example of an article in a magazine and one related to a similar topic in an academic journal. What differences do you notice in the writing styles?
6. Identify a topic that interests you. Find two articles related to this topic. Synthesize the information and report it in an organized fashion using no more than two double-spaced pages.
7. What is an effective practice or program that you support or that you believe should be instituted in your classroom or in schools? Find an article in an academic journal that supports your view and write one to two paragraphs to make your case using objective, academic language.

POSSIBLE RESEARCH QUESTIONS FOR ACTION RESEARCH PROJECTS

1. How does your school identify students for gifted education programs? How does this compare with most current definitions of intelligence? How does this compare with most definitions of giftedness?
2. How does your students' writing change throughout the year? Are there changes in structure, themes, organization, topics, or mechanics? To what might these changes be attributed?
3. How do students perceive themselves as learners?
4. How do students identify themselves? To which group or groups do they seem to relate?
5. What are the demographics of your students in terms of gender, ethnicity, culture, SES, religion, ability, and family size? Why is this important? How do these data appear in your classroom?
6. How do students solve problems? When given a task, what steps or processes are used?
7. What types of thinking are used in open-ended class discussions? What types of thinking are used in small-group discussions?
8. What management issues are of concern to most teachers in your school or district? What strategies do successful teachers employ in maintaining an effective learning environment?
9. How does competition appear in your classroom and in your school? What seem to be the positive and negative effects?
10. How does cooperation appear in your classroom and in your school? What seem to be the positive and negative effects?
11. What decisions are made by the school board over the course of a year? What values seem to be used in making these decisions?
12. What educational decisions are made by you or your colleagues? What values seem to be used in making these decisions?
13. What issues are parents most concerned about?
14. What issues are students most concerned about?

CHAPTER SIX

METHODS OF COLLECTING DATA

This chapter contains practical suggestions related to data collection techniques. Many of these techniques are also forms of authentic assessment that can be used as part of your classroom teaching practice.

DATA COLLECTION

The goal of action research is to understand some element of your classroom by collecting data. Data (plural) are any form of information, observations, or facts that are collected or recorded. Collecting data is what separates the action research project from a newspaper editorial. As stated previously, action research is not simply writing about what you think to be true; rather, it is collecting data and making conclusions based on that data.

Systematic

In reviewing the literature related to action research, the one descriptor that is used in almost every book and article is the word *systematic*. Action research is systematic. This means that before the research begins a plan is in place that describes what data you will collect and when, how, and how often you will collect them. However, action research is a dynamic process; thus, it is common to abandon certain forms of data collection and adopt others as you are conducting the study.

One way to ensure that you are collecting data on a regular basis is to use a calendar or a checklist. Figure 6.1 shows a simple checklist that can be used to record which data were collected and when. This ensures that data are collected systematically and that all types of data are equally represented.

Type of Data	Dates Collected						
Individual quiz scores	8/18	8/25	9/2	9/9	9/16		
Audiotapes	8/13	8/19	8/26	9/2	9/17		
Student writing samples	8/17	9/9	10/1				
Homework	8/17	8/18	8/23	8/27	9/2	9/10	9/16
Student journals	8/27	9/17					
Small-group conference/focus group	8/20	8/27	9/3	9/10	9/17		

FIGURE 6.1   Checklist for Collecting Data

Data Collection and Soil Samples

Collecting data in an action research project is not a snapshot of a single incident like a test score. Nor should data collection rely on a single type of data, for example, collecting only survey data or only homework scores. Rather, action research is a series of quick looks taken at different times and in a variety of ways. In this sense, data collection in action research is much like collecting soil samples: You collect little bits of soil in different places over time.

A Television Sports Analyst

In your action research project you are the lens through which a bit of classroom reality is described. It is a given that this reality will be filtered through your own experiences and perceptions; however, you have the responsibility to present an accurate portrayal and to be as unbiased as possible. Any biases you are aware of should be stated up front so that readers of your report are able to take this into account. You are not creating a brochure for the Chamber of Commerce, nor are you advocating a particular methodology or approach; rather, you are examining what is happening in your classroom and letting us read your thoughts as you analyze what you are perceiving and experiencing. In this sense, you act as a television sports analyst for a football game as you describe what is happening and break it down so that others can understand it.

TYPES OF DATA COLLECTION IN ACTION RESEARCH

A wide variety of data to collect and methods used to collect them exist. This section describes 13 data collection methods. I would encourage you to select only two to four types of data to collect to keep your research focused. Nothing is more confusing than trying to read research that seems to go off in all sorts of directions.

Keep your action research simple and focused. Trying to collect too many kinds of data is a good way to make your life miserable. Often, my graduate students find

a lot of interesting ideas as they start their projects and want to go off chasing all of them. Those who do this usually end up making a mess of their research projects.

Finally, you may notice that some overlap or commonality exists between the methods described in the following sections. The goal is not to have categories and labels with precise edges; rather, it is to generate some ideas with fuzzy borders. In all cases in this chapter, and as I have continued to emphasize throughout this book, find or adapt the methods that best suit your research question or your teaching situation and that seem to make the most sense to you.

Log or Research Journal

A research journal is a notebook used to record thoughts and observations related to all parts of your research. Use this to describe each step of your research process. It is an important source of information to use when trying to piece together the chronology of your research project. You may choose to include a variety of data, such as observations, analyses, diagrams, sketches, quotes, student comments, scores, thoughts, or even feelings and impressions.

How you use your research journal and the form it takes is a matter of personal preference. Some choose to use their research journals to collect field notes and other forms of data, whereas others keep their field notes separate and use the research journal to record their impressions and ideas related to the research process. I sometimes use a computer file as my research journal. The advantage of this is that it is quick and easy to organize and read, and I can print copies or share files with colleagues. The disadvantage is that I can usually see only 30 lines of print at any one time, I have to scroll up and down in linear fashion, I cannot draw or sketch, and it is less spontaneous. I suggest you choose the method that you will most likely continue using.

Field Notes—Your Observations

Field notes are the written observations of what you see taking place in your classroom. Beginning action researchers are often unsure of what they should record. My advice is to stop thinking and just write what you see. Once you start recording, you begin to see things that are interesting or important. In this way field notes help you notice details you might not otherwise have noticed. And as you make many observations over time, patterns begin to emerge from the data. Also, as stated in the previous chapter, a review of the literature may give you clues as to the kinds of things you might attend to in your field notes. Field notes can be of either of three types: thick descriptions during, quick notes during, and notes and reflections after.

Thick Descriptions During.   The first type of field notes involves taking notes while teaching is taking place. However, few teachers are able to disengage during their teaching to become an objective observer recording thick descriptions of ongoing classroom events. Most need to be fully engaged in the teaching process and thus are not able to enter an effective researcher/recorder mode during teaching. Also, by becoming a researcher during your teaching, you run the risk of

becoming a nonteacher and thus becoming a foreign entity in your research environment. That is, by transforming yourself from a teacher who regularly responds to students' immediate concerns into an impartial researcher who observes and takes careful notes, you introduce something into the classroom environment that does not reflect what is normally there.

You can, however, observe another teacher's classroom or observe your own when somebody else is teaching. I have spent considerable time observing classrooms and taking field notes as both a researcher and a supervisor of preservice teachers in their field experiences. In this process I have learned much by watching master teachers at work. Providing training in some basic action research techniques and creating opportunities for teachers to do this each year is a very economical and effective form of teacher development. Here are five tips for observing a classroom and taking field notes:

1. *Enter the classroom as quickly and quietly as possible.* Move quickly to a spot in the classroom that offers the least distraction and sit down. Usually this is in the back or to the side.

2. *If students ask you who you are, answer them.* "I'm Mr. Johnson. I'm here to look at interesting things happening in your classroom." Students will attend to you for a short time, but you will quickly begin to fade from their consciousness.

3. *Begin taking notes without looking directly at students.* A person writing with his or her head down is much less distracting or imposing than a person staring and recording. Also, it is not always important that you see to know what is going on. It is possible to observe by listening and still get a good sense of a classroom setup, feelings, general impressions, and emotional tone. You can also record interesting or important dialogue by the teacher or students simply by listening.

4. *Smile.* A person smiling is much less threatening.

5. *Do not think—write.* Start by recording the time in the margin of your notes and then simply describe what you see happening. Whenever a new event or circumstance appears, record the time to provide a sense of chronology. Then write quickly without thinking. Working memory has a limited capacity, and it is difficult to perceive, record, process, and analyze information simultaneously. Writing quickly without thinking or analyzing frees up space in working memory and enables you to perceive more things.

Quick Notes During. Whereas it is difficult to record thick descriptions while you are teaching, it is possible to make quick notes to hold your ideas. Three tips for you to use are described.

1. *Keep a file in your desk drawer for every student with his or her name on it.* If something interesting occurs related to a particular student, make a quick note on the nearest scrap of paper, record the date, and put it in that student's file. Along with observations and field notes, these files can be used to collect representative samples of students' work, checklists, and test scores. The student file is a good data-collecting technique for action research, and at the same time it helps you become a more knowledgeable teacher when assessing growth, planning instruction, or speaking with parents about their children's progress.

2. *Keep a file related to the research project.* Whenever an idea, observation, or insight occurs to you during the day related to your research, make a quick note to yourself, record the date, and put it in your research file.

3. *Take notes on the margins or back of your lesson plans.* Often I am hit with a unique insight in the middle of a lesson. I find it most effective to make little notes to myself in the margin of my lesson plan. I use just enough words to hold the idea, then revisit it after class or after school when I am ready to record and write more fully. The more you do this, the better you will become at finding your original thoughts with single-word clues.

Notes and Reflections After.   Like many teachers, I prefer to record my observations after the lesson or at the end of the day. I am more relaxed, I am not rushed for time, and I find that I am able to think and remember much more clearly. There are three ways you might do this:

1. *After each lesson, make a quick note to yourself in your research journal.* In my college classroom, I go back to my office after a class, shut the door, and scribble a few quick notes in my journal. When I have more time, I use these jottings to make more extensive field notes.

2. *Record your insights and observations at the end of the day.* It requires a certain amount of discipline to ensure that you do this on a regular basis. Set aside 10 minutes every day and make that time sacred.

3. *Reflect on the back of your lesson plans.* This becomes a good source of data telling you what was taught, when you taught it, how it was taught, how it went, and insights for change.

Checklists

Checklists come in many forms. A checklist is a list that specifies certain attributes, such as behaviors, traits, assignments, or skills. When that attribute is seen, some method is used to either check it off or indicate the number of times it was present.

Student Checklists.   Student checklists are created by the teacher and filled in by the students. Ping Hew was using action research to study writing workshops in her fifth-grade class. As part of this, all students had portfolios they were required to maintain that included, among other things, the weekly checklist in Figure 6.2. Each day of the workshop, students used tally marks to indicate the activities they participated in that day. The bottom three boxes are open ended, allowing for a variety of responses related to topics, skills, and questions. As the quarter progressed, these checklists gave Ping a good sense of where her students were spending the majority of their time, of their writing topics, of the skills learned, and of the skills that needed to be taught.

Weekly Checklist for September 2010

At the end of each class, put a tally mark beside any activities done in that session.

Generating/prewriting	
Drafting	
Revising	
Editing	
Conferencing/talking	
Reading	
Other	

Writing topics:

Special skills learned or used:

Things I have questions about:

FIGURE 6.2   Student Checklist for Skills and Activities

Teacher Checklists.   Checklists can also be designed for use by teachers to indicate exactly what skills have been introduced or mastered and when. Checklists like these are also helpful in guiding instruction and providing evidence that skills have been covered. Figure 6.3 contains a teacher checklist for writing skills. One checklist for each student is kept in a three-ring binder. The skills necessary for successful second- and third-grade writers are listed in the first column. During writing time or in individual writing conferences, it is a simple matter to take out this checklist and make a quick assessment.

An important note when using a teacher checklist: Do not try to cover all attributes during a single session; rather, look for a few attributes during each observation. One observation tells you little; however, many short observations over time tell you much. Plan on using one checklist each quarter.

Writing Checklist for Second- and Third-Grade Students

Student: _____

Describe the student's progress using the following key:
3 = very much, 2 = some, 1 = very little, 0 = not at all.

Attributes	Dates				
1. Uses invented spelling to hold ideas					
2. Can spell most words on the 100 MFW list					
3. Uses capital letters for beginning of sentences					
4. Uses periods and question marks					
5. Displays a willing attitude toward writing activities					
6. Is able to write attentively for about 15–20 minutes					
7. Is able to brainstorm ideas for writing					
8. Knows what nouns, verbs, and adjectives are					
9. Has ideas to share					
10. Is able to organize ideas					
11. Is able to talk about his or her writing					
12. Is able to write an acceptable rough (first) draft					
13. Is able to edit or revise the rough draft effectively					
14. Uses complete sentences					

Words per fifty (WPF) spelling scores:

Observations or comments:

FIGURE 6.3   Teacher Checklist for Writing

Teacher checklists can also be used to document when you taught particular skills or concepts. A scope and sequence chart or curriculum guide can be used to help you design these. The checklist in Figure 6.4 was used to document literacy skills taught in a first-grade classroom.

Open-Ended Checklists.   An open-ended checklist contains a list of skills with enough space for students to describe their ability, understanding, or usage of each skill (see Figure 6.5). This provides you with an accurate indicator of students' levels of understanding and also enables you to plan instruction to meet specific needs.

Dates Taught

Key: I = introduced, L = learning, P = practice/reinforce

Skill	10/13	10/15	10/30	11/1		
SHORT VOWELS						
a				P		
e	I	L	L			
i				I		
o						
u						
y						

FIGURE 6.4   Teacher Checklist to Document Skills/Concepts Taught

Writing Skills

Skill	Explanation of How You Use Each Skill
Capitalization of names	
There versus *their*	
Adjectives	
Writing dialogue	
Paragraphs	
Commas	

FIGURE 6.5   Open-Ended Checklist

Rating Checklist

A rating checklist specifies traits you are looking for in a product or performance and allows the observer to assign levels of performance to each trait. This is similar to a rubric (see following section); however, whereas a rubric uses a sentence or more to provide a description of each level, a rating checklist uses one-word indicators (see Figure 6.6). I find rating checklists to be a more pragmatic method to use for collecting data for action research and for use in classroom assessment. The rating checklist in Figure 6.6 was used at the end of a science unit. Students evaluated their own level of performance on one side, and the teacher evaluated their performance on the other.

Science Skills

Key: 4 = outstanding, 3 = very good, 2 = average, 1 = low

STUDENT	SKILL	TEACHER
	Observe and describe	
	Create a graph	
	Weighing	
	Predicting	
	Organize data—create groups	
	Conclude	
	Use a lab report	

Student: _____

Teacher: _____

Grade: _____

Comments:

FIGURE 6.6   Rating Checklist for Science Skills

Rubrics

A rubric describes specific traits you are looking for in a student product or performance (like the preceding checklists). It also describes the various levels of performance for each trait (see Figure 6.7). That is, instead of just assigning a number to each level (4 = outstanding, 3 = very good, etc.), it contains a description of each level. The purpose of a rubric is to provide consistency and accuracy of scoring. However, they are very time intensive in their construction and use.

Conferences and Interviews

There is an important difference between conferences and interviews. In a conference one or more students talk about their work or some aspect of classroom functioning. Prompts may be used to get students talking about a particular topic; however, lists of planned questions are not used. Conferences can be conducted individually or in small groups (focus groups). In an interview students respond to planned questions, which are best conducted on an individual basis.

Individual Student Conferences.   Students should always do the majority of talking and lead the conversation in a conference. The exchange is open ended, and teacher questions are used simply as prompts to get students talking. Conferences

Oral Communication Activity

	4 = well above criteria	3 = meets all criteria	2 = meets some criteria	1 = meets few criteria
1. Eye contact	Maintains eye contact with audience throughout the speech, focus includes all audience members	Eye contact with audience in most of the speech, focus includes most audience members	Eye contact with audience in some of the speech, shifts focus to include some audience members	Maintains little eye contact with audience, shifts focus to include audience members
2. Inflection and pauses	Uses inflection and pauses effectively to maintain interest and attention	Uses some inflection and pauses to maintain interest and attention	Uses little inflection and pauses to main interest and attention	Uses a flat, monotone voice with no pauses throughout
3. Structure	Structure is very apparent and is used to organize ideas; all ideas within a section are related	Structure is apparent and is used to organize ideas; most ideas within a section are related	Some structure is used to organize ideas; some ideas within each section are related	Little or no structure is used to organize ideas; few ideas within each section are related
4. Preparation	Draft looked like a finished product, handed in on due date, all revisions were made	Draft was mostly complete, handed in on time, some revisions were made	Draft had some important parts included, handed in near the due date, few revisions were made	Draft was incomplete, handed in late, few or no revisions were made

FIGURE 6.7   Rubric for a Speech

How's it going?

What are you working on? (Tell me about that.)

What is something that you seem to do well?

What might be something that gives you problems? (Tell me about that.)

Read part of your story.

Do a long division problem, and talk out loud as you are doing it.

Tell me what you do when you work in a cooperative group.

What skills have you learned?

What part of science is most interesting to you?

What is something interesting or important that you have learned in our social studies class?

FIGURE 6.8   **Questions and Prompts for Student Conferences**

can last anywhere from 2 to 15 minutes. Figure 6.8 contains a list of possible confer-ence questions that can be used as prompts.

When conferencing with a student, take notes but do not try to get a verbatim transcript of the conference. Instead, record only the items you think are impor-tant, such as strengths, weaknesses, general impressions, skills learned, progress, insights, or what the student is currently working on. You may want to design some kind of a checklist to use for taking notes during conferences. Again, this is a matter of personal preference. It is normal to feel a little unsure of this process at first; however, after you have done it a few times you will get a good sense of what to record and how to best record it.

As a teaching tool, individual conferences are also an effective way to touch base with each student in a personal way. For example, in Jason Hinkle's ninth-grade biology class, his students are assigned conference times to talk about their projects, which include a series of experiments and lab reports. Knowing they are going to meet with him, students are able to prepare and make sure they have something to say. In these short conferences, Jason listens, takes notes, asks ques-tions, gives responses, encourages, and makes one or two suggestions for improving their experiments or lab reports. He schedules no more than three to five confer-ences in any day because conferences can be tiring. This allows him to see each student every 2 weeks.

A checklist can be used to keep track of students and conference times (see Figure 6.9). Conferences such as these can be used across the curriculum as you work on teaching specific skills. They can also be used as a means of checking in and staying in touch with your students. Finally, conferences might also be used to address social issues or interpersonal issues within your classroom. You are limited only by your imagination.

Small-Group Conferences/Focus Groups.   In a small-group conference (some-times known as focus groups) you meet with three to eight students at one time. This is an effective data-collecting method that allows you to see a number of

Checklist for Individual Student Conference Dates

Billy A.	8/23	9/13	10/4				
Sally B.	8/23	9/13	10/4				
Amy C.	8/23	9/13	10/4				
Molly D.	8/24	9/14	10/11				
Michael E.	8/24	9/14	10/11				
Thomas F.	8/24	9/14	10/11				

FIGURE 6.9   Checklist of Individual Conferences

students fairly quickly and watch them interacting with each other. It is also a valuable teaching tool because students are able to hear and respond to the thoughts of other students. As in the individual conference, the teacher should talk as little as possible.

Small-group conferences can be adapted for use in a variety of situations. For example, it may be used to discuss subjects such as good books, current or historical events, research projects, writing projects, moral dilemmas, math skills, problem-solving skills, textbook reading assignments, homework problems, and personal issues. You cannot, however, assume that students instinctively know how to function in small groups. Thus, structure must be provided so that they know how to speak and respond to each other (see Figure 6.10). It is common to spend a few class sessions teaching students how to interact in small groups and to use students to help model the process. Each group can use a checklist to report its progress. This helps the group focus on the key elements of successful group behavior and provides you with another form of data (see Figure 6.11).

In-Person Interviews.   An interview differs from a conference in that an interview consists of a specific set of questions prepared in advance and is teacher directed. The questions should be asked in the same order each time to maintain consistency.

Before
1. Be prepared.
2. Bring all materials with you.

Speaking
1. Only one person talks at a time.
2. Say what you have to say, then let others respond.
3. Do not dominate the conversation.
4. Listen.

Responding
1. Ask a question.
2. Find something you like.
3. Ask for clarification.
4. Find something it reminds you of.
5. Offer suggestions or ways to do it differently.
6. Do not make put-downs or personal remarks.

FIGURE 6.10   Rules for Small-Group Conferences

Group: _____   Date: _____

	yes	no	some
1. The group stayed on task.			
2. Everyone responded or asked a question.			
3. The group used time wisely.			
4. Everyone was prepared for the conference.			

Interesting or Important Ideas: _____

1.

2.

3.

FIGURE 6.11   Checklist for Small-Group Conferences

Figure 6.12 demonstrates a hierarchy of questions, going from lower-order closed-response questions to higher-order open-ended questions. Make sure to include both types in your interview.

A common mistake most beginning interviewers make is having too many questions. Keep your interviews short (you can always ask follow-up questions). End each interview with an open-ended question, such as, Is there anything else that you want to say about . . .? Finally, do not try to take detailed field notes during the interview; rather, write down only a few interesting ideas or impressions. Keep your focus on the responses and follow-up questions. Use an audiotape to record the interview (videotape is too obtrusive), then go back and take detailed notes.

E-mail Interviews. Because they are not dependent on time or space, e-mail interviews can be a very effective method to use to get data from parents, teachers in your school or school district, and even teachers all over North America and the world. As an example of this, in one of my teacher preparation classes here at

1. Which would you rather read? (a) fiction, (b) science fiction, (c) nonfiction, (d) historical fiction, or (e) mysteries   closed-response
2. What is your favorite reading genre?
3. Name a very good book or your favorite book.
4. Tell me what you like to read.
5. Tell me about your reading.   open-ended

FIGURE 6.12   Hierarchy of Interview Questions

Minnesota State University, Mankato, I have designed a Teacher Interview Project (TIP) where students are asked to interview two special education teachers. The goals of this project are to (a) develop a greater understanding or gain new insight in regard to the populations or grade levels students will be teaching, (b) develop greater understanding of the teaching–learning process, and (c) connect concepts and skills covered in class with real-world humans and classroom situations.

Students are asked to identify specific interests and design interview questions around their interests. A list of possible interview questions is given to them to use (see Figure 6.13). Then they do a little Internet detective work to find teachers in various parts of the state, country, or world. Next, they submit a proposal to me for approval before beginning this project.

To create effective e-mail interviews, students plan five to eight initial questions. If they use too many questions respondents are less likely to answer or possibly give only superficial answers. As well, students are encouraged to plan possible follow-up questions to ask in separate e-mail conversations.

1. What advice do you have for students coming into special education?
2. What do you wish you would have known before your first year?
3. What do you like about your job?
4. What part or parts of your job do you wish you could change?
5. What special insights have you gained as a result of being a special education teacher?
6. What has been a joyful or meaningful experience you have had as a special education teacher?
7. What resources would you need to be able to be more effective in your role as a special education teacher?
8. What are your thoughts related to the inclusive classroom? Do they work? If they do, what makes them successful? If they don't, why?
9. What are your thoughts related to pull-out services or programs? Do they work? If they do, what makes them successful? If they don't, why?
10. What are the traits of an effective special education teacher?
11. What special skills do effective special education teachers need to have or develop?
12. How do you stay current with knowledge related to teaching and learning? Special education?
13. What recommendations do you have in regard to professional development? What do you see as the best ways to grow as a teacher?
14. What advice or insights can you share in regard to communicating and working with parents?
15. What advice or insights can you share in regard to communicating and working with other teachers?
16. What community services do you use to foster learning?
17. What books, journals, or conferences would you recommend?
18. Other...

FIGURE 6.13   Possible Interview Questions

Skype and Other Technologies. New technology is appearing at a rapid rate and is becoming less expensive, more available, and easier to use. I am able to do things today that just 2 years ago seemed far-fetched. Keep this in mind as you begin to think about possible interviews for your action research projects. Skype, webinars, and other types of Internet communication can be used to conduct face-to-face interviews across great distances as well as being used for focus groups and surveys. Also, chat rooms, discussion groups, blogs, texts, tweets, and even virtual reality can also be used for interviews and to collect a variety of other data. You are limited here only by your imagination.

Video and Audio Recordings

Video recordings (videotape and digital) provide information related to students' nonverbal behaviors, their location or movement throughout a lesson, and a general overview of your performance or pedagogical techniques. However, a video camera is an obtrusive instrument, and thus it creates a nonreal teaching environment. One way to diminish this effect is by videotaping a great deal so that students get used to the camera. Another way is to use audio recordings (audiotape and digital). Audio recordings are quicker, easier, less intrusive, more natural, and easy to listen to in a car or with a small handheld unit. Although you might miss nonverbal behaviors and movement, you will find that you get just as much important information with an audiotape. Chapter 15 describes a variety of strategies for using video and audio recordings to examine your own teaching practice for professional development.

Data Retrieval Charts

Data retrieval charts (DRCs) are graphic organizers that are used to help you (or your students) collect and organize information. These come in a variety of forms. Bob Larson was teaching his sixth-grade students the positive discussion elements (PDEs) as part of his social studies class (Johnson, 2009). He gave students a question related to an important current event topic and then put them in groups of five to discuss this topic. Each day he chose one group to observe during that day's discussion. The DRC in Figure 6.14 was used to record the number and types of

Allow others into the conversation.	
Affirm and encourage others.	
Find areas of agreement and disagreement.	
Ask questions.	
Seek clarification.	

FIGURE 6.14   DRC for Analyzing Positive Discussion Elements

	Male	**Female**
Allow others into the conversation.		
Affirm and encourage others.		
Find areas of agreement and disagreement.		
Ask questions.		
Seek clarification.		

FIGURE 6.15   DRC for Analyzing Positive Discussion Elements Sorted by Gender

PDEs that occurred. This DRC provided data that could then be quantified and compared across grade level or over time. Gender differences can easily be compared by including an extra column (Figure 6.15).

Maps

Maps are a form of DRC that can be used to record where things occur in physical space or students' paths as they move about the classroom, school, or playground. To do this, create a simple map of that physical space. Record where behaviors occur by putting an X in those observed spots. Record the paths students use by creating lines on that map.

Artifacts: Students' Products or Performances

Samples of students' work (artifacts) can be used as data sources. Remember that you do not need to collect every bit of students' work; rather, take only representative samples at different time periods to give you a feel for students' performances and their changes over time. It is often helpful to create a flexible schedule to determine when you will collect students' work before you begin.

Product and Performance.   Figure 6.16 shows a product and performance assessment form (PPAF). This rating checklist can be used to analyze and evaluate any type of product or performance, such as science projects, inventions, dramas, dances, or experiments. Incidentally, all forms described in this chapter can be used by both students and teachers. Just like teachers (Watts & Johnson, 1995), students who analyze and assess their own work become more critical and skillful practitioners.

Writing Samples.   Figure 6.17 contains a rating checklist that can be used to analyze and evaluate any type of writing. This is also a good teaching tool in that it forces you to define exactly what is expected, and it puts the onus on you to teach each skill associated with those expectations. Students appreciate knowing the requirements and getting the precise feedback that this form provides.

Product and Performance Assessment Form

Student: _____   Age: _____

Grade: _____   Type of Product or Performance: _____

Key: 5 = very high, 4 = high, 3 = average, 2 = low, 1 = very low

When compared to other students of a similar age, rate the product or performance on the following criteria:

1. Creativity ____

2. Integration of ideas ____

3. Technical merit ____

4. Sophistication and level of detail ____

5. Aesthetics: artistic expression, emotion, feeling ____

6. Overall effect ____

Comments:

FIGURE 6.16   Product and Performance Assessment Form

Independent Research Projects.   Figure 6.18 shows a rating checklist used for students' independent research projects. Notice that all the elements of action research are found on this checklist. Understanding action research will enable you to incorporate more effectively methods of science, inquiry, and research into

Writing Assessment Form

Writing prompt:

Key: 5 = very high, 4 = high, 3 = average, 2 = low, 1 = very low

content, ideas _____	mechanics: spelling, grammar, punctuation _____	met deadlines; fulfilled assignment requirements _____
organization, structure _____	fluency, communication _____	appearance _____

Ideas or insights:

Skills to work on:

FIGURE 6.17   Writing Assessment Form

Checklist for Independent Research Projects

Key: 3 = trait is present to a high degree, 2 = trait is present,
1 = trait is present to a low degree, 0 = trait is not present

____ A question was asked, a problem was identified, or an area of exploration was defined.

____ Data collection was systematic.

____ Data was analyzed in a way that made it credible and trustworthy.

____ The results were described clearly and accurately.

____ Recommendations or conclusions were made based on the results.

____ The research project was linked to a theoretical context (or background information).

____ The research was communicated in a way that was understandable.

____ Met all deadlines and requirements.

Research topic or focus:

Major results and conclusions:

FIGURE 6.18   Checklist for Independent Research

your own teaching, and also provide you with a variety of ideas to use in getting students to create their own independent research projects.

Scores and Other Quantifiable Data.   Students' scores on tests, homework, quizzes, grades, and standardized assessment measures can also be used as a data source. However, they should never be used as the only source of data.

Students' Creative Work.   An examination of students' creative writing, journaling, visual art, sketchbooks, creative dramatics, or other open-end products and performances can provide a picture of how they view the world or perceive certain issues and life events. They are also very effective in helping you to understand students' attitudes, emotional states, self-concepts, or social perspectives. Here you can either analyze students' work already created looking for themes or patterns to emerge or you can hone in on specific issues by examining their responses to specific prompts or questions. Figure 6.19 shows some examples of the types you might use here. These might also give you some ideas for possible action research projects. When using specific prompts or questions, I would recommend that you allow students to submit their work anonymously. Finally, students' creative work or personal accounts can be used to examine the effect of a particular strategy or intervention or changes that might occur over time.

The Arts

The arts are another way of seeing the world and can be used to bring a different level of understanding to your action research. Elliot Eisner (1998) suggested that

1. How do you like to learn?
2. What brings you joy?
3. What is your favorite part about school?
4. What makes you nervous?
5. What do you do when you have a hard decision to make?
6. Describe school life.
7. Topic: drugs or alcohol.
8. Topic: peer pressure.
9. Topic: fitting in.
10. Topic: relationships.
11. Topic: having sex.
12. Topic: people who are gay and lesbian.
13. What would you like your future to look like?
14. What are plans for after high school?
15. Who are you?
16. What are you good at?
17. What do you like about you? What would you like to change about you?
18. What is a good friend?
19. What do you do when you have a problem?
20. What problems do you have in your life?

FIGURE 6.19   Questions and Prompts for Students' Creative Work

literature and poetry be used as a research device to capture and illuminate some portion of reality. Artists and researchers are very much alike in that the work of both is like lenses through which reality is interpreted and translated.

You will be using your artwork here to illuminate or bring to life some aspect of school or classroom life. Certain kinds of art lend themselves naturally to action research. These are (a) two-dimensional visual art, such as sketches, collages, paintings, drawings, and photography, and (b) the language arts, such as poetry, creative writing, short story, drama, and written dialogue. You might also include students' use of these media along with your analysis. I would encourage you to experiment with the arts as one of your data sources. Your credibility will not be diminished if you collect multiple forms of data and if you include an analysis of your artistic data.

Archival Data

Archival data include such things as past grades, test scores, cumulative folders, health records, parental occupation, disciplinary actions, or attendance records. Make sure you follow your school procedures for obtaining access to this data, and that they are used and reported in an ethical manner.

Surveys

Surveys allow you to get a variety of information quickly. They can be designed using both closed-response or open-ended questions.

Closed-Response Questions.   A closed-response question provides a number of choices for respondents to select. An example follows:

What is your favorite reading genre? (a) history (b) comedy (c) science fiction (d) mystery

Do you like to read science fiction? (a) yes (b) no (c) sometimes

The advantage of this type of question is that you can ask a number of questions and get quantifiable data on many types of issues. For example, after surveying a group of students with the first question shown here, one could safely report that 84.4% of students surveyed preferred comedy as a reading genre. The problem with these kinds of questions is that they can be inaccurate, misleading, or controlling. What if the first reading choice of a respondent was not even listed in the question? Or what if a respondent liked to read three or four different kinds of books equally well?

Open-Ended Questions.   An open-ended question allows respondents unlimited choices. An example follows:

What kinds of books do you like to read?

These questions provide a more accurate sense of what respondents are actually thinking. Some respondents may report four or five different kinds of books, whereas others may report only one. The researcher would then create categories from all the books listed and report the number of books in each category (see inductive analysis in Chapter 9). This data might be reported as in the following:

Forty-five students provided 152 responses to the survey question. The greatest number of responses (49%) indicated realistic fiction as the preferred genre.

Problems with open-ended survey questions are that they are somewhat messy in terms of analysis, and you can generally ask fewer of them.

Tips for Preparing Surveys.   The following tips will help you in preparing surveys:

1. *Identify the purpose for your survey.* Define, in a very general sense, what you want to find out or are interested in. This keeps the survey focused. Do not include any questions that do not support your survey purpose.

2. *Do not use too many questions or questions that are not necessary.* I have found that using four to eight questions is most effective. Too many questions frustrate respondents. A frustrated respondent will not complete the survey or will not give you accurate information. Err on the side of using too few rather than too many questions.

3. *Make your questions short, concise, and reader-friendly.* If a reader has to work to figure out exactly what you are asking, chances are that the question will not be

read, or if it is, it will be misunderstood. Read your questions out loud to see if they make sense. Avoid double negatives.

1. Example of a poorly worded question: Which of the following do you not like doing the most?

    a. keeping from eating candy.
    b. staying inside on a sunny day.
    c. doing sit ups.
    d. bullies who always try to hurt you.

4. *Proofread your questions several times.* Make sure the questions say exactly what you intend.

5. *Be very clear with your questions.* Make sure they are unambiguous and give you the information you are looking for.

1. *Example of an unclear question:* Do you spend a lot of time on your homework each day?

2. *Example of a more precise question:* How much time do you usually spend working on your homework each day?

    a. 0-30 minutes
    b. 30 minutes to 1 hour
    c. 1-2 hours
    d. 2 or more hours.

6. *Do not use leading questions.* A good survey is completely objective. Respondents should not know your position on any of the issues asked about. Do not use terms or questions that might bias the respondent.

1. *Bad example:* Do you support Dr. Murray's generous offer to enhance literacy by providing good books for all our classrooms?

7. *Avoid specialized words or unusual words germane to a particular field.* This is especially true when communicating with or surveying parents. The goal is not to show how smart you are; rather, to communicate effectively and to get data that is valid and reliable.

8. *Always include at least one open-ended question.* If you are using closed-response questions, provide an opportunity for respondents to make comments at the end.

9. *Create a neat, professional-looking document.* The presentation should be attractive, well organized, and easy to read.

Attitude and Rating Scales

Attitude and rating scales provide respondents with a question or statement for which they are asked to select one of several answers that determine the strength of their response.

Attitude Scales.   Students' attitudes are assessed by asking them to respond to a series of statements in a way that indicates their level of agreement or disagreement. Attitude scales like this can quickly provide you with information about students' attitudes and yield quantitative data that can be used to make comparisons. A 5-point rating scale is usually most effective for students in grades 3 and above.

> **Key:** SA = strongly agree, A = agree, NO = no opinion,
> D = disagree, SD = strongly disagree
>
> **1.**   Reading is fun. SA . . . A . . . NO . . . D . . . SD

These responses can also be numbered to provide you with quantitative data.

> **Key:** 5 = strongly agree, 4 = agree, 3 = no opinion,
> 2 = disagree, 1 = strongly disagree
>
> **1.**   Reading is fun.   5 . . . 4 . . . 3 . . . 2 . . . 1
> **2.**   I know how to use science skills. 5 . . . 4 . . . 3 . . . 2 . . . 1

With younger students, provide fewer choices and use graphics.

> **1.**   I like to read: very much ☺, some ☺, little ☹

Rating Scales.   A rating scale is used to determine the strength of a response. These are often used to determine how much, how often, or how many times something occurs.

> **Key:** 4 = often, 3 = some, 2 = little, 1 = not at all
> **1.**   I read at home each day.   4 . . . 3 . . . 2 . . . 1
> **2.**   I watch TV at home each day.   4 . . . 3 . . . 2 . . . 1
> **3.**   I complete my homework at school.   4 . . . 3 . . . 2 . . . 1
> **4.**   I use some sort of prewriting strategy.   4 . . . 3 . . . 2 . . . 1

Online Surveys and Rating Scales

There are a variety of web-based surveys, polls, questionnaires, forms, or ratings tools that can be used for your action research projects. Here are some sites that are free or offer free basic packages:

- Zoomerang at www.zommerang.com
- SurveyMonkey at www.surveymonkey.com
- FreeOnlineSurveys at www.freeonlinesurveys.com
- Bzoink at www.bzoink.com
- Polldaddy at www.polldaddy.com
- Questionform at www.questionform.com
- Questionpro at www.questionpro.com

You can find additional web-based survey tools by using the search terms: *online-surveys-free.* These are the questions you should ask when selecting a web-based survey tool: Is it easy to use? Can I use and apply this tool with minimum of time and effort? Is it easy for respondents to access and use? Is it flexible? Does it fit my particular needs and research question? Does it give me the results in a way that is easy to understand and use?

Online Platforms and Class Journals

Online platforms and class journals are effective methods to use in getting to the underbelly of classroom discourse. However, you may need to provide some guidelines and check in quite often so that this does not turn into a form of graffiti that might be highly offensive to some.

Online Platforms.   Chat rooms, discussion groups, and blogs can be used to create a living, dynamic classroom entity. These are good data sources for certain types of action research questions. Here students are able to share their ideas on a given topic and respond to what others have said. These transactions can be printed out for a more thorough analysis.

You can also have students analyze or participate in chat rooms, discussion groups, and blogs found on the web. There are some that are appropriate for inter-mediation, middle school, and high school students. However, extreme caution must be used here. Students should be supervised and be given very strict parameters and instruction on Internet safety.

If your district does not have an online platform, free chat rooms, blogs, and discussion groups can be found on the Internet using the search terms: *free-chat-rooms-online, free-discussion groups-online,* or *free-blogs.* Again, use extreme caution here. Make sure you get approval from a building principal or administrator before proceeding with one of these.

In using a chat room all participants must be on at the same time. I have found it most effective to create chat rooms consisting of three or four students. It is easier to communicate and find a common time with small groups, and you tend to get more and better information from all participants. It is hard to hide in a chat room of three or four.

Discussion groups or blogs are asynchronous. Students do not have to be on at the same time for them to be used. You tend to get a different type of information here as the responses do not have to be immediate. Students are able to think about and discuss topics over time. You can use both whole-class and small-group discussion groups. I have found that both are effective in action research projects. Blogs are best used for whole class discussions.

Class Journals.   The class journal is a nontechnical version of the online platforms above. Simply provide a blank notebook that is passed around the class or put in a learning center for several weeks. Students then enter their thoughts, ideas, impressions, or any other forms of response such as pictures or diagrams.

SUMMARY

- Data are any form of information, observations, or facts that are collected or recorded.
- A flexible plan for collecting data should be in place before you begin collecting them.
- The data collected in action research should be varied and collected in different ways over time.
- There are a wide variety of data that could be collected; however, selecting only two to four kinds will keep your action research focused.

QUESTIONS AND ACTIVITIES

1. Go to an interesting place. Practice taking field notes by recording what you see. Plan on spending at least 30 minutes at this place on two or more occasions.
2. Pick an assignment or project that you have your students do or that you plan to do with them. Create a checklist that has the specific skills or attributes necessary to complete the assignment.
3. Create a short open-ended checklist for students and experiment by using it with one class or subject area.
4. Think of an area or topic you are interested in. Create an interview with four to eight questions. Interview one or more students or adults using follow-up questions you feel are appropriate. Tape-record your interview.
5. Use an audiotape to record one of your classes. What did you discover? Based on this tape, create a DRC to indicate the number and type of some observation. For example, the level of questions, the gender of those who were asked or who responded to the questions, the number of times you said the word *um*, or the number of positive statements.
6. What are five characteristics or qualities of a good movie? Use these to create a ratings checklist. Evaluate two to four recent movies. You may want to do this in small groups. This can be extended to TV shows, dramas, or any other performance.
7. Create a rating checklist for a student product or performance that you plan to have your students do.
8. Create a survey related to any topic that interests you. Experiment with different types of questions and have at least five people respond to it. If you are reading this book as part of a class, you may want to bring your survey to class and practice with your classmates by responding to each other's surveys.
9. Go to an interesting place. Describe that place using visual art or a form of language art.

POSSIBLE RESEARCH QUESTIONS FOR ACTION RESEARCH PROJECTS

1. How are your lessons going? What things seem to be working? What things could be done more effectively?
2. As a teacher, what things do you need to focus on or pay more attention to?
3. As a human being, what things do you need to focus on or pay more attention to?
4. What takes place during small-group discussions?
5. What social skills do students in your room seem to lack?
6. What are the social expectations of children in your classroom? How are children coping? What are the common traits among those who seem to be having trouble in this area?
7. What does it feel like to have a learning disability? What things make learning more difficult? What things help learning with this group? What do students with learning disabilities wish teachers would understand?
8. What makes school difficult for students with emotional/behavioral disorders?
9. How do students in your classroom define themselves?
10. What types of misconduct occurs most often on the playground? In the cafeteria? In the hallway? In your classroom?
11. What common traits do you see among the highly creative students in your classroom? What would make school more interesting for this group? What would they like included in their learning experience? What types of projects or performances would they like to engage in?
12. How do students' concepts of themselves change across grade levels or across ability levels?
13. Whom do you see as the unpopular children? Why do they seem to be having trouble with peer relationships?
14. Given moral dilemmas or problems involving values, how do students in your class tend to solve them? How do they decide what is right and wrong?
15. What do students perceive as the qualities of an effective teacher? What do teachers believe to be the qualities of effective teachers? What do administrators believe to be qualities of effective teachers? What do parents believe to be qualities of effective teachers?
16. What life issues are of most concern to students in your classroom? What school issues are of most concern to students in your classroom?
17. What type of school experiences do the parents in your school desire for their children?
18. Are teachers in other classrooms or schools using inclusive strategies in their general education classrooms? If so, what strategies are being used?
19. Who do students turn to when they have a problem?
20. Who do students admire or see as heroes and role models? What traits do these figures have?
21. What are students' attitudes and behaviors related to alcohol and other drugs?

CHAPTER SEVEN

METHODS OF ANALYZING DATA

This chapter describes data analysis. Analysis means to break something down into its component parts so that it can be understood. In action research, data are analyzed and organized into categories so that others might come to understand the reality you are trying to represent. Three elements related to data analysis are presented in this chapter: (a) accuracy and credibility; (b) validity, reliability, and triangulation; and (c) inductive analysis.

ACCURACY AND CREDIBILITY: THIS IS WHAT IS

The ultimate goal of action research is to use your findings to make effective changes or choices. To this end, the collection and analysis of data must be accurate and credible. Accuracy in action research means that the data you are collecting create a fairly true picture of the bit of reality you are observing. This helps you make decisions that are best for your particular situation. Credibility in action research means trustworthy or capable of being believed. This enables you and others to use your data with confidence. The following seven tips will help you establish more accuracy and credibility as you collect and analyze your data.

1. *Record your observations carefully and precisely.* Always double-check to make sure you are recording exactly what you are seeing.
2. *Describe all phases of data collection and analysis.* In your recording, recount all the steps used in collecting and analyzing the data. In your eventual reporting you want to create a level of clarity whereby another person could duplicate your steps.
3. *Make sure you record and report everything that is of importance.* Record and report fully; do not omit data that may be counter to what you believe. The goal is to understand fully all aspects of what you are observing.
4. *Be as objective as possible in describing and interpreting what you see.* Pronounced biases and hidden agendas are fairly easy to spot and prevent you from

seeing all aspects of what you are trying to study. They also make your action research less accurate and credible.

5. *Use enough data sources.* (See discussion of triangulation in the next section.) Your observations and analysis will be much more accurate and credible if you are able to find similar patterns using two or more forms of data. For a short observation (2 to 4 weeks), I usually ask my students to use a minimum of two sources. For longer action research projects, the number of sources is dictated by the question and the kinds of data you are trying to collect.

6. *Use the right kinds of data sources.* (See the discussion of validity in the next section.) The type of data you choose to collect should provide as accurate an understanding of your research topic as possible. For example, if I were interested in understanding how middle school students use humor, I might interview classroom teachers. Although this could provide some interesting information, the data would be a poor reflection of the reality I was trying to observe. A much more accurate and credible view would be obtained by using audiotapes of actual conversations, by observing middle school students and taking descriptive field notes, and by creating a survey form in which students self-report to indicate the kinds of humor used and the instances in which it was used.

7. *Look long enough and deep enough.* A 3-week observation might provide some interesting data; however, a 3-month observation would make your data even more accurate and credible. Longer observations provide more chances to see and confirm patterns than do shorter observations. Again, the length of your observation and data collection is dictated solely by your question. The final criterion should always be the degree to which you have created an accurate picture of what was studied.

VALIDITY, RELIABILITY, AND TRIANGULATION

Three essential parts of establishing accuracy and credibility in any research project are validity, reliability, and triangulation. In action research, they take on a different form than they do in traditional experimental research.

Validity

How do we know your data actually assess and describe what they say they do? Validity is the degree to which a thing measures what it reports to measure. For example, in trying to assess the writing ability of elementary students, I could give them a standardized test of grammar and punctuation in which they would read a series of questions and choose one of four responses. This would produce some fairly accurate results that could be quantified and used to make comparisons; however, this type of measure does not look at writing in an authentic context, and thus it is not a very valid measure of students' ability to organize and communicate their ideas using writing. A more valid assessment would be to look at students' actual writing samples and use the writing assessment form described in Chapter 6 to rate specific elements.

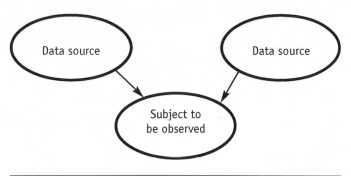

FIGURE 7.1   Triangulation

Triangulation

Triangulation means looking at something from more than one perspective. Think of a triangle with the subject to be observed as one point and the various data sources as the other two points (see Figure 7.1). Triangulation ensures that you are seeing all sides of a situation. It also provides greater depth and dimension, thereby enhancing your accuracy and credibility. In action research, triangulation is achieved by collecting different types of data, using different data sources, collecting data at different times, and having other people review your data to check for accuracy and adjust your findings.

Reliability

Reliability is the degree to which a study or experiment can be repeated with similar results. Unlike action research, traditional experimental research strives to create a hermetically sealed world with all the variables controlled so that X can be said to cause Y beyond all doubt. If the experiment is reliable, X should cause Y each time it is repeated. If this is indeed the case, the experiment is deemed reliable, the results are generalized to similar situations, and the researcher is granted tenure at a major university.

Action researchers, however, observe messy, real-world events in which humans are mucking about. These humans are inherently and wondrously unpredictable and not at all inclined to exist in hermetically sealed worlds. Thus, each time we search and research, we expect to see different things. The closest we come to repetition is in noticing recurring items, themes, or patterns that emerge from our data. (See the discussion of inductive analysis that follows.) Therefore, action research findings are not generalized broadly; instead, they are used to help understand particular situations as well as inform similar situations.

INDUCTIVE ANALYSIS

Inductive analysis means to look at a field or group of data and try to induce or create order by organizing what is observed into groups. This should occur as you begin to collect data. Look for recurring items, themes, or patterns to emerge.

Similar things should be coded and moved into initial categories. These categories, however, should be very flexible as later data may change their nature and composition. It is helpful to begin this process while you are collecting data because the categories that form initially inform further data collection.

Larry, Moe, and Curly Help with Inductive Analysis

Let me use the Three Stooges to illustrate inductive analysis. I watched a Three Stooges video to understand the Stooges and their humor. My initial questions were, What kind of humor is found? What do these episodes comprise? Who are the Stooges? Note how these questions help inform and provide focus for my search.

I watched a 15-minute episode on videotape called *Grips, Grunts, and Groans* (Columbia Pictures, 1937) and began to look for instances of humor. The events in a Three Stooges episode happen much faster than in real life; thus, I used the pause button often to suspend video reality to make notes. As I watched, I used field notes to record those funny things I saw. Funny things (humor), in this instance, was defined as those elements inserted into the movie for the express purpose of creating a comedic effect. As I watched, my notes began to look like the following:

Bump, stumble, kick, punch, slap, poke, twist ear, word play silly, absurd silly, word play silly, absurd silly, etc.

After the first time through the video, I saw that the types of humor recorded in my notes could be put into four categories.

Thing-to-Head Violence.   This violence represents instances in which a non-human thing hit or was dropped on somebody's head. For example, Larry hits Moe on the head with a board, or an anvil falls on Curly's head.

Human-to-Human Violence.   A part of somebody's body was struck, twisted, or otherwise violently engaged by a part of somebody else's physical being. This violence included instances of eye poking, ear twisting, kicks, chokes, punches, pushes, slaps, or general violence such as twisting one's foot.

Self-Mishap.   These are instances in which characters cause their own mishap, including stumbles, bumps, and falling episodes.

Silly Stuff.   Silly stuff represents items, events, phrases, or actions that are incongruous, apart from what is normally expected, or an exaggeration of normality. An example of situational silliness would be the Stooges accidentally pulling off the pants of a drunk wrestler while trying to drag him, revealing funny, long underwear with garters. An example of verbal silliness would be what is said after a man throws water on the Stooges, who were just knocked unconscious by blows to the head. Curly yells out, "Man the lifeboats." Moe says, "Women and children first." The implication is that the Stooges acted as if they were on a boat that was sinking.

Each category contained different types of humor. Once I had my initial categories and subcategories, I created a version of an open-ended checklist (see Figure 7.2). I then viewed the episode a second time and put a tally mark next to each type of humor every time I observed it. I was thus able to break down

SILLY STUFF		HUMAN-TO-HUMAN VIOLENCE		THING-TO-HEAD VIOLENCE		SELF-MISHAP	
Situational silliness	26	General hurt	5	Things dropped on head	12	Bump or stumble	9
Verbal silliness	7	Slap	5	Things hit on head	11		
		Kick	4				
		Twist ear	2				
		Poke eye	2				
		Punch	2				
		Choke	1				
		Push	1				
Total	33	**Total**	22	**Total**	23	**Total**	9

FIGURE 7.2 Three Stooges Humor

the humor into its component parts and get a good sense of what the total episode comprised. It looks as if, more than anything, the Three Stooges material was violent. Forty-three instances of humor were violence inflicted on another person (human-to-human and thing-to-head violence); however, silliness was the largest single category of humor. In this episode, the Stooges were sillier than I had imagined they would be; however, the amount of violence stands out to the viewer watching in the 21st century. To add credibility to my observation and analysis, I viewed this particular video several times. I also had somebody else view it to see whether they came up with similar categories and numbers.

This inductive analysis gave me a good understanding of this single episode of the Stooges and their humor. To extend this study, I would need to observe several Stooges episodes and use the same categories to collect and organize data. These data would then be put in the form of a bar graph for easy consumption by the reader. This would also allow me to compare various Stooges episodes or to compare the Stooges to other comedians of that era or today. I might also choose to investigate further to see whether early Stooges and late Stooges differ. I might want to pursue other questions: Did the type of humor change over time? Did the Stooges get more violent over time? Did they get sillier over time? Do HPM (humor-per-minute) ratios of the Stooges differ in various eras? Do males react differently than females to Stooges humor? You may notice that a good study usually creates as many questions as answers.

Case Studies or Representative Samples

In my report I will use representative samples to bring further understanding to the Stooges reality that I observed. I will include a few examples of the funny things in each category so that the reader fully understands what that category entails. Including representative samples also allows the reader to go beyond the numbers, to make the research come alive.

Verbal Silliness

The scene opens with two railway security guards walking, clubs in hand, by a train car marked horses. One foreman taps on the door and says, "Anybody in there?" Curly's high, whining voice is heard, "Nobody here but us horses." The two guards, having gotten an answer to their question, begin walking away. After two steps, they realize the incongruity, stop, do a double take, and wait for the door to open.

Verbal Silliness

A gangster has made a big bet on Gustov, a professional wrestler. The Stooges have been paid by the gangster to keep him from getting drunk for that evening's match. Gustov is about to drink a large container of something when Moe says, "Listen, Gustov, you can't drink that. That's alcohol." Gustov snorts and says, "That's not alcohol. That's just a little tequila, vodka, and cognac." Curly says, "Oh, that's different. Go ahead." Gustov pours the jug down his throat. The bit of incongruity is that although tequila, vodka, and cognac are not referred to as alcohol, they all contain it.

Situational Silliness

Curly goes mad every time he smells wild hyacinth. In a restaurant, a woman accidentally pours some on him. Curly begins making high-pitched "woo, woo, woo" sounds. He slaps his forehead repeatedly, barks, and makes wild twisting, dancing motions with his legs. He goes crazy, trips over a table, and starts breaking a chair, then yells, "Moe, Larry, tickle my foot!" Larry and Moe tackle him, twist his legs, yank off his shoes, and begin tickling his feet. There is much flopping around and manic laughing by Curly, and he eventually comes to his senses.

Self-Mishap

Running from the two railway guards, the Stooges round a corner. Two women are standing next to a baby carriage. In unison, the Stooges trip over the baby carriage and fall face first on the sidewalk.

Human-to-Human Violence

Moe tells Curly to put up his hands. He then hits him in the stomach. When Curly makes a sound in protest, Moe uses his fist to pound him on top of the head, twists and slaps his nose, and slaps his forehead. Curly yells in a loud, high voice, "Ow, ow, ow . . . ohhhh!"

Thing-to-Head Violence

In the locker room before the big wrestling match, Larry, Moe, and Curly have finally succeeded in getting Gustov, the drunk professional wrestler, ready to go out and wrestle. They then accidentally knock him into a set of lockers. Five dumbbells that are on top of the lockers fall, one at a time, on Gustov's head.

Vision Quest

As another example of inductive analysis, I was interested in examining the idealized visions of the undergraduate students in my literacy methods course. That is, how did they see themselves teaching literacy when they got their own classroom teaching position? During student teaching I have often noticed a certain amount of stress when the idealized teaching visions of student teachers do not match their current teaching reality. For this action research project I was interested in seeing what the initial idealized vision was and how it changed throughout the semester as a result of my instruction and their field experiences.

Twenty-five students were in my undergraduate literacy methods course, 22 females and 3 males. Most of the students were in their early twenties; however, two females and one male were in their late thirties or early forties. To get at their idealized visions, I gave them the following writing prompt: "Imagine yourselves 5 years from now. You are in a regular classroom teaching some aspect of literacy. What do you see? What's going on? What does it look like?"

Students wrote one to two paragraphs on a sheet of paper. I collected them and analyzed these data, looking for patterns. This was repeated at 1-month intervals four times during the semester. I called this Vision Quest. The following are some examples of students' responses:

8/31/99

I see myself stressing meaning and feeling within the message and words of books. I will probably assign or suggest books with these characteristics—books that share good family ties, struggle, success, hard work, etc. [female]

In 5 years I see my students participating in short skits or role plays to share what a book was about or an individual chapter. The plays will be written and directed by the students themselves (with help as needed). [female]

In 5 years I see myself modeling quiet reading time for my students. I also see myself incorporating reading into other subject areas. I do not see myself doing comprehension sheets or book reports. [female]

I see myself teaching second grade. The students are seated on the floor next to me while I introduce our book. They listen to me read while they follow along in their book. Then they have the opportunity to explain the story in their own words, with a storyboard, or acting it out. Later, they will be able to write about the story, perhaps including themselves. They will be able to draw pictures. These will be displayed. [female]

As I read through students' descriptions, I looked for patterns, themes, or similar kinds of things. For instance, many students described aspects of creating a warm, inviting classroom environment. In my notes I jotted down warm-fuzzy, environment, atmosphere as an initial category. Every time I found something related to creating a warm, comfortable environment, I put a tally mark by this

I. **Warm Environment**		**6**
II. **Holistic/Nontraditional Activities**		**16**
A. Reading choices	4	
B. Creative projects	3	
C. Student-centered activities	4	
D. Class library/books	2	
E. Independent reading	3	
III. **Skills-Oriented/Traditional Activities**		**23**
A. Vocabulary instruction	4	
B. Basals and worksheets	8	
C. Teacher-led discussion	3	
D. Round-robin reading	8	
IV. **Teacher Reading to Class**		**8**
V. **Specific Pedagogical Methods**		**2**

Figure 7.3   Vision Quest, First Month

descriptor. I read all the selections and made adjustments to my initial categories. Figure 7.3 shows which categories and subcategories I used. I then went through the data a second time and once again put a tally mark every time an instance of an activity fell within that category. This twice-through approach allowed for more accuracy.

Defining and Describing Categories

One cannot expect the reader to have complete understanding of my categories, so, as with the Three Stooges, I must define and describe each category. To demonstrate, I have included the following examples:

HOLISTIC OR NONTRADITIONAL

This category represents activities that might fit within a whole language classroom, specifically, activities that would not reflect a basal or skills-based approach. The subcategories include the following:

Reading Choices

Students would be able to make choices about the kinds of books they want to read.

Creative Projects
Activities would include drama, role play, art, games, and puppets.
Student-Centered Activities
Students would be in charge of a process or a final product or performance. For example, students would write and direct their own plays, or students would be able to retell a story in their own words using a storyboard.
Class Library/Books
A prescribed place in the classroom with lots of books would be set aside as a reading area.
Independent Reading
Time would be scheduled for students to read books of their choice independently.

Following is an example of how I might put the data into categories:

I see myself sitting in a cozy chair with my students sitting on a large soft rug in front of me [Warm Environment]. In my hands I hold a brand-new book. I introduce the book to the children and I begin to read aloud [Teacher Reading to Class]. When I have finished reading, we discuss the book [Teacher-Led Discussion]. [female]

I see myself in 5 years with a large selection of books that I have read and am comfortable with [Class Library/Books]. Students choose their own books [Reading Choices]. I will allow ample class reading time [Independent Reading]. [female]

I see myself helping students learn new words by using overheads. As a class we would read the words together, then use them in sentences [Vocabulary Instruction]. I just think it will be exciting to have them learn new words. [female]

I see myself reading to students every day [Teacher Reading to Class]. Students in my classroom will have free time to read every day [Independent Reading]. Perhaps there will be a special reading corner [Warm Environment]. I plan to use trade books in reading class and across the curriculum. I really like that idea. I would like to have a large library in my classroom [Class Library/Books]. [female]

I see myself setting up a small library in my classroom where children are able to read when they are done with their work [Class Library/Books]. I would make my library full of color, pictures of books, and many comfortable chairs to create an inviting reading environment that would make children look forward to reading [Warm Environment]. [female]

I. **Warm Environment**		11
II. **Holistic/Nontraditional Activities**		64
A. Reading choices	24	
B. Creative projects	12	
C. Student-centered activities	5	
D. Class library/books	5	
E. Independent reading	18	
III. **Skills-Oriented/Traditional Activities**		9
A. Vocabulary instruction	1	
B. Basals and worksheets	3	
C. Teacher-led discussion	5	
D. Round-robin reading	0	
IV. **Teacher Reading to Class**		15
V. **Specific Pedagogical Methods**		17

FIGURE 7.4   Vision Quest, Second Month

The Next Month

The next month, the same categories were used. As you might expect, the change reflects my instruction, the literacy philosophy I was proposing, and students' interaction with these ideas (see Figure 7.4). In Chapter 9 you can see how this data was reported in graph form. One final thought: Methods used for inductive analysis vary and are a matter of personal preference. Although it might seem messy at first, you will get more comfortable with this process by doing it.

SUMMARY

- Analysis means to break down something into its component parts so that it can be understood.
- The collection and analysis of data must be accurate and credible to be of use in making effective changes or choices.
- Validity is the degree to which a thing measures what it reports to measure.
- Triangulation means collecting more than one form of data or looking at something from more than one perspective.
- Reliability is the degree to which a study or experiment can be repeated with similar results.
- Action researchers recognize that the universe they are observing is a messy, unreliable entity, and thus they look for repeating patterns and themes to help them understand it.

- Inductive analysis means to observe a field and create order by organizing items into groups or categories.
- In using inductive analysis, initial categories should be flexible as later data may change their nature and composition.

QUESTIONS AND ACTIVITIES

1. Cut out a newspaper article, a description of research, or a research article that you think lacks credibility. Tell why.
2. Find an interesting person or student to observe for a short time. Use two of the data sources described in Chapter 8 to create understanding.
3. Cut out an ad in a newspaper or magazine that you think lacks validity. Tell why.
4. Practice inductive analysis by randomly generating a list of 25 nouns. Then, in a small group or individually, put order to this field by moving them into groups or categories. Describe your field in terms of categories and numbers in each category.
5. Go to a place that is interesting and unique where you can observe people. Use field notes to record the behaviors you see. Then use inductive analysis to put order to your data. Report your data in terms of categories and numbers in each category.
6. Extend the previous activity by creating a checklist or data retrieval chart that uses the categories described. Go back to your interesting place at a different time of day. Use tally marks to record the instances of behaviors you observe. Add new categories if you need to. Create a graph to compare and report your observations and conclusions.
7. To extend the previous activity further, use the same checklist or data retrieval chart to observe a different but similar place. Create a bar graph to compare and report your observations and conclusions.

POSSIBLE RESEARCH QUESTIONS FOR ACTION RESEARCH PROJECTS

1. There are three types of learning: individualistic, competitive, or cooperative. How much of each occurs in your classroom in an average week? How could you create more cooperative learning tasks? How might this affect learning?
2. How do students view themselves? Ask students to provide written descriptions of themselves. Examine the adjectives used. Use inductive analysis to look for groups and quantify the numbers in each group. Look for differences between male and female, across ability levels, and across cultural and ethnic groups.
3. In what areas are students currently given choice and responsibility in your classroom? To what degree are these given? How would the learning environment differ if you provided more opportunities for choice and responsibility?

4. What would students like to learn about as part of a social studies curriculum? How would they like to learn?

5. What would students like to learn about as part of a science curriculum? How would they like to learn?

6. How can social studies be connected to students' lives outside of school? Does this affect the perception of social studies? Does it affect learning in any way?

7. What forums are presently available in your class for students to discuss or debate the issues of the day? To what degree are students allowed to come to their own conclusions? To what degree are they told what they must conclude?

8. How do students use the Internet?

9. Where do your students get their news about the world? To what degree do they read magazines, newspapers, watch television news, or get their news from the Internet?

CHAPTER EIGHT

QUANTITATIVE DESIGN IN ACTION RESEARCH

Quantitative research is based on the collection and analysis of numerical data. Earlier it was said that action research falls clearly in the realm of qualitative research because it does not manipulate the environment to isolate variables and prove cause-and-effect relationships. This chapter will backtrack a bit. There are three quantitative research designs that can fit within the action research paradigm: correlational research, causal–comparative research, and quasi-experimental research. This chapter discusses all three designs.

CORRELATIONAL RESEARCH

Correlational research seeks to determine whether and to what degree a statistical relationship exists between two or more variables (Gay & Airasian, 2008). It is used primarily to describe an existing condition or something that has happened in the past. This means that it examines a group of people and two or more things (variables) that have already happened to them to determine whether there is a relationship between these two things. For example, correlational research found a strong relationship between the amount of independent reading students do outside school and their scores on standardized achievement tests (Allington, 2002). Those students who did a great deal of reading seemed to have high scores on standardized achievement tests. Thus, there was a fairly high co-relation, or correlation, between these two variables. When one score went up, the other also went up, and when one score went down, the other also went down.

To determine this correlation, researchers examined the achievement test scores of a large number of students and then looked at the amount of time spent reading at home. Both of these variables (reading time and test scores) were things that had already occurred. There was no need to manipulate an environment to produce these.

Correlation Coefficient

The degree or strength of a particular correlation is measured by a correlation coefficient. A positive correlation means that when one variable increases, the other one also increases. A negative correlation means that when one variable increases, the other one decreases. A correlation coefficient of 1.00 would indicate a perfect one-to-one positive correlation. This rarely happens. A correlation coefficient of .0 means that there is absolutely no correlation between two variables. A correlation coefficient of −1.00 would indicate a perfect negative correlation. This also rarely happens.

Misusing Correlational Research

A word of warning here: Correlation does not indicate causation. Just because two variables are related, we cannot say that one causes the other. There may be other variables that have not been accounted for. In the previous example, we cannot say that lots of reading causes test scores to increase, although we may suspect as much. Likewise, we cannot say that higher standardized test scores cause an increase in reading. We can say, however, that the two seem to appear together. A true experiment would then be used to isolate variables with controlled populations. However, in this case a true experiment would be unethical because you cannot deny one group of students the pleasure and benefits of reading while encouraging another.

You can find many examples in the popular media of people (usually with a political agenda) who misuse correlational research by trying to attribute cause and effect. To illustrate this misuse, note that when the water temperature goes down, far fewer people drown. An increase in water temperature correlates fairly strongly with an increase in drowning. It would be spurious to try to say that water temperature causes drowning. A variable not accounted for here, but associated to both, is that when the water temperature gets cold, people are much less likely to be swimming. Also, when the water really gets cold, it turns to ice. It is very hard to drown on an ice-covered lake. (Another misuse of correlational research is described in the section on whole language in California.)

Negative Correlation

Sometimes an increase in one variable causes a decrease in another. This is an example of a negative correlation. An example of a negative correlation would be television watching and GPAs. As the amount of television watching goes up, students' GPAs go down. There is a negative correlation in that an increase in one seems to be related to a decrease in the other. Again, we cannot say that one causes the other; however, we can make predictions based on the strength of the correlation coefficient.

Making Predictions

Correlation coefficient is identified by the symbol r. When $r = 0$ to .35, the relationship between the two variables is nonexistent or low, and it is useless for making predictions. When $r = .35$ to .65, there is a slight relationship. This level is useful for limited predictions, usually with larger groups. When $r = .65$ to .85, there is a strong relationship. This would be useful for making predictions for large groups. We could say with some certainty that an increase or decrease in one variable is related to an increase or decrease in the other. In the television example, if $r = -.75$, we could reasonably predict that an increase in television would lead to a decrease in GPA. If $r = -.40$, we would be less confident of a prediction. A correlation coefficient of $r = .86$ and above shows evidence of a very strong relationship. Again, keep in mind that correlational coefficient describes the strength and direction of a relationship, not cause and effect.

CAUSAL–COMPARATIVE RESEARCH

Causal–comparative research is used to find the reason for existing differences between two or more groups (Creswell, 2004). It is used when the random assignment of participants for groups necessary for the true experiment cannot be met, which is certainly the case in most classrooms. Like correlational research, it is used to describe an existing situation. That is, it looks at conditions that have already occurred and collects data to investigate why one group is different from the other (Leedy & Ormrod, 2001). It is called causal–comparative research because it compares groups to find a cause for differences in measures or scores.

Like correlational research, causal–comparative research uses statistical analysis to describe conditions that already exist. However, whereas correlational research examines one group of participants using two or more variables, causal–comparative research examines two or more groups that differ on one or more variables. For example, if a principal was interested in looking at the effectiveness of a new math program, he or she could use causal–comparative research to make an informed decision. The math scores of several schools, some of which used the new program and some of which did not, would be compared and analyzed. The independent variable would be the type of math program. The dependent variable would be the average math scores on similar standardized tests from each school. If the schools using the new math program demonstrated higher test scores, and the differences in scores were statistically significant, it would be reasonable to assume that the new math program was more effective.

Whole Language in California

In California in 1996, some critics claimed that whole language approaches to reading instruction were causing reading scores to go down (McQuillan, 1998). These critics wanted all California schools to abandon whole language practices and instead adopt phonics-only reading instruction. The fallacious logic used was that whole language approaches were being used in California schools and reading scores on standardized tests were decreasing (although this was not the case); therefore, whole language approaches must have caused the decrease in scores. Remember again that correlation does not imply causation. In this case there was a whole host of unidentified variables that may have attributed to the decrease in standardized scores, such as an increase in class size, a decrease in funding available for school libraries, an increase in immigrant populations, and others.

Causal–comparative research was used in this situation to parse out three different groups and make comparisons. The groups consisted of fourth-grade students' scores in reading whose classroom teacher identified the primary mode of reading instruction as whole language, literature based, or phonics. The independent variable was the type of reading instruction. The dependent variable was the average score on the NAEP standardized reading tests. The results of this research are shown in Table 8.1.

The results show there was a difference in the groups favoring both teachers who identified their approach to reading instruction as literature based and whole language over those teachers who identified their approach to reading instruction as phonics. Statistical analysis found that this difference was statistically significant. However, again we must be careful in how we interpret these results. This was not a true experiment in that randomized selection of participants into groups was not used. Also, there are many variables, called confounding variables, that could have accounted for the difference in scores. For example, we have no way of knowing whether the initial scores of students in each group were equal, or whether the sample of classroom teachers was representative of the entire population. Also, the difference in scores could be a result of teachers instead of approaches. That is, it may be that more effective teachers tend to use newer approaches such as whole language, whereas less effective teachers tend to use more traditional approaches. And finally, only fourth-grade teachers were surveyed here. The results may have been different if primary teachers were included.

As you can see, when reading research reports you always have to go beyond the report to look for confounding variables. This report concludes that there was no evidence to support the notion that whole language methods caused reading test scores to decrease; however, there may be a link between literature-based and whole language instruction and positive performance on standardized reading tests.

TABLE 8.1   Approaches to Reading Instruction

APPROACH TO READING INSTRUCTION	PERCENTAGE OF TEACHERS REPORTING	AVERAGE NAEP READING SCORE
Literature based	49%	221
Whole language	40%	220
Phonics	11%	208

QUASI-EXPERIMENTAL RESEARCH

The third type of research design that can be used is the quasi-experimental research design. This is the closest to the true experiment; however, in a quasi-experimental design there is no random assignment of subjects to groups. Random selection ensures that the groups being compared are relatively similar, that you are not comparing apples and oranges. As stated earlier, in most schools and classrooms, random selection is not possible; therefore, other ways must be used to ensure that the comparison groups are relatively similar. The two most common methods are pretests and matching.

In using pretests to compare groups before an investigation, simply give a test to comparison groups on the variable you are looking to examine. If they are relatively similar, you can continue with the research. If there is a significant difference between groups, there are three options: (a) find another group to compare, (b) reconfigure your existing groups so that they match, or (c) take the dissimilarity of groups into account when describing findings and conclusions.

Matching is used to create relatively similar groups. Here again a pretest is given to the entire population on the variable you are looking to examine. Based on the test results, students are matched with others who have relatively similar scores. Groups are then created by putting each person in the match in a separate group. For example, one would go in the experimental group, and the other would go in the control group.

Quasi-Action Research

As you can see from the previous descriptions, quasi-experimental research involves the manipulation of the environment. Thus, it has to be used with caution in an action research setting. With this type of research you are not observing an authentic classroom environment, but rather one that has been manipulated to examine a particular variable. In this sense, quasi-experimental research is also quasi-action research.

This is a good place for a reminder of what action research is: Action research is a systematic observation of one's own teaching practice. The goal is to understand what is happening in a particular classroom or school. Some types of quantitative research methodologies can be of use to this end. However, action research is not designed to prove or disprove a hypothesis, nor is it meant to provide data that can be generalized to a larger population. Quantitative methodologies in an action research project should be used simply to provide a picture of what is happening in a particular situation.

The following sections describe five different quasi-experimental designs. Figures are used to provide a clear view of the structure of each design. In these figures, Exp = experimental group, Cnt = control group, O = observation or measure, and T = treatment.

Pretest–Posttest Design

The pretest–posttest design is the most primitive quasi-experimental design. Here one group is given a pretest, a treatment, and a posttest (see Figure 8.1). Pretest

Group	Time →		
Exp	0	T	0

FIGURE 8.1   Pretest–Posttest Design

and posttest scores are compared. This is often done before and after a particular unit. The variable that cannot be accounted for here is maturation. That is, simply by cognitive maturation and exposure, most students make some academic gains, regardless of the technique or methodology.

Pretest–Posttest Control Group Design

This is the same as the preceding design except that a control group is used (see Figure 8.2). This allows the researcher to control for the variable of time and maturation. Groups can be compared based on both final scores and gain scores from pretest to posttest. There are many variables that cannot be controlled, the most significant of which is the administration of the treatment. If different teachers are teaching in the experimental and control group, it is hard to account for teaching style.

Time Series Design

Time series design examines one group over time, both before and after the treatment (see Figure 8.3). This is essentially an elaborate one-group pretest–posttest design except that here the researcher collects an extensive amount of data to look for patterns over time. An example of this would be a teacher who gave a spelling test each week for several weeks using traditional methods of spelling instruction. In the middle of the semester a new method was instituted and observations continued. Here the teacher looked for dramatic increases or decreases in spelling test scores over time.

Time Series Control Group Design

Time series control group design is the same as the time series design except that it allows you to conduct a parallel series of observations on experimental and control groups (see Figure 8.4).

Group	Time →		
Exp	0	T	0
Cnt	0	—	0

FIGURE 8.2   Pretest–Posttest Control Group Design

Group	Time ➔									
Exp	0	0	0	0	T	0	0	0	0	0

Group	Time ➔									
Exp	T1	0	0	0	0	T2	0	0	0	0

FIGURE 8.3   Time Series Design

Group	Time ➔								
Exp	0	0	0	0	T	0	0	0	0
Cnt	0	0	0	0	—	0	0	0	0

Group	Time ➔									
Exp	T1	0	0	0	0	T2	0	0	0	0
Cnt	T1	0	0	0	0	T1	0	0	0	0

FIGURE 8.4   Time Series Control Group Design

Equivalent Time-Sample Design

Using equivalent time-sample design, the treatment is sometimes present and sometimes not (see Figure 8.5). It is presented at irregular intervals; however, the measures or observations are made at regular intervals. This allows the researcher to account for and control outside influences.

THE FUNCTION OF STATISTICS

Statistical analysis can serve two functions: to describe and to infer. It is beyond the scope of this text to describe the specifics of statistical analysis; however, if you understand the concepts and limitations behind these two approaches, software programs can be used to help you with the statistical analysis. I also recommend the following books: *Educational Research: Competencies for Analysis and Applications* (Gay & Airasian, 2008) and *Educational Research: Planning, Conducting, and Evaluating Quantitative and Qualitative Research* (Creswell, 2004).

Group	Time →							
Exp	T	0	—	0	T	0	—	0

FIGURE 8.5   Equivalent Time-Sample Design

Descriptive Statistics

Descriptive statistics are statistical analyses used to describe an existing set of data. There are three major types of descriptive statistics: (a) measures of central tendency, (b) frequency distribution, and (c) measures of variability.

Measures of Central Tendency.   Measures of central tendency are a way of describing a set of data with a single number. The three measures of central tendency are the mode, the median, and the mean.

The *mode* is the score that is attained most frequently. For example, Mr. Smith gave the same 100-point math test to the 66 students in eighth grade at his school (see Figure 8.6). On this 100-point test the scores ranged from 50 points to 99 points; however, 12 students had a score of 80 out of 100. Even though the statistical average is higher than this, the mode is 80.

The *median* is the observation where 50% of the scores are above and 50% are below. There were 66 total scores on Mr. Smith's test. The median is 79. Approximately half the scores are above this and half the scores are below this.

The *mean*, the most common measure of central tendency, is the arithmetic average. In this case it is 75.7, or 76 points.

Frequency Distribution.   Frequency distribution is not so much a statistical procedure as it is a way of organizing information. It tells you all the scores that were attained and how many people attained each score. Frequency distribution provides a visual sense of your data and is fairly easy to do. First create a two-column table. Then list all the scores in the left column from highest to lowest (see Table 8.2). Finally, list the number of students represented by each score in the right column.

If there are a large number of scores, put them in groups of 5 or 10 for easier comparison. For example, when Mr. Smith gave the same math test to all the eighth-grade students in his school district, he used the frequency distribution for these scores in Table 8.3.

To make this information more visual and to put it in a form that is more amenable to comparison, a frequency polygon can be created (Figure 8.7). This is a frequency distribution represented in a line graph.

50, 54, 54, 55, 56, 57, 59, 59, 65, 65, 65, 67, 67, 68, 68, 68, 68, 68, 69, 69, 69, 69, 75, 75, 75, 75, 78, 78, 78, 78, 78, 78, 79, 79, 79, 79, 79, **80, 80, 80, 80, 80, 80, 80, 80, 80, 80, 80, 80**, 83, 83, 83, 83, 83, 83, 84, 84, 84, 84, 85, 85, 90, 92, 92, 97, 99.

FIGURE 8.6   Scores from Mr. Smith's Eighth-Grade Math Test

TABLE 8.2	Frequency Distribution
SCORES	NUMBER OF STUDENTS
99	1
97	1
92	2
90	1
85	2
84	4
83	6
80	12
79	5
78	6
75	4
69	4
68	5
67	2
65	3
59	2
57	1
56	1
55	1
54	2
50	1

TABLE 8.3	Frequency Distribution for a Large Number of Scores
SCORES	NUMBER OF STUDENTS
95–100	6
90–94	10
85–89	25
80–84	35
75–79	15
70–74	10
65–69	9
60–64	7
55–59	4
50–54	2
45–49	1
40–44	1

Measures of Variability.   Measures of variability tell us about the spread of scores or how close the scores cluster around the mean. There are three measures of variability: range, variance, and standard deviation.

Range is simply the difference between the highest and lowest score. For example, Mr. Smith's eighth-grade students had scores from 50 to 99. This range for these scores is 49.

Variance is the amount of spread among the test scores. If the variance is small, the scores are bunched together. Figure 8.8 shows scores with a small variance. If the variance is large, the scores are spread out. Figure 8.9 shows scores with a large variance.

FIGURE 8.7   Graph for Frequency Distribution

			XX	XX	XX	XX	XX	XX			
				XX	XX	XX	XX	X			
				XXX		XX					

FIGURE 8.8   Scores with a Small Variance

| X | X | X | X | X | X | X | X | X | X | X | XX | XX | X | X | X | X | X | X | X | X | X | X |

FIGURE 8.9   Scores with a Large Variance

Variance can be described with a number. For example, five children went out trick-or-treating for Halloween. They got the following numbers of candy bars: 25, 35, 40, 45, and 55. The variance can be calculated using the following steps:

1. Find the mean for all scores (second column in Table 8.4).
2. Find the difference between the raw score and the mean for each score (third column).
3. Square this difference value for each score (fourth column).
4. Add the squared scores to find the total (500).
5. Divide by the total number of scores (500 divided by 5 total scores = 10). This indicates that on average, the difference or variation between the numbers of candy bars is 10. (Note: This is different from the average spread between numbers, which in this case is 5.)

TABLE 8.4   Calculating Variance

RAW SCORES	MEAN	DIFFERENCE BETWEEN RAW SCORES AND MEAN	DIFFERENCE SQUARED
25	40	−15	225
35	40	−5	25
40	40	0	0
45	40	5	25
55	40	15	225

Total of differences squared: 500

The variance score is of little value by itself; however, it can be used to calculate the standard deviation. Standard deviation is the square root of the variance. It is the most frequently used index to describe variability or the dispersion of scores. Whereas variance tells you how tightly the scores are clustered, standard deviation tells you how tightly the scores are clustered around the mean in a set of data.

Figure 8.10 shows what a normal distribution of scores would look like if these were plotted on a graph. This is the bell-shaped curve with which you are most likely familiar. The highest part of the bell is the mean. In a given sample, if the scores are normally distributed and that data were put on a graph, it would look like this. The majority of scores would fall in the middle. This is the large part of the bell, known as the average. Fewer scores fall on the top and bottom. These are the smaller parts of the bell on each side, known as above average and below average.

When scores are tightly clustered around mean as in Figure 8.11, the standard deviation is small. When scores are spread out as in Figure 8.12, the standard deviation is large.

If the mean and standard deviation of a normal distribution are known, it is possible to compute the percentile rank of any given score. On the graph in Figure 8.13, the zero point in the middle represents the mean or arithmetic average. Zero in this

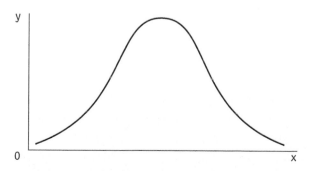

FIGURE 8.10   Bell-Shaped Curve for Normal Distribution of Scores

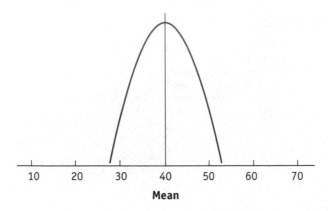

FIGURE 8.11   **Small Standard Deviation: Closely Distributed Scores**

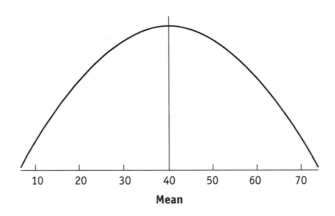

FIGURE 8.12   **Large Standard Deviation: Widely Distributed Scores**

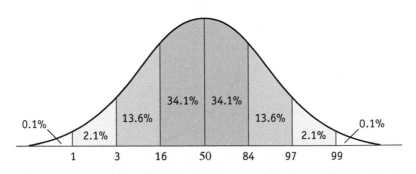

FIGURE 8.13   **Standard Deviation**

case means zero standard deviations from the mean. This is the 50th percentile. Half the scores fall above and half fall below. The first standard deviation (–1 and 1) represents 68% of the total population. In a normal distribution of scores, about 34% are approximately 1 standard deviation above the mean, and about 34% are below the mean. This means that if you gave a 100-point math test to all Americans, 50% of the total population would score 50 points or above, and 50% would score 50 points or below. About 34% would score between 50 and 84 points, and about 34% would score between 16 points and 50 points. Thus 68% of the population would score between 16 and 84 points. Both 16 points and 84 points represent one standard deviation from the mean.

Two standard deviations away from the mean (about 13.6% above the first standard deviation) represent 95% of the population. This means that about 95% scored between 3 and 97 points on this mythical math test. About 47% of the population scored between 3 and 50 points; about 47% of the population scored between 50 and 97 points.

Three standard deviations away from the mean (about 2.1% above the second standard deviation) represent about 99% of the population. This means that about 99% of the population would score between 1 and 99 points on this test. About 2% would score between 1 and 3 points; about 2% of the population would score between 97 and 99 points.

INFERENTIAL STATISTICS

Inferential statistics are statistical analyses used to determine how likely a given outcome is for an entire population based on a sample size. These analyses allow the researcher to make inferences to larger populations by collecting data on a small sample size. The most common inferential statistical analyses are the t-test, analysis of variance (ANOVA), and chi square.

The t-test is used to determine whether the difference between two different means is statistically significant. Statistical significance tells us that it is very unlikely that difference in mean was caused by chance or sampling error. If the difference between two means is not statistically significant, it tells us that the differences between them are so small, we cannot say for certain whether it was due to chance or an error in selecting the initial sample populations. It must be pointed out also that there is a difference between statistical significance and practical significance. A difference in scores may be statistically significant; however, if this difference does not mean anything or does not have any practical effect, it is not practically significant. For example, there may be a statistically significant difference between two test scores, but if they both fell within the B range, there would be no practical significance between the two.

In educational research, two different levels of significance or probability are generally used: $p = .05$ and $p = .01$. A level of $p = .05$ means that we can be reasonably certain that only 5% of the differences might be due to chance or sampling error. A level of $p = .01$ means that we can be reasonably certain that only 1% of the differences might be due to chance or sampling error. Smaller sample sizes make it harder to find statistical differences and larger ones easier. For example, it is much easier to find a statistically significant difference in two groups of 3,000 than it is between two groups of 30. The *t*-test automatically adjusts for sample size.

Whereas the *t*-test is used to compare the difference in mean between two groups, ANOVA is used to compare the difference in mean between or within three or more groups. This is a more general form of a *t*-test. If you want to compare frequencies within categories, a chi square is the best choice. For example, if you wanted to compare how many female and male students enjoyed a particular activity, a chi square would be used to compare the number of favorable and unfavorable responses within each gender category.

SUMMARY

- Two quantitative research designs that can be used with teacher action research projects are correlational research and causal–comparative research.
- Correlational research looks at one group to find a relationship between variables.
- Correlation coefficient describes the strength of the relationship between two variables.
- Correlation does not indicate causation.
- Predictions can be made based on the strength of the correlation coefficient.
- Causal–comparative research looks at two or more groups to compare the differences in one variable.
- Correlational research and causal–comparative research are not true experimental research designs because they do not manipulate variables or use random populations for sample groups.
- Both correlational research and causal–comparative research are used to examine existing conditions.
- Quasi-experimental design is a true experiment without random selection of participants.
- Pretests and matching are two ways to ensure groups are relatively similar before a quasi-experimental research project.
- Because quasi-experimental design manipulates an environment, it should be considered quasi-action research.
- Quasi-experimental design in action research should be used to understand a particular situation; it should not be used to prove or disprove a hypothesis or to make generalizations to a larger population.
- Descriptive statistics are used to describe an existing set of data.
- The four major types of descriptive statistics are frequency distribution, measure of central tendency, measures of variability, and measure of relationship or correlation.
- Frequency distribution tells you the scores that were attained and how many attained each score.
- Measures of central tendency (mode, median, and mean) use a single number to describe a set of data.

- Measures of variability (range, variance, and standard deviation) describe how spread out a set of scores is.
- Inferential statistics are used to make predictions for a general population based on a small sample size.

QUESTIONS AND ACTIVITIES

1. Find and evaluate an example of correlational research found in the popular media.
2. What are some examples of common correlations that seem to have become fact?
3. Describe three correlations that you would like to examine in a school or classroom.
4. Find an example of causal–comparative research. Identify three or more possible confounding variables.
5. Find and describe examples of quasi-experimental research. Identify three or more possible confounding variables.

POSSIBLE RESEARCH QUESTIONS FOR ACTION RESEARCH PROJECTS

1. Use one of the quasi-experimental designs described in this chapter to examine the effectiveness of a new approach or methodology. For example, instead of reading the stories from a basal reader, encourage a group of students to select the books they want to read during reading class. Are there differences in reading scores, fluency, or perception of reading? Alternatively, encourage students to work on math problems together; one person does the problem and thinks out loud while another watches, listens, and guides. Is there any difference in students' abilities to solve problems? Is there any difference in students' perceptions of math or math class?
2. Is spelling instruction effective in moving words into students' productive, writing vocabulary? Analyze students' writing. Look for instances of words from weekly spelling lists. Are they spelled correctly? Are there any differences among any of the following groups: gender, ability, SES, age?
3. Is spelling instruction more effective than allowing students to choose their own words for their weekly spelling? Find two relatively similar classrooms. Before the study collect samples of students' writing. Randomly pick 100-word passages from each sample and record how many words per hundred (WPH) were spelled correctly. This would be their WPH score. For a month, allow one group to choose their own words to study during spelling instruction while the other class receives the traditional spelling instruction. At the end of a month, are there differences in the WPH scores of the two groups?
4. How much time do students spend reading for pleasure during the school day? How much time do they spend at home? Are there any differences among any of the following groups: gender, ability, SES, age?

5. What types of books, genres, or topics do children like to read? Are there any differences among any of the following groups: gender, ability, SES, age?

6. What strategies are used to teach children how to comprehend expository text in your school? How often or to what extent are these strategies used?

7. What opportunities does your school or district provide for professional development? How does this compare to other schools? Are there recommendations related to professional development from the U.S. Department of Education or other national organizations?

8. Approximately how many hours a night do your students spend doing homework? Are there any differences among any of the following groups: gender, ability, SES, age? How do these hours compare with homework recommendations or guidelines outlined by the U.S. Department of Education or other research-based national organizations?

9. What homework policies are used by your school your district? How do these compare with other schools or districts? (Note: The Internet has a lot of good information here.)

10. What do teachers perceive to be the purpose of homework?

11. What types of extracurricular activities do students participate in each week? How many hours a week are spent doing extracurricular activities? To what degree are these activities school related and non–school related? Are there any differences among any of the following groups: gender, ability, SES, age?

12. How many students are working? How many hours a week do students spend working? What types of jobs do they have? When do they work? How might this affect their school performance? Are there any differences among any of the following groups: gender, ability, SES, age?

13. How many hours a week do students spend watching TV? What types of shows do they watch? When are they most likely to watch? How might this affect their school performance? Are there any differences among any of the following groups: gender, ability, SES, age?

14. What is the average class size in your school or district? How does this compare with state or national averages? How does this compare with recommendations by the U.S. Department of Education or other national researched-based organizations?

15. What types of professional development activities does the teaching faculty in your school or district engage in? What new skills or types of knowledge are learned? How are these new skills implemented, or in what form does this knowledge appear in the curriculum? That is, what is the effect of teacher professional development? Can a case be made for a school or district paying for this?

16. What is the makeup of the teaching faculty? How many years of experience do they have? What levels and types of education do they have? Are their differences related to gender, age, or ethnicity?

17. How would students' perception of reading or reading class change if they were allowed to choose their own books to read?

18. Other than using test scores, how do you know learning is taking place in your classroom or school? What products or performances indicate growth, learning, curiosity, inquiry, exploration, and creativity?

19. In a particular subject, what do teachers think is important for students to know or be able to do? What products or performances might indicate this? Are students in a school or class able to do these things? To what degree or at what level?

20. Does students' writing change if they are allowed to choose their own writing topics? Use the writing assessment form in Figure 6.17 (p. 82) to note change. Do students' perceptions of writing change, or are there changes in self-efficacy if students are given autonomy in the choice of writing topics?

CHAPTER NINE

EVALUATING, DESCRIBING, AND PROPOSING RESEARCH

By now you should have an understanding of some of the basic concepts related to educational research. Next we will look at evaluating, reporting, and proposing research. By the end of this chapter you will see how these are all related.

EVALUATING RESEARCH

My primary goal in writing this book is to help you understand and be able to implement action research. A secondary goal, however, is to enable you to become better consumers of educational research. To these ends, this section examines some basic concepts related to evaluating educational research. I would highly recommend the book, *Reading Educational Research: How to Avoid Getting Statistically Snookered* by Gerald Bracey (2006). Bracey's book describes, in very simple terms, the uses and misuses of research and statistics in education.

Buyer Beware

Claims about practices, products, and procedures in education are often bolstered by words such as, *"Research shows that …"* or *"Scientists have found that …"* or *"Studies indicate that …"* or *"A recent report confirms that …"* [insert claim here]." However, these words alone are meaningless. To be of real value there must be something behind the words. A few of things to keep in mind in this regard are listed here.

Saying So Does Not Make It So.   If there is research or a body of research to support a claim, the claimant has the responsibility of citing the source. If a research-based claim is made in print, the author must cite and include the full reference citation. This enables you to see if the research was peer-reviewed and to retrieve it to check the accuracy of the author's claims. If a research-based claim is made as part of an oral presentation you should always ask the claimant to supply you with reference citations.

True Scientific Research is Peer-Reviewed. Be very wary of research that has not been subjected to some form of peer review. Doing a study or collecting data may produce results that are of interest and value; however, unless it has been peer-reviewed by experts in the field, these results should not be generalized to other situations or used to understand issues outside a specific context. (Note: I would urge you to consider submitting your action research projects to professional journals for peer review and publication and at professional conferences. This will enable your voice to be part of the grand conversation in education.)

You can find studies posted or disseminated by the U.S. Department of Education and other government agencies. As described in Chapter 5, these should always be approached with a healthy degree of skepticism because they are often created without peer review. As well, studies that originate from think tanks, non-profit groups, and for-profit organizations are often designed to promote a particular view, practice, product, or program and, as such, do not go through the peer-review process. You should also be very wary of these types of studies as well.

There is No Such Thing as the Perfect Research Study. In education there is no research that "proves" conclusively for all time that a thing is so. Be wary of any universal claims based on one study. As well, when dealing with human subjects it is impossible to control all the variables. Every research study has some limitations, flaws, or confounding variables (described later). This is why published research studies always include a description of the methodology and the statistical analysis that were used. These enable readers to accurately assess and evaluate them.

You Cannot Make Research Say Anything You Want. You may have heard the expression, "You can manipulate research to make it say anything you want to." This is not quite correct. You might be able to find one study that may support a particular claim, but when you look at a body of research in an unbiased fashion you see definite patterns form. This is why a review of the literature includes analyses of more than one article or research study.

Using Research is Like Sighting in a Target Rifle. People who engage in target shooting sight in their rifles to see if they are shooting accurately. One year as I was sighting in my rifle it dawned on me that what I was doing perfectly illustrated the process of using research to get an accurate picture of reality. My question was this: Is my rifle shooting accurately? To answer this question I needed to get some data. I did this by setting up a paper plate at 100 yards, aiming for a dot in the center, and then recording where the bullet hit. However, I could not rely on one shot to determine the accuracy of the gun. I may have wiggled or flinched when I shot. Thus, I took several shots until I noticed a pattern. When looking at the holes in various places on the target, I began to see a cluster. This gave me a sense of where my gun was shooting.

The analogy is this: Each one of the holes appearing on the target was like a single research study (see Figure 9.1). Had I taken only one or two shots, I could not be very confident of the accuracy of my rifle. This illustrates the importance

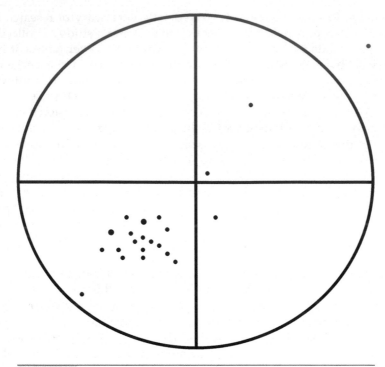

FIGURE 9.1   **Research Is Like Target Shooting**

of looking at a number of research studies. Although it may be possible to find research to support a variety of positions on any given question, one must look at a body research to see a pattern or general trend.

Show Me the Data.   In the popular media it is common to hear people make conclusive statements about the state of education or the effectiveness/ineffectiveness of a program, strategy, or approach without any supporting data. If these claims are repeated often enough they frequently become perceived as accepted fact. Examples of some of these sorts of broad claims in education include the following: Our schools are failing. Teachers are doing a terrible job. Teachers' unions are ruining education. We need to get back to the "basics." More phonics instruction will cure all the reading problems that students have. A longer school year will result in more learning. Starting formalized reading instruction in kindergarten will result in long-term reading gains. More standardized tests will improve the quality of education. School vouchers and competition will enhance public education. Private schools do a better job than public schools at education students.

Claims like this are often made based solely on *anecdotal evidence* and *I-think-isms*. Anecdotal evidence is when a general conclusion is based on a single incidence or experience. For example: "This is what happened when I tried [insert teaching strategy]. Therefore this will happen if anybody tries [insert teaching strategy]."

Or, "I knew a person, and this is what was true for that person; therefore that same thing must be true for all people."

An I-think-ism is when conclusions are drawn or decisions are made based on what one thinks or what seems to make good sense. Examples: The quality of a teacher can be determined by looking at gain scores on standardized achievement tests. Cutting recess will result in more learning. Schools run by private, for-profit companies will result in a better quality of education. Assigning more homework will result in higher levels of learning. Test scores are an accurate way to compare American schools to schools in other countries.

Personal experience and logic are powerful determinants in shaping our view of the world but they can create a view that is misshaped. Imagine the state of things if decisions in science and medicine were made this way. Science is a systematic observation used to remove personal bias and rise above preconceived ideas to arrive at some semblance of truth. Sometimes what science finds contradicts personal experience and is the exact opposite of what makes good sense. In all situations, if a claim is made the response should be, "Show me the data."

Scientifically Based Research

So we want to use research to inform our teaching practice, and we want that research to be of high quality. The NCLB Act calls for teaching practices that are based on "scientifically based research." Other federal mandates call for teaching practices that are "research based." What exactly do these terms mean? How do we know if research is "scientifically based"? Does this mean only quantitative research studies are to be used in making decision in education?

First, the National Research Council described scientifically based research as being defined by a set of principles not by research methods (quantitative or qualitative). In education these principles are the same regardless of method (Eisenhart & Towne, 2003; see Figure 9.2).

The specific research standards based on these principles are in Figure 9.3. These are at the core of evaluating any type of research in education. Specific criteria for quantitative and qualitative research are described in detail later.

Principles of Scientifically Based Research

Scientifically based research should

1. Post significant questions that can be investigated empirically.

2. Link research to relevant theory.

3. Use methods that permit direct investigation of the question.

4. Provide a coherent and explicit chain of reasoning.

5. Replicate and generalize across studies.

6. Disclose research to encourage professional scrutiny and critique.

FIGURE 9.2   Principles Used to Define Scientifically Based Research in Education by NRC

Scientifically Based Research Standards

1. **The term "scientifically based research standards" means research standards that—**
   A. apply rigorous, systematic, and objective methodology to obtain reliable and valid knowledge relevant to education activities and programs; and
   B. present findings and make claims that are appropriate to and supported by the methods that have been employed.

2. **The term includes, appropriate to the research being conducted—**
   A. employing systematic, empirical methods that draw on observation or experiment;
   B. involving data analyses that are adequate to support the general findings;
   C. relying on measurements or observational methods that provide reliable data;
   D. making claims of causal relationships only in random assignment experiments or other designs (to the extent such designs substantially eliminate plausible competing explanations for the obtained results);
   E. ensuring that studies and methods are presented in sufficient detail and clarity to allow for replication or, at a minimum, to offer the opportunity to build systematically on the findings of the research;
   F. obtaining acceptance by a peer-reviewed journal or approval by a panel of independent experts through a comparably rigorous, objective, and scientific review; and
   G. using research designs and methods appropriate to the research question posed.

From the Education Science Reform Act of 2002

FIGURE 9.3   Scientifically Based Research Standards in Education

EVALUATING QUANTITATIVE RESEARCH

This section describes things to consider when evaluating quantitative or experimental research. As described in Chapter 1, experimental researchers seek to isolate or manipulate one or more variables to study its effect on others.

Independent and Dependent Variables

A variable in quantitative research is an item, characteristic, attribute, or factor that can be measured or observed. Variables are things that can change in a study or things that you change to determine cause–effect relationships (see Figure 9.4).
Here is a quick review of independent and dependent variables with examples.

Independent Variable.   In quantitative research the *independent variable* is the thing that the researcher isolates or tries to make independent of all other forces. It is what is manipulated or selected and then compared to see if there are differences. It comes first and influences what comes later.

Dependent Variable.   The *dependent variable* depends on the independent variable. It is what happens as a result of the independent variable and is what is measured. The independent variable is the cause; the dependent variable is the effect.

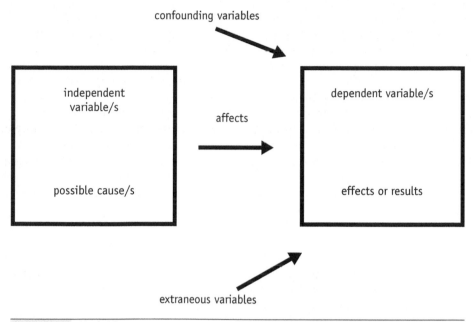

FIGURE 9.4   Variables

In educational research the teaching method is often the independent variable, and student achievement or test scores are often the dependent variable. In non-experimental research (descriptive or correlational research), variables cannot be manipulated. That is, they have already occurred. In this type of research you are looking at the condition, experience, or category as an independent variable and then some sort of related measure as a dependent variable

Examples.   Following are some examples of independent and dependent variables. These are purposefully simplistic to enable you to see their salient elements and to illustrate the concept of confounding variables that follow.

- Researcher Mary Jones wanted to examine the effect of structured conversations related to chapter content on students' ability to comprehend expository text. Students in two fifth-grade classrooms were asked to read chapters in a social studies textbook. As a postreading strategy one group used a structured conversation strategy after each chapter. The other group completed worksheets related to chapter content. After three chapters students were tested on chapter content. The independent variable here was the postreading strategy used. The dependent variable was students' test scores.
- Researcher James Smith wanted to examine the effect of saying the Pledge of Allegiance every day on students' moral reasoning. Three elementary schools that said the pledge every day were identified. Three elementary schools that did not say the pledge were identified. At the end of the year, students at each grade level were given moral dilemmas in which they were asked to

determine the appropriate behavior or course of action in response to a situation and explain their supporting reasons. Their answers and reasons were recorded and transcribed. The independent variable here was the pledge. The dependent variable was students' answers and their reasoning.

- Researcher Patricia Williams wanted to see if teaching writing using the process approach was more effective than using a skills-based approach. Specifically, she wanted to know if there were any differences between the two approaches on the quality of students' writing (organization, coherence, and word choice) and their ability to use and apply mechanics (grammar, spelling, and punctuation). Two sixth-grade classrooms were identified that used each approach. At the end of the year writing samples were analyzed and rated. The independent variable here was the approach to writing instruction. The dependent variable was the rating scores on students' writing.

- Researcher John Martinez wanted to see if there was a relationship between social economic status and students' ability to learn biology. The National Testing Corporation Biology Test was given to all ninth-grade students in Burnett County in Wisconsin. The scores on this test were sorted into three categories based on parents' level of income (low, middle, and high) and were compared. The independent variable here was social economic status. The dependent variable was the test scores.

Confounding Variables

Confounding Variables.   *Confounding variables* (sometimes referred to as extraneous variables) are independent variables that are unknown or have not been controlled and which affect the results or dependent variables. In this way they mess up or confound the experiment and make it possible for other interpretations of the results. This means that things other than the independent variable could account for the effect on the dependent variable.

- For example, students' comprehension test scores in the Mary Jones study noted earlier could have been influenced by differing interests in social studies or the topic, ability levels of students in each class, incidents that may have occurred on the day of testing, the time of day the tests were given, the proximity of the test to the reading assignment, or the time between reading assignments. (Did they read three chapters in three days or three weeks?)

  Using large sample sizes and randomized assignment to control and experimental groups are both ways to limit the effects of extraneous variables. However, as stated in the Chapter 8, randomized assignment to groups is often not possible in education. That is why much of the experimental research in education is defined as quasi-experimental research.

- In James Smith's study, the small sample size increases the possibility of confounding variables affecting students' answers and reasoning in the moral dilemma. Confounding variables might include students' cultural or religious background, community values and norms, gender, or experiences with situations similar to that used in the moral dilemma.

- In Patricia Williams' study, differences in rating scores on students' writing could be attributed to the teaching style, personality, knowledge related to grammar and punctuation, past writing experience, or the experience and expertise of each teacher.
- In John Martinez's study, students' scores on the National Testing Corporation Biology Test could have been influenced by the knowledge and expertise of their teacher, the amount of science and biology included in students' curriculum, district resources, or class size.

Common Confounding Variables

Following are descriptions of typical confounding variables.

Dropout or Experimental Mortality.   This is when subjects in an experiment or study drop out while the experiment is in progress.

Concurrent Events.   This is when there are coinciding events outside the experiment or study that may affect the results.

Unequal Samples.   Samples here refer to the subjects or participants in experimental and control groups or in the different populations being compared. If one group is larger than the other or if the groups are not similar in terms of demographics, ability, age, or other types of variables, the interpretation of the results should be questioned. Two common methods are used to control confounding variables here: One is random selection using a large sample size. Subjects are randomly put in control and experimental groups. As described earlier, this is often problematic for research in education. The other is matching. Here groups are matched in terms of variables. For every subject put in one group, a similar subject is put in the other.

A rule of thumb in research: When comparing two things you must first make sure the two things are comparable. Figure 9.5 contains a list of some of the variables that could affect student achievement. If not controlled or accounted for, these could affect any research looking at student achievement. As an example of this, in recent years there have been a variety of studies or reports showing that private schools are more effective than public schools. However, private and public schools differ on many variables including demographics, curriculum, and class size. Gerald Bracey (2000) found that when variables are controlled the resulting comparisons most often favor public schools.

Maturation.   Sometimes when you are looking at change over time the results are not due to any treatment or independent variable but to maturation. That is, as students grow and learn, measures of learning are naturally going to increase. Change in achievement cannot always be attributed to teacher performance or the type of instruction received.

Sampling or Selection Bias.   This is when the types of subjects or participants included or excluded in a study affect the results. When looking at the effect of a

- Parent level of education
- Class size
- Enrollment by grade level
- Teacher quality/proficiency
- Teacher certification
- Teacher professional development opportunities
- Expectations of teachers, parents, or peers
- Number and types of books in classroom and school library
- Diet
- Parent SES

- Level of technology in classroom
- Percent of English language learners
- Teacher attitude
- Inclusion vs. segregation curriculum
- Type and amount student writing instruction and opportunities
- Amount of free reading time
- Access to health care
- Stress or anxiety factors
- Economic base
- Unemployment rate

- Percent of special education students
- Class size
- School size
- Research-based strategies used
- Gender differences
- The use of standardized testing
- Safety at school
- Amount of study time
- Parent involvement and support

FIGURE 9.5   Some Variables that Can Affect Student Achievement

treatment or condition, did the samples chosen to be in various groups selectively favor a particular outcome?

For example, Dr. Peggy Brown conducted a study that compared the effects of social studies instruction using traditional lecture-activity methods with social studies instruction using guided-discovery on student achievement. Teachers in the state of Minnesota who taught social studies were identified. They were put into groups based on the method used to teach social studies. The results of this study showed that students who were taught using guided-discovery methods scored significantly higher on the National Testing Corporation Social Studies Test than those who were taught using traditional methods of instruction. One interpretation of the results could be that guided-discovery is more effective than traditional methods in teaching social studies. However, this might be a spurious conclusion, as the results might be more strongly related to the type of teacher who taught each method. Because guided-discovery is a high-level teaching strategy, teachers who would learn and use it might be more creative, more motivated, more experienced, or better educated than those who used traditional methods.

Hawthorne Effect.   Sometimes participants in a study behave differently because they know they are in a study. Here the difference in effects is not a result of treatment; but rather, it is a result of getting special attention and recognition for being part of a study. When participants' behavior is affected by the knowledge that they are participating in a study and not by any particular treatment, this is called the *Hawthorne effect*. As well, subjects in an experiment may also be responding to the novelty of the treatment and not the treatment itself.

Validity of the Measure.   In quantitative research validity is related to the dependent variable and the measurement or instruments. Do the data collected actually determine what it is intended to measure? Does the instrument measure what it purports to measure? Is it a valid measurement? For example, a study looking at the effects of a particular treatment on students' ability to write used scores on a language arts achievement test. Although this data may be reliable, it is not a valid measure of students' ability to organize ideas and create meaning with text. In the same way, many want to use achievement test scores to measure teachers' effectiveness, but by itself this is not a valid measure of a teacher's ability to create effective learning experiences.

EVALUATING QUALITATIVE RESEARCH

This section describes things to consider when evaluating qualitative or descriptive research. As described in Chapter 1, qualitative research uses systematic observations to study naturally occurring phenomena to better understand a bit of reality. Following are some elements to consider when evaluating qualitative research. (Generally, one or two sentences should be used to describe each of the elements.) The description of these elements is based on Leedy and Ormrod's (2010) nine criteria for evaluating qualitative research:

Purposefulness. The purpose, question, or area of study should be clearly defined. In the report, everything that precedes and follows the research question should be directly related. Also, the question should be one that can be answered by qualitative types of data. And the methods used to collect data should be the best ways to get at the research question.

Explicitness of assumptions and biases. Any biases the researcher has should be stated up front. Preconceived ideas, beliefs, or values that may influence what is being seen and how data are interpreted should also be described.

Rigor. There should be a systematic plan used to collect and analyze the data. The type of data collected should be of sufficient quality to accurately answer the research question. The number of observations, their duration, and the quantity of data collected should be sufficient to accurately understand what is being studied. The duration of the study should be sufficient to accurately answer the research question. And multiple types of data should be collected. (Remember, however, that rigor is different from complexity. Complexity can be used to mask bad research.)

Open-mindedness. The researcher should not start with an answer. You should get a sense that the researcher will let the data collected inform or change his/her belief system.

Completeness. All relevant aspects of the environments should be described in a way that enables you to understand the phenomena being studied. The description should provide an accurate and complete picture of the person, place, event, or experience. The researcher should describe how his or her presence in the setting influences what is being observed. And the researcher should describe any people or events that may have influenced the study or change what is observed and how data are collected.

Coherence.   The description should make sense. You should be able to understand the report. The literature review, research question, methodology, findings, and discussion or conclusions should be in alignment. There should not be too much data described. (Too much information can be just as confusing as too little information.) And the data should be analyzed and reported in a way that is clear and comprehensible.

Persuasiveness.   The researcher should use sound logic to analyze and interpret the data. Also, recommendations or conclusions should be a logical extension of the data collected.

Consensus.   The research should be set in a sound theoretical context. And it should be aligned with previous research or linked with what others have found or experienced.

Usefulness.   You should be able to use the findings to better understand and accurately interpret similar people, places, events, or experiences.

DESCRIBING RESEARCH

Being able to knowledgeably evaluate research will enable you to make good decisions in selecting particular research to inform your teaching practice. It will also enable you to select the best research studies to use with your action research projects. This section describes how to describe these research studies. These types of descriptions are used in literature reviews (Chapter 5), annotated bibliographies (described later), and action research proposals (described later). Here the following elements are usually described and presented in the following order:

Question or purpose of the study.   Use one statement to describe the research questions and/or the purpose of the study.

Subjects or participants.   Describe the number of subjects or participants and any relevant demographics or characteristics.

Treatment, criteria, or conditions.   For a quantitative study describe the independent variable. For descriptive research describe the criteria used to select the various data. For a qualitative study describe the general setting, environment, or condition in which the data were collected.

Measures or instruments.   Describe what data were collected, how it was collected, and what was used to collect it.

Results.   Describe the relevant results of the study.

Conclusions or findings.   Describe, in general terms what the results mean.

Limitations. Describe any limitations of the study or relevant confounding variables. (Note: This element is not always included in an annotated bibliography or research proposal.)

Examples of Research Descriptions

Fruit

This section describes two studies related to Fruit.

Abbot Study

Abbot (1947) examined the effects of kumquats on working memory. For this study, 80 subjects were chosen from a pool of 250 college students and randomly assigned to either a treatment or control group. The treatment group ate 3 kumquats every day for a week, and the control group ate no kumquats. Both groups were given the Imperial Testing Corporation Memory Test (ITCMT) as a posttreatment measure. It was found that the kumquat experimental group scored significantly higher than the nonkumquat control group in this measure. It may be inferred that kumquats have some positive effect on memory.

Costello and Abbot Study

Costello and Abbot (1952) wanted to see if muskmelons had any effect on reasoning ability. For this study 250 adult subjects were selected from a shopping mall and randomly put into treatment and control groups. The Imperial Testing Corporation Reasoning Test (ITCRT) was given as a pretreatment measure and showed no statistically significant differences between the two groups. Over a six-month period, the treatment group was given half a muskmelon to eat each day. The control group ate no muskmelon during this time. Posttreatment measures showed no difference between the two groups.

Summary Of Fruit Studies

The results of these two studies show the following:

1. Kumquats have been shown to positively affect memory (Abbot, 1947).
2. Muskmelons have no significant affect on reasoning ability (Costello & Abbot, 1952).

Do not include every aspect of the study in your description of research; just include those elements or results that are relevant to your action research project. Also, some descriptions are one to two paragraphs, whereas more complicated studies require more in-depth descriptions. Following is an example of one such study.

Robins And Mayer Study

Robins and Mayer (1993) compared the effects of four instructional methods on students' ability to acquire and transfer analogical reasoning skills. Three identical experiments were conducted. The subjects were 93, 97, and 86 college students randomly assigned to one of four treatment methods.

A computer system was used to provide subjects with training on 20 practice analogies in one of four instructional methods: (a) schematic/high load, (b) schematic/low load, (c) nonschematic/high load, and (d) nonschematic/low load. The length and duration of each training program were not reported.

Schematic instruction consisted of practice problems grouped by type and accompanied by direct instruction, which described the problem type. Nonschematic instruction consisted of practice problems arranged in random order without a description of the problem type. High-load instruction or problems that utilized a high cognitive load consisted of practice problems presented as exercises without examples of the correct solutions. Low-load instruction or problems that utilized a low cognitive load consisted of worked-out examples, which emphasized the formation of correct relational schemas.

After the training programs were completed, subjects were asked to solve new analogy problems of the same relational type (near or low-load transfer), solve new analogy problems of a new relational type (far or high-load transfer), and take a recognition test of the terms from the previously presented analogies (recognition memory). Measures of students' error rates and response times were used to compare the effectiveness of each instructional method.

The results indicated that (a) schematic/low-load instruction was the best condition for learning problem solving initially and for transferring this knowledge to similar or near-transfer problems, and (b) there was no significant difference in the types of instruction for problems considered far-transfer and for measures of memory recognition.

These results seem to suggest that thinking skills are best learned when the schema or problem type are identified and accompanied by direct instruction, the cognitive system is not overloaded, and there is an adequate amount of modeling and practice.

AN ACTION RESEARCH PROPOSAL

Descriptions of several related research studies is called an *annotated bibliography*. These come in various forms and are used in literature reviews and research proposals. Research proposals are used to get permission for or approval to conduct research projects. However, you will find that designing your research proposal will be helpful in defining your research question and thinking through all parts of your intended project. Proposals come in varying forms but usually contain some or all of the following elements.

Title or heading. The title or heading should be in boldfaced and centered with title caps (see Figure 9.6). Put your name centered on the line below followed by the date on the following line.

Topic. What are you interested in? What problem do you see in your school, classroom, or education setting? What would you like to know more about? Is there an area in which you might wish to become more knowledgeable or proficient? Your topic should not be what you want to do or create (application), but an area in which you are interested. Also, tell why it is important. Example of a topic: *Meeting the needs of gifted elementary readers in a general education setting.* The topic section is generally two to three sentences. Here you will use one sentence to describe your topic followed by one but no more than two sentences to tell why your topic is important.

Question. Put your topic in the form of one to three questions. The question or questions will define and guide your data collection and your review of research articles. Do not start with the answer, as this will make your search much more difficult. Example of research questions: *(a) What special needs do readers with learning disabilities have in the elementary grades? (b) How can general education teachers meet these needs within the confines of reading instruction?* Keep this simple. Again, more complexity does not mean more rigor. One precisely worded research question is often much better than two or three overly wordy, nebulous questions.

Annotated bibliography. This is where you describe two or more studies that are directly related to your research project (this number will vary). Keep in mind that this is not a literature review. Instead it is a short description of research that supports your study or project. At the end of your annotated bibliography you need to make the link between the studies described and your research project.

Methodology. Here you will briefly describe your plan for collecting data. Included here will be a description of the participants (number, age, gender), special material you will be using, the type of data, how and when you will collect the data, and how your data will be analyzed.

Use a Level I heading (see Chapter 12) for the title and Level II headings for the four elements just described. Use Level III subheadings as you find necessary. Here are two examples of action research proposals. Other proposal examples along with proposal forms and IRB information can be found on my website (www.AR-Johnson.com).

Research Proposal
Sally S. Student
July 27, 2009

I. Topic

II. Question/s

III. Annotative Bibliography

IV. Methodology

FIGURE 9.6 Basic Structure of an Action Research Proposal

Annie Oftedahl, Northfield, Minnesota

PROPOSAL FOR ACTION RESEARCH PROJECT
Annie Oftedahl
July 25, 2009

I. Topic

My topic is effective parent education programs. Parent education programs are an important element when designing a family-centered early intervention program for young children with special needs and their families. Parent education programs can provide knowledge and support that can alleviate some of the difficulties associated with caring for a child with special needs.

II. Question

My research-related question is this: What are the features of an effective parent education program?

III. Annotated Bibliography

Akai, Baggett, Guttentag, and Noria Study. This study was conducted by Akai, Baggett, Guttentag, and Noria (2008) and designed to assess the impact of the *My Baby and Me* program. This program was intended to improve early parenting skills by enhancing parents' understanding of infant developmental needs, promote maternal responsiveness, increase positive behavioral support, and decrease psychological control. Study participants consisted of 48 mothers of diverse ethnic identities between the ages of 15 and 38.

Mothers were identified as being at-risk and qualified for the study based on either low maternal education (no high school diploma) or low family income (eligible for WIC or TANF). Participants were randomly assigned to either a treatment group involved in the *My Baby and Me* program or the nontreatment group receiving only parenting literature and community referrals. The treatment group participated in the program for 12–14 weeks focusing on responsive training, developmental knowledge training, and loving touch training. A pre-intervention and post-intervention assessment battery was completed by all of the participants. The assessments included: the child abuse potential inventory, the adult–adolescent parenting inventory, and the mother–infant observation.

The results suggest that *My Baby and Me* was successful in improving mothers' use of language with their infants, direct teaching and demonstration of skills to their infants, and acceptance of responsibility for their appropriate parental role. Those mothers receiving intervention also decreased negative parenting behaviors. Beneficial results such as the impact on parents' attitudes and interaction with their infants may be due to the weekly attention and support received by the mothers.

Hirsch and Wolfe Report. This report was written by Hirsch and Wolfe (2003). It reviewed the results of two studies involving the impact of the *Listening to Children* (LTC) parent education program. The purpose of the first study was to evaluate the effectiveness of the LTC program on middle-class families. The first study involved 25 middle income, married mothers that had at least one child under the age of five. A pretest/posttest/follow-up model was used with 11 participants randomly assigned to the treatment group and the remaining 14 were assigned to the nontreatment comparison group. The participants were involved in an 8-week course, meeting weekly for 2½ hours in the evening. The pretest consisted of the Hereford Parent Attitude Survey and the Parenting Stress Index Short Form. The posttest and follow-up included an additional questionnaire, the Evaluation of Program Content and Impact, to assess parents' opinions regarding the program. Data were collected from these self-report questionnaires to gauge maternal esteem, parent–child interaction, confidence in parental role, acceptance of child's feelings and behavior, parenting practices, and stress level before and after the program.

The purpose of the second study was to evaluate the effectiveness of the LTC program among diverse populations. The second study included 12 low-income families of diverse ethnic identities. A different parent attitude survey was used in the second study to address issues of subscale reliability. A questionnaire on parenting practices was also added to the second study.

Positive effects were observed in both studies, some of which were maintained at the follow-up. The results suggest that LTC contributes to improved parental attitudes, reduced parenting stress levels, and encourages authoritative parenting practices. Generalizing results to a larger population should be done with caution due to the small sample size.

Summary. The results of these studies suggest that the *Listening to Children* program and *My Baby and Me* program were successful. The participants in the studies have shown increased knowledge of child development, reduced stress levels, improved parenting practices, and have instilled the sense of parental responsibility. In addition to these positive effects, the parenting programs have helped to decrease negative behaviors such as the authoritarian parenting style. This information will be useful while continuing research related to the components of an effective parent education program.

IV. Methodology

For this action research project I will be using three forms of data collection. The first one will be a literature review regarding the components of effective parent education programs. The second will be interview data from two early childhood special education teachers in each of the participating school districts. Questions here will be related their experience with parent education programs and their effectiveness (see Appendix A). The teachers completing the open-ended interview questions will be those who have students with participating parents on their caseload. The third data source will be interviews with the parents participating in the parent education course (see Appendix B). Participation will be determined by recommendations from early childhood special education teachers. There will be 10–20 parents interviewed in each of the participating districts.

After reviewing the literature, inductive analysis will be utilized to find common themes or patterns related to the characteristics of an effective parent education program. Program curriculum will be determined by research concerning effective parent education programs. Interview data from early childhood special education teachers and parents will be collected and organized into tables to look for similarities in answers.

References

Akai, C., Baggett, K., Guttentag, C., & Willard Noria, C. (2008). Enhancing parenting practices of at-risk mothers. *Journal of Primary Prevention, 29*, 223–242.

Hirsch, B., & Wolfe, R. (2003). Outcomes of parent education programs based on reevaluation on counseling. *Journal of Child and Family Studies, 12*, 61–76.

APPENDIX A

Teacher Interview

1. Do you believe this program was effective?
2. What do you believe made this program effective?
3. What changes did you see in the lives of your student's families participating in the program?
4. How are parents interacting with their children after participating in the program?
5. What changes did you see in your students of whom had parents participating in the program (academically/emotionally/behaviorally)?
6. What do you believe would make this program more successful?

APPENDIX B

Parent Interview

1. Do you believe this program was effective?
2. What do you believe made this program effective?
3. What changes have occurred in your family since participating in this program?
4. What changes have you seen in your child since participating in this program (academically/emotionally/behaviorally)?
5. What things can you do at home to support your child's development?
6. What topics (i.e., parenting practices, child development, education) are you interesting in learning more about?
7. What do you believe would make this program more successful?
8. What did you enjoy most about the program?

Ann Schmitz, Garden City Minnesota

PROPOSAL FOR ACTION RESEARCH PROJECT

Department Of Special Education
Ann R. Schmitz
June 23, 2009

This is a proposal for my action research project. I plan to conduct this research project from August 3 to August 20, 2009

Proposed Topic

The topic for this action research project is free for all preschool students identified with developmental delay. Information about children's play can help teachers to understand development and apply it to interventions.

Related Questions

The research questions I am interested are:

1. What areas of the room do children with developmental delays spend the most amount of time in during free-play?
2. How much time do children with developmental delays spend interacting with a teacher during free-play?
3. How much time do children with developmental delays spend interacting with peers during free-play?

Annotated Bibliography

This section describes two studies related to preschool children with developmental delays and free-play in inclusive classrooms.

Knotos, Moore, and Giorgetti Study. Knotos, Moore, and Giorgetti (1998) studied the experiences of children with disabilities as compared to children without disabilities during free-play in inclusive classrooms. Forty children with mild to moderate disabilities participated in the study. Sixty-six typically developing children, 1 boy and 1 girl from each of the classrooms, were randomly selected to participate in the study. Scan sampling observations were conducted by a trained graduate student during free-play periods. Each observation was rated and placed in categories, these categories include teacher involvement, interaction with objects and peers, activities, and social context.

This study found that children with developmental delays (DD) or disabilities were mostly involved in nonplay activities, art, and manipulatives than their typically developing peers during free-play in inclusive classrooms. They were also more likely to be in a group of children with a teacher. Children with DD engaged in less peer play and more object play. It may be inferred that children with disabilities use play areas, peers, and teachers differently than peers without disabilities.

Malone Study. Malone (2006) The purpose of this study was to match developmental age (DA) and sequential play observed during home-based independent play and in an inclusive classroom during free-play. Seventeen preschool children with cognitive disabilities and 17 preschool children without cognitive disabilities were matched on developmental age and sex. Children's behaviors observed were coded and placed into play categories.

Malone found that the patterns of play during home-based independent play correlated more closely with DA for children with cognitive disabilities. Children who are typically developing, play patterns during free-play in a preschool classroom more closely matched their DA. Information about the different ways children play and how it matches to developmental age is meaningful for practitioners in the field to provide insight for the implementation of curriculum and teaching strategies.

Summary of Journal Articles. These studies reviewed seem to indicate the following:

1. Inclusive preschool classrooms provide children with developmental delays and disabilities the opportunity to play in a variety of situations that promote growth and development.
2. The examination of where, with, and how long children play can provide information about development, teaching strategies, curriculum implementation, and effective interventions.
3. Free-play in the inclusive preschool classroom is experienced differently by children with and without developmental delays or disabilities.

Application. These two studies use observation and rating scales to help us understand preschool children's play activities. They tell me that where children play, whom they play with and in what kinds of play they engage can provide information about their levels of development, socially, academically, and emotionally. Preschool years are a critical time in a child's development, teachers must have the ability to gather information about children and apply it to the child's intervention program and classroom curriculum. The information I gather from this action research project will help me to understand children with disabilities play and apply that information to their IEPs and the general curriculum and instruction within my classroom.

Methodology

This section describes the methodology used in this research project.

Participants. There will be 8 children participating in this study. They are between the ages of 3 and 5 years old and are diagnosed with two or more developmental delays. Five are male and three are female. They are all a part of an Extended School Year Preschool Program.

Materials. The materials used in the study will be a teacher survey (see Appendix A). This survey will contain three open-ended questions to gather information related to children's free-play. A data retrieval chart (see Appendix B) will be used to collect information about where and for how long children spend in specific areas of the classroom. This DRC is a map of the classroom where the children will be observed. Eight different DRC will be copied, one for each student, each chart will be color coded with each child given a color to identify them. A stopwatch will be used to record time.

Data. Data collected will be collected using field notes, teacher survey, and a data retrieval chart. Observations of the children during free-play will be done for 4 days and recorded on the data retrieval chart. Data from the chart will be analyzed and organized to determine the amount of time the children spend in specific activities, or areas of the room and whom they spend that time with (peer, teacher, solitary).

Procedures. During each day in a preschool classroom some time is devoted to open/free-play. During this time children are allowed to play or participate in any area or with materials of their choice. I will be observing and recording the participating children's choices of play areas, the amount of time they are involved in these choices and whom they are spending this time with. For this study I will select 4 consecutive days to observe the children. Two children will be observed during separate 15-minute intervals on each of the four days. Data for each child will be collected on a separate DRC/map of the classroom. If a child spends more than 1 minute in an area the time will be recorded on the DRC as will an indication of whom they were with during that time. If the child was in an area for less that 1 minute a minus mark (−) will be placed in that area.

Organization and Analysis of Data

In examining the data I collect from the observations, I will be looking to see what areas and how much time the children spend in particular areas of the room. I will also be interested whom they are spending their time with and for how long.

Field notes will be examined and used to examine patterns of play, organize and create the data retrieval chart. The teacher survey will include three questions to determine what types of activities and play spaces are available to the children in the preschool classroom. It will also be used to find out when and for how long free-play is offered during each school day.

Inductive analysis will be used to describe the patterns and time children spend in play, tasks, or activities of choice and with whom they spend their free-play time.

References

Kontos, S., Moore, D., & Giorgetti, K. (1998). The ecology of inclusion. *Topics in Early Childhood Special Education, 18,* 38–48.

Malone, D. (2006). Contextually influenced patterns of play-development as associations for preschoolers with and without mental retardation. *Early Childhood Education Journal, 34,* 215–225.

APPENDIX A

Teacher Survey

1. When and how long do children participate in free-play during your normal day?
2. List specific areas of activities in your classroom.
3. List areas or activities children are allowed to use during free-play.

APPENDIX B

Data Retrieval Chart

Classroom Map

In this area I will have a map of the classroom with each area labeled and an area to record each child's movement and time spent in each area.

Total time spent in each area in minutes:	Time spent with each in minutes:
Blocks___ Art ___ Manipulatives ___	Peers___
Sand/Water___ Books___ Dramatic Play___	Teachers___
Large Motor___ Writing Center ___ Non Play___	Solitary___

SUMMARY

- Research should be used to inform both our teaching practice and our action research projects; however, we must be knowledgeable consumers of research if we are to use it effectively.
- In evaluating quantitative research a variety of possible confounding variables must be considered.
- Qualitative research can be evaluated by considering the following criteria: purposefulness, explicitness of assumptions and biases, rigor, open-mindedness, completeness, coherence, persuasiveness, consensus, and usefulness.
- In literature reviews, annotated bibliographies, and research proposals research is described by included concise depictions of the following: Question or purpose of the study; subjects or participants; treatment, criteria, or conditions; measures or instruments; results; conclusions or findings; and limitations.

- Action research proposals are used to get permission for your action research projects.
- Action research proposals are helpful in defining your research questions and thinking through all phases of your project.

QUESTIONS AND ACTIVITIES

1. As you consume various media, TV, radio, the Internet, magazines, and newspapers, see how many instances you can find of research claims being made without reference to particular studies.
2. Identify a teaching practice, strategy, or program that you commonly use. See if you can find research to support it.
3. Why do we give students in elementary schools weekly spelling tests? See if you can find research to support that this is effective in helping them spell words in authentic writing situations.
4. Select a quantitative research study in an area of interest in education. Evaluate it using the criterion presented in this chapter. Describe it using the guidelines described in this chapter.
5. Select a qualitative research study in an area of interest in education. Evaluate it using the criterion presented in this chapter. Describe it using the guidelines described in this chapter.
6. Find research in an area of interest outside education. Evaluate it using the criterion presented in this chapter. Describe it using the guidelines described in this chapter.
7. Identify a controversial area related to education, schools, or classroom practice. See if you can find research to support a particular view.

POSSIBLE RESEARCH QUESTIONS FOR ACTION RESEARCH PROJECTS

1. Do weekly spelling tests improve students' ability to spell under authentic writing conditions?
2. Whom do you see as the unpopular children? Why do they seem to be having trouble with peer relationships?
3. Given moral dilemmas or problems involving values, how do students in your class tend to solve them? How do they decide what is right and wrong?
4. What do students perceive as the qualities of an effective teacher? What do teachers believe to be the qualities of effective teachers? What do administrators believe to be qualities of effective teachers? What do parents believe to be qualities of effective teachers?
5. What life issues are of most concern to students in your classroom? What school issues are of most concern to students in your classroom?
6. What type of school experiences do the parents in your school desire for their children?

7. Are teachers in other classrooms or schools using inclusive strategies in their general education classrooms? If so, what strategies are being used?
8. Who do students turn to when they have a problem?
9. Who do students admire or see as heroes and role models? What traits to these figures have?
10. What are students' attitudes and behaviors related to alcohol and other drugs?

CHAPTER TEN

REPORTING FINDINGS IN ACTION RESEARCH

This chapter describes how to present qualitative and quantitative data in your action research report.

REPORTING QUALITATIVE DATA

Presenting the data you collected in your action research project may comprise the bulk of your report. Your data will be used here to create a picture that describes what you found. The goal is to transform your field notes and other data into a form that can be easily digested (Taylor & Bogdan, 1998). Do not try to recount and report every bit of data collected because you will overwhelm and bore your reader. Instead, describe the meaningful trends, patterns, and categories you found and include representative samples so that the reader gets a sense of what you discovered. In this sense you are representing a particular view of reality (yours).

Tips for Presenting Qualitative Data

You can be creative in how you present the data as long as you describe your experiences fairly and adequately. Five tips can help you create an effective writing tone and style.

1. *Try to be an impartial reporter.* Action researchers realize that it is impossible to be totally impartial; however, you should fairly represent all aspects of what you are studying. In your writing tone, avoid letter-to-the-editor syndrome. You create a more credible document when you simply state and support your ideas and avoid using value statements.

Less Effective
The observations in this study clearly demonstrate the absurdity of those misinformed educators who insist that time spent reading good books in reading class is wasted time.

More Effective

The observations showed that allowing time for voluntary reading in reading class has some very positive effects.

2. *Include yourself when it is warranted.* It is acceptable to use the I pronoun when describing something that you did or observed (McNiff, Lomax, & Whitehead, 1996). You are, after all, a part of the study; thus, you should refer to yourself in a personal way instead of using an impersonal form, such as "the researcher."

Less Effective

For this study, the researcher spent 7 weeks observing students in a second-grade classroom.

More Effective

For this study, I spent 7 weeks observing students in my second-grade classroom.

3. *Take readers along with you in all phases of your study.* Let them inside your head so they know exactly what you did and why you did it. To do this, your action research report should describe some or all of the following: (a) your question or focus, (b) the present environment or conditions, (c) what data you plan to collect, (d) the methods used to collect the data, (e) the data, (f) your thoughts along the way, and (g) how the data might be applied or used to understand other situations. The rule of thumb is that a reader should be able to replicate your procedure. Teresa Van Batavia wrote in such a way that we knew exactly what she was doing (her complete project is included in the Appendix):

Writing Workshop

My first-grade students at Eisenhower Elementary are involved in a writer's workshop setting at least 3 times a week. My concern is that children may be slipping through the cracks—doing little or no writing and not being noticed.

Data Collection

The first form of data collection that I used was that of a weekly checklist. As I circulated among students during the 2-week period from November 15 through December 3, 1999, I carried a clipboard and checked off each type of writing activity that I observed (see Figure 1). This checklist became an effective tool for helping me to choose mini-lesson topics for the children. I will continue to use this on an informal basis throughout the year.

In addition to the checklists, I met individually with each student and also collected their writing folders for further study of their writing habits. Following are my notes of these conferences.

Writer's Workshop Checklist, Week of November 15–19, 1999

Generating/prewriting	|||| ||||	
Drawing/sketching	|||| |||
Drafting	|||| |||| |||| |||| |||| ||||	
Revising	||||	
Editing	|||
Conference/talking		
Reading		
Other	|||| ||

FIGURE 1   Writer's Workshop Checklist

4. *Write clearly and precisely.* As stated previously, too many words are as damaging to comprehension as too few words. Be selective in what you choose to report. The goal is to achieve maximum communication using a minimum of words. A clear, concise paper is more apt to be read. A long, rambling paper is more apt to be ignored.

5. *Organize your paper.* You have a certain amount of freedom in the structure or form of your research report. That is, you are not bound by the same confines that dictate empirical research studies; however, the onus is on you to create a paper that can be easily understood. One way to do this is to organize your paper so that the structure is readily apparent to the reader. The next section describes this.

THE IMPORTANCE OF STRUCTURE

Structure is the essence of all things. In writing, structure is the skeleton used to carry your ideas.

Structure and Inductive Analysis

One way to create structure for your paper is to use the process of inductive analysis described in Chapter 7:

1. Gather data and collect notes.
2. Spread out your notes in front of you.
3. Look for common ideas.
4. Move common ideas into groups to create sections.
5. Within each section, look for similar items to create paragraphs or subsections.

Using Headings to Create Structure

Using headings makes a report easier to read. Following is a writing sample that does not use headings. To the reader it appears as a large blob of text. Large blobs like this are less reader friendly because the structure is indistinct.

MS. BAKER'S WRITING WORKSHOP

In November 1996, I spent 2 weeks in Ms. Baker's second grade classroom watching her writing workshop. Here writing was taught as a process consisting of five stages: prewriting, first draft, revising, editing, and publication. Student choice was integral to this process. Ms. Baker said that allowing students to choose their own writing topics seemed to result in a better quality of writing. Students' writing often reflected events going on in their lives, thus increasing feelings of ownership and emotional attachment. They seemed eager to share their ideas and experiences using writing.

Conversation was an integral part of the writing workshop. Students talked about possible writing topics, about their current writing projects, and about things happening in their lives. More formal conversations related directly to students' writing occurred in individual and small-group conferences and in large-group sharing sessions.

Skills identified in language arts manuals and unit tests were taught using explicit instruction in short mini-lessons lasting 5 to 10 minutes. After each skill was presented, students moved into small groups to create examples of that skill. This allowed students to help each other generate ideas and hear the thinking processes of others. For documentation, checklists were created that listed each skill and the date it was taught. Students' work was also used to determine those skills used in mini-lessons. When unit tests were given, it was found that these students performed just as well on tests of basic skills as students in other second grade classrooms. Thus, it appeared that students in this writing workshop were learning literacy skills using far less instructional time than did other classes while more time was spent writing and composing.

Ms. Baker said that management was going better than she had expected. She put more responsibility on students for correcting tests, organizing the classroom, and choosing writing topics. This made the room more student-centered and resulted in her having fewer behavior problems. The time spent teaching routines and procedures led to fewer distractions and helped her workshops run smoothly. Also, creating writing experiences that tapped into students' interests and valued their ideas seemed to contribute to much of her success with classroom management. My observations showed few incidents of off-task behavior during writing workshops. Ms. Baker created structure while giving students choices and a sense of autonomy within this structure.

Notice how the same large blob of text becomes more reader friendly when I insert some headings and add a short introductory paragraph at the beginning. The structure becomes readily apparent and, thus, comprehension is enhanced.

MS. BAKER'S WRITING WORKSHOP

In November 1996, I spent 2 weeks in Ms. Baker's second grade classroom watching students in her writing workshop. Following are described (1) the writing process, (2) student talk, (3) teaching skills, and (4) behavior management.

Writing

Here writing was taught as a process consisting of five stages: prewriting, first draft, revising, editing, and publication. Student choice was integral to this process. Ms. Baker said that allowing students to choose their own writing topics seemed to result in a better quality of writing. Students' writing often reflected events going on in their lives, thus increasing feelings of ownership and emotional attachment. They seemed eager to share their ideas and experiences using writing.

Talk

Conversation was an integral part of the writing workshop. Students talked about possible writing topics, about their current writing projects, and about things happening in their lives. More formal conversations related directly to students' writing occurred in individual and small-group conferences and in large-group sharing sessions.

Skills

Skills identified in language arts manuals and unit tests were taught using explicit instruction in short mini-lessons lasting 5 to 10 minutes. After each skill was presented, students moved into small groups to create examples of that skill. This allowed students to help each other generate ideas and hear the thinking processes of others. For documentation, checklists were created that listed each skill and the date it was taught. Students' work was also used to determine those skills used in mini-lessons. When unit tests were given, it was found that these students performed just as well on tests of basic skills as students in other second grade classrooms. Thus, it appeared that students in this writing workshop were learning literacy skills using far less instructional time than did other classes while more time was spent writing and composing.

Behavior Management

Ms. Baker said that management was going better than she had expected. She put more responsibility on students for correcting tests, organizing the classroom, and choosing writing topics. This made the room more student-centered and resulted in her having fewer behavior problems. The time spent teaching routines and procedures led to fewer distractions and helped her workshops run smoothly. Also, creating writing experiences that tapped into students' interests and valued their ideas seemed to contribute to much of her success with classroom management. My observations showed few incidents of off-task behavior during writing workshops. Ms. Baker created structure while giving students choices and a sense of autonomy within this structure.

Using Subheadings to Create More Structure

Subheadings can be used to further organize large sections of text. Subheadings are italicized, flush left, with the first letter of the principal words capitalized. Example:

Skills

Teaching

Skills identified in language arts manuals and unit tests were taught using explicit instruction in short mini-lessons lasting 5 to 10 minutes. After each skill was presented, students moved into small groups to create examples of that skill. This allowed students to help each other generate ideas and hear the thinking processes of others.

Assessment and Evaluation

For documentation, checklists were created that listed each skill and the date it was taught. Students' work was also used to determine those skills used in mini-lessons. When unit tests were given, it was found that these students performed just as well on tests of basic skills as students in other second grade classrooms. Thus, it appeared that students in this writing workshop were learning literacy skills using far less instructional time than did other classes while more time was spent writing and composing.

CASE STUDIES OR REPRESENTATIVE SAMPLES

Including samples of students' products, quotes, or excerpts from your research journal makes your data come alive. Again, the goal is to convey to the reader a sense of being there.

It's Alive!

When I was doing my doctoral work at the University of Minnesota, I taught writing courses in the composition department. To inform my teaching practice, one quarter I used a technique called dialogue journaling (Watts & Johnson, 1995). I recorded and analyzed my thoughts and feelings after each class on a computer disk (journal). Michelle, a colleague, did the same. At the end of each week we exchanged disks and responded to what the other had written. This had three positive effects: (a) it provided a good sense of what was going on in our classes, (b) it gave us another viewpoint, and (c) we could see how the other was organizing and teaching the writing course. This is an extremely informative practice and one that I would highly recommend to all teachers.

Notice in the following sample how the inclusion of just a few journal entries gives you a sense of what I was seeing and experiencing. My entries are in lowercase. Michelle's responses are in uppercase. We both agreed to write without worrying about spelling, grammar, punctuation, or word choice.

1/2/99

Good to start this journal. It is very helpful for me to communicate with somebody else what does and doesn't work and also to hear the triumphs and tribulations of another. It helps also to know what other instructors are doing in their classes and also what they're thinking and feeling. We are human beings dammit!

Also, as teachers of writing we will be practicing what we preach. We will write to see what it is we have to say. We will write to extend and analyze our thoughts. Writing will affect our thinking.

ANDY—THANK YOU FOR ASKING ME TO DO THIS. JUST READING THROUGH YOUR COMMENTS ABOUT THE FIRST WEEK MAKES ME PLEASED TO BE INVOLVED IN THIS VENTURE. I AM LEARNING ALREADY FROM HEARING ABOUT EXPERIENCES YOU'RE HAVING IN YOUR CLASS. THIS IS A GOOD THING.

1/5/99

They're so quiet. Not like my other class at all. I miss the busy bustle of voices when I come into the room. I love to hear students chattering away. I like when students tell me things, tease me gently, or ask me questions. I like when there's a gosh darn relationship. Teaching starts with a relationship. Until then I'm just some clown dancing in front of the classroom.

I have to remember that it's only week 1. It will take me awhile to get there. Students have to learn to trust me and to trust each other. Like petting a strange dog: you have to let him/her smell your hand before you pet him/her.

"Arf!"

Building community—I can't demand instant community. Trust is earned.

ANDY—IT'S THE THIRD WEEK AND MY STUDENTS ARE STILL QUIET AT THE BEGINNING OF THE HOUR. THIS BOTHERS ME. I LIKE WALKING INTO A ROOM

WHERE EVERYONE IS TALKING, SHARING STORIES ABOUT OTHER CLASSES OR THE COMMUTE TO SCHOOL. LAST QUARTER WHEN MY STUDENTS WOULD FALL SILENT AS I CAME INTO THE ROOM, I WOULD SAY, "TALK, TALK. THERE'S NO REASON TO BE QUIET JUST BECAUSE I'M HERE. I WANT TO HEAR YOUR VOICES!" I WOULD SAY THIS LIGHTLY AND IT OFTEN WORKED. BUT LAST QUARTER I TAUGHT IN A SMALL ROOM WITH ONLY THREE ROWS OF DESKS, SO STUDENTS WERE ALREADY CLOSE TO ME AND TO ONE ANOTHER. THIS QUARTER I'M IN A FISH BOWL (302 LIND HALL) WITH MANY ROWS AND A GREAT DEAL OF DISTANCE BETWEEN ME AND THE STUDENTS WHEN I FIRST WALK IN THE ROOM. SOMEHOW I HAVE A LESS EASY TIME MAKING JOKES OR LIGHTENING THE TONE AT THE BEGINNING OF CLASS. ARE YOUR STUDENTS TALKING MORE NOW?

1/9/99

In group work I allow for chatter-time. Groups are more expensive in terms of time, but the payoff is great in terms of tapping into a diversity of ideas and talents and creating a positive social climate.

My all-female group has done a great job of getting to know each other. I looked up to see them passing pictures around. One of my all-male groups is having a hard time with this. You can insert your own gender generalizations here:

ANDY—I'M EAGER TO KNOW MORE ABOUT HOW YOU BUILD COMMUNITY IN GROUPS. I HAVEN'T STARTED ANY PARTICULAR COMMUNITY BUILDING EXERCISES, ALTHOUGH MOST OF MY GROUPS ARE WORKING OKAY. I'D BE EAGER TO HEAR ABOUT ANY ACTIVITIES YOU HAVE UP YOUR SLEEVE.

PERHAPS YOU COULD ASK YOUR ALL-MALE GROUP TO BE RESPONSIBLE FOR REPORTING BACK TO THE CLASS ON SOME ASSIGNMENT OR FOR MAKING A PRESENTATION? MAYBE THEY WOULD BOND THROUGH THE EXPERIENCE OF HAVING TO ASSUME A MORE PUBLIC ROLE IN THE CLASS? I'M NOT SURE.

1/12/99

Ryan is a male student. I read faces pretty well. I got anger from him. He gave me stone face. Sullen, almost challenging at times. I'm beginning to see this as a defense mechanism. He's scared, wondering if he measures up. I know I've sometimes put on a tough exterior to protect my soft inner core . . . Funny the things we do to protect our inner core.

ANDY—I REMEMBER ONE STUDENT FROM LAST QUARTER WHO LITERALLY GLOWERED AT ME. I THINK HE HAD REASON TO BE FRUSTRATED, BUT I COULDN'T FIGURE OUT HOW TO MAKE THINGS BETTER. DON'T YOU WANT TO INTERVENE WHEN YOU SEE A STUDENT LOOKING SO ANGRY? I WANT TO ASK HIM OR HER WHAT'S THE MATTER? BUT THEN I WORRY THAT IT WOULD NOT BE THE PROFESSIONAL THING TO DO.

1/29/99

So it's Monday . . . I'm sure every writing instructor has the same feelings that I'm having this week. Am I doing any good? Are students learning anything? Am I just standing up here wiggling my arms, getting excited for nothing? Are they just nodding their heads like dogs in the back of car windows just so they can get their five credits and move on down the road?

ANDY—IT'S INTERESTING THAT WE'RE BOTH HAVING THESE SAME WORRIES THIS WEEK. IN MY JOURNAL THIS PAST WEEK I MENTIONED THAT TEACHING IS HARD WORK PRECISELY BECAUSE IT IS DIFFICULT TO MEASURE HOW "GOOD" WE ARE. WE DON'T SEE A BUSINESS DEAL GO THROUGH OR CURE A PERSON OF A RASH. INSTEAD, WE HOPE THAT WE'LL PLANT SEEDS . . . OR, EVEN MORE INDIRECTLY, THAT WE'LL FOSTER SOME SORT OF EXCITEMENT ABOUT LEARNING.

Inductive analysis was used to analyze the wealth of data in my dialogue journal. I went through and found the patterns emerging in the types of responses and reported the categories and their frequency. I was then able to report these data in terms of numbers (see Chapter 18). I mixed this with my insights and representative samples to create a good sense of being there.

APPENDICES

Appendices (plural form of appendix) contain information that interrupts the flow of the text. These are placed at the end of your report and comprise information such as data retrieval charts, surveys, questionnaires, tests, interview questions, detailed descriptions that may be too distracting if inserted in the body of your report, or longer samples of your data. Information should be indicated in the body of your text by a reference within parentheses.

REPORTING QUANTITATIVE DATA

In an action research report, you may need to describe quantifiable data. In these instances, when do you use numbers and when do you use words to express these arithmetic concepts? The following information is taken from the *Publication Manual of the American Psychological Association* (2009).

Using Numbers

Use numerals to express arithmetic concepts in the following cases:

1. Numbers 10 and above

   - The class generated 27 different ideas in the space of 5 minutes.

2. Dates

    • This study took place on May 5, 2009.

3. Ages

    • She is 7 years old.

4. Time

    • The subjects reported to the laboratory at 1:00 p.m. They stayed there for 2 hours and 7 minutes.

5. People in a study

    • There were 15 students in this study: 8 males and 7 females.

6. Grade level

    • Most children begin grade 2 with a thorough knowledge of consonant sounds. (Note: It is grade 2 but second grade.)

7. Chapters

    • Most would agree that Chapter 17 is the most fascinating chapter of the book.

8. Pages

    • Page 1 of this text begins with a fascinating review of the writing process.

9. Scales or rating systems

    • He scored a 7 on a 10-point scale.

10. Money

    • The subjects in this study were paid $8 for participating.

11. Numbers grouped for comparison with other numbers 10 and above

    • The study showed that 9 of 15 students were able to improve their grade averages significantly by learning how to read critically. Of the 15 students participating, 6 received a grade of A, 5 received a grade of B, and 4 received a grade of C.

Using Words

Use words to express arithmetic concepts in the following cases:

1. Numbers below 10

    • He sank three of seven free throws.

2. Numbers that begin a title

    • Mr. Higgins read the book *Seven Silly Swans* to his second-grade class.

3. Numbers that begin a sentence

   • Fourteen children fell asleep during the story. (Try to avoid starting sentences with numbers.)

4. Numbers grouped for comparison with other numbers below 10

   • In reading class, seven out of the nine boys preferred action stories.

5. Numbers in a hyphenated word

   • The Minnesota Vikings are four-time Super Bowl losers.

Reporting Arithmetic Data

Four rules apply for arithmetic data numbers.

1. Arithmetic data are reported in descending order (from greatest to least). In the following example, in which some numbers are above 10 (27 walruses), I used numbers instead of words throughout to remain consistent even though some numbers are below 10 (9 kangaroos and 3 white-tailed deer).

   • The mosaic contained 27 walruses, 14 elephants, 9 kangaroos, and 3 white-tailed deer.

2. Tell what you are observing first.

   • This study was designed to determine the types of movie genre that were popular among elementary students.

3. Tell the total number before you report categories. Both the examples here are correct. The second one, however, seems a little less repetitive.

   • Of 99 total responses, 47 preferred action movies, 31 preferred comedies, 14 preferred science fiction, and 7 preferred historical movies.

   • Respondents in this study reported their favorite movie genre. Of 99 total responses, the following preferences were noted: 47 action movies, 31 comedies, 14 science fiction, and 7 historical movies.

4. Stay consistent with the order of gender or other categories. Always report numbers in descending order; however, when reporting gender or other categories, the order of the first example must remain consistent throughout. In the following example, I start with the largest total category (Caucasians). The order is 9 males and 2 females. In the categories that follow (Black and Asian), even though the number of females is greater than the number of males, they are reported second to maintain a consistent order.

   • There were 28 students in the class: 14 males and 14 females. Nine males and 2 females were Caucasian, 3 males and 7 females were Black, and 2 males and 5 females were Asian.

TABLES

Tables are a quick, visual way to organize and report information. They are especially useful if you have a great deal of numerical data to report. Tables are meant to replace information written in the text. Thus, you might refer to data in the text, but do not duplicate table information in the text. For example, in a study looking at the leisure reading habits of high school students, the following data could appear in the text in written form:

- A study was conducted to determine the leisure reading preferences of high school students. Of the 250 students surveyed, 140 were females and 110 were males. The responses were as follows: action or adventure was preferred by 35% of the males and 5% of the females; mysteries were preferred by 10% of the males and 25% of the females; histories were preferred by 0% of the males and 35% of the females; biographies were preferred by 5% of the males and 20% of the females; fantasies were preferred by 20% of the males and 0% of the females; comedies were preferred by 15% of the males and 3% of the females; technical reading was preferred by 5% of the males and 10% of the females; and science fiction was preferred by 10% of the males and 2% of the females. Total responses were as follows: 40% preferred action or adventure, 35% preferred mysteries, 35% preferred history, 25% preferred biography, 20% preferred fantasy, 18% preferred comedy, 15% preferred technical reading, and 12% preferred science fiction.

This paragraph is certainly correct; however, it is not easy to digest this amount of information in this form. A table can be used to report the same information (see Table 10.1). For each gender, the preference is listed from greatest to least. Use parentheses to refer to a table in the text (see Table 10.1). Because it is a title,

TABLE 10.1 Percentages of Leisure Reading Preferences of High School Students

MALES		FEMALES	
Action/adventure	35	Historical	35
Fantasy	20	Mystery	25
Comedy	15	Biography	20
Science fiction	10	Technical	10
Mystery	10	Action/adventure	5
Biography	5	Comedy	3
Technical	5	Science fiction	2
Historical	0	Fantasy	0

TABLE 10.2   Percentages of Leisure Reading Preferences of High School Students

GENRE	MALE	FEMALE	TOTAL
Action/adventure	35	5	40
Mystery	10	25	35
Historical	0	35	35
Biography	52	0	25
Fantasy	20	0	20
Comedy	15	3	18
Technical	5	10	15
Science fiction	10	2	12

the word *Table* is capitalized. In your action research report the title should be listed on the next line, also flush left. The title should be listed on the next line, also flush left. This lets readers know quickly and easily exactly what they are reading. If you are using chapters, merge the table and figure numbers with the chapter numbers. For example, Table 10.1 means Chapter 10, Table 1.

In Table 10.2 the leisure reading preferences of high school students are again reported; however, the data are grouped and listed in descending order according to the genre totals. (Note: Because I referred to Table 10.2 in the sentence, I did not have to put "see Table 10.2" in parentheses.)

Tables help organize information and make it readily available to the reader. Consider the following example:

> This study was conducted to see what kind of footwear middle school students wear. For this study 127 middle school students were observed. The findings are shown in Table 10.3.

FIGURES

Figures include lists, graphs, diagrams, or pictures. Figures are labeled differently than tables. The figure number is bold, flush left, and followed by a period. In the title, only the first letter is capitalized and the last word is followed by a period (see

TABLE 10.3   Type of Footwear Worn by Middle School Students

TYPE OF SHOE	MALE	FEMALE	TOTAL
Athletic or court shoes	25	20	45
Hiking boots	20	21	41
Sandals	10	20	30
Dress shoes	5	6	11

Playground Games

1. Jump rope
2. Soccer
3. Playground equipment
4. Football
5. Chasing games
6. Softball
7. Other

FIGURE 10.1   Playground Games

Figure 10.1). Figures are not the same as tables and should be counted differently. For example, I have used three tables thus far in this chapter, but this is the first figure, so it is labeled Figure 10.1.

Graphs

Graphs are listed as figures. Bar graphs are used to show comparison. Most word processors have options that allow you to make high-quality graphs quickly and easily. The Vision Quest data described in Chapter 9 is displayed in Figure 10.2. Line graphs are used to show change over time. Figure 10.3 shows how the types of responses in my Vision Quest study changed over time.

Other Visuals

Pictures, photographs, maps, illustrations, or sample products are all examples of figures and should be referred to in the same way as those figures just described.

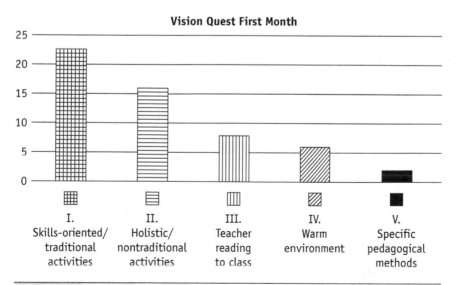

FIGURE 10.2   Vision Quest Bar Graph

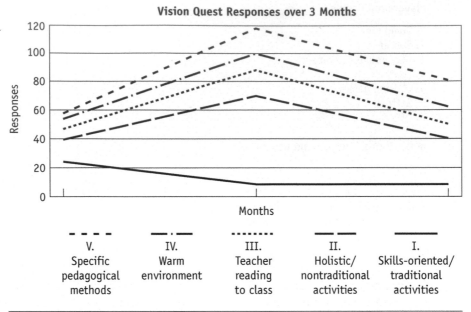

Months

- - - - V.
Specific
pedagogical
methods

— · — IV.
Warm
environment

· · · · · · · III.
Teacher
reading
to class

— — II.
Holistic/
nontraditional
activities

——— I.
Skills-oriented/
traditional
activities

FIGURE 10.3 **Vision Quest Line Graph**

If you have an abundance of these, they should be included in an appendix at the end of your report and simply referred to in the body of your text.

SUMMARY

- Reporting your findings usually comprises the bulk of your action research report.
- Your data should be converted into a form that can easily be read and understood.
- In writing your action research report the onus is on you to be fair and impartial.
- You are part of the research and should include your thoughts and actions in your report.
- When you write your report, let the readers hear your thoughts as you go through all phases of your research.
- Write as concisely as possible.
- Creating structure using headings and subheadings improves the comprehension of your report.
- Important information that seems to interrupt the flow of your report should be put in an appendix.
- Numbers and words are both used to express arithmetic concepts.
- Tables are an effective way to organize information and are especially useful in reporting a large amount of arithmetic data.

- Do not duplicate table information in the text of your action research report.
- Figures are different from tables and include lists, graphs, diagrams, pictures, photographs, maps, illustrations, and various kinds of examples.

QUESTIONS AND ACTIVITIES

1. Find and share a piece of qualitative research related to an area of interest. What do you notice about the writing style?
2. Find and share a piece of quantitative research related to an area of interest. What do you notice about the writing style?
3. Do a quick survey asking at least 25 people to name their favorite book or books. Use inductive analysis to find groups and numbers within each group. Report your data using a table or figure.
4. In the activity in #3, report your data without using a table or figure.
5. Do a quick survey of at least 25 people to determine their preference for movie genre. Report your data. In your report, describe how the data were collected, what you found, possible differences related to gender, and what those data might mean or how they might be applied.
6. Repeat the previous activity, except compare adults' preferences to adolescents' (ages 12–19) and children's (ages 6–11).
7. Find an area where you can observe many people. Observe to get a feel for the different kinds of shoes people wear, then find categories and use a data retrieval chart and tally marks to determine what kind of shoe is most often worn. Report your data. In your report, describe how the data were collected, what you found, possible differences related to gender, and what those data might mean or how they might be applied.
8. Repeat the previous activity, except find a different place to collect the same information. Compare the kinds of shoes worn at the two places.

POSSIBLE RESEARCH QUESTIONS FOR ACTION RESEARCH PROJECTS

1. How many hours a night do your students spend doing homework?
2. How many hours a night do your students spend watching TV?
3. How many hours a night do your students spent on the computer?
4. How many text messages per day do your students send? Receive?
5. What personal characteristics, traits, or attributes do students value? Examples: honesty, compassion, friendliness, humor.
6. What research-based strategies do teachers currently use? What research-based strategies would they like to know more about or be able to use?
7. What topics or strategies would teachers like to be included in their professional development?
8. What kind of books do your students like to read?
9. What are your students' favorite books?

10. Identify a class in which students seem to be struggling. Create a simple open-ended survey using the following two questions: What things help you learn in that class? What could be done differently to help you learn?

11. What do teachers consider to be their strengths or special talents as teachers and as human beings?

12. What do students consider to be their strengths or special talents?

13. What do students consider to be their passion? What are they very much interested in? What would they like to know more about?

14. What do teachers consider to be their passion? What are they very much interested in? What would they like to know more about? What would they like to be able to incorporate into their learning curriculum?

15. What do your students value? What physical things do students value or see as important? What traits or personal characteristics do students value? What experiences do students value?

16. What do your colleagues value? What physical things do your colleagues value or see as important? What traits or personal characteristics do your colleagues value? What experiences do your colleagues value?

17. Who are your students' heroes? What traits do these heroes have in common?

18. Who are your colleagues' heroes? What traits do these heroes have in common?

19. Whom do your students identify as villains or adversaries? What traits do these villains have in common?

20. Whom do your colleagues identify as villains or adversaries? What traits do these villains have in common?

21. What do students consider to be the important events in their lives? What does this tell you about your students?

22. What do your colleagues consider to be the important events in their lives? What does this tell you about your colleagues?

23. What dreams do your students have? Where do they see themselves at age 25, 35, and 45?

24. What do teachers and parents see as the purpose of schools in our society? Why do they think we educate students? To what end? How does this compare with different philosophical orientations toward education such as those of Plato, John Dewey, Paulo Freire, Rudolph Steiner, Maria Montessori, or Neil Postman?

CHAPTER ELEVEN

DISCUSSION: YOUR PLAN OF ACTION

Although it may not be as long as the other parts of your paper, everything in your action research report leads up to the section in which you discuss your findings and make your conclusions and recommendations based on the data collected. This is followed by what most consider to be the most important part of an action research project—your plan describing the actions you will take based on your findings. Although they are described in three separate sections here, these items do not need to appear in this order or in this exact form and may even merge in your action research report.

Also, I am making the assumption that an action research project will result in some sort of written document or report. This report may vary in length and formality, depending on the purpose of your research. Even if you are doing action research simply for your own edification as a classroom teacher, I would encourage you to create a short written document of your findings and describe ideas for change. Writing helps to clarify and organize your thinking and enables you to see patterns or associations you may have missed. Also, a written report documents your professional development. In most states teachers periodically have to engage in some kind of continuing education to maintain their teaching license. An action research report can be used for this purpose. Finally, having a written account of your findings and ideas allows you to share them with others, either in oral or written form. In this way you can help to keep the field of education evolving and moving forward.

CONCLUSIONS AND RECOMMENDATIONS

A conclusion is a reasoned deduction. That is, you come to believe one thing based on another thing or series of things. Based on the data you have collected and reported, what does it all mean? What is it that you now know to be true? What can we deduce from the data you have presented? Your conclusion is often no more than a paragraph or two describing your current state of knowing or a list of things you have come to believe as a result of your study. It should bring together the important data and explain what they mean. As you write your conclusion, be aware that it will be the basis for your recommendation. You are making a case for a particular plan of action.

A recommendation is a general suggestion for what is believed to be an effective choice or action based on your findings. You tell how your findings might be used or provide advice as to what should be done differently. Keep in mind, however, that the line between conclusions and recommendations is often blurred. Some action research papers have only conclusions; others have only recommendations. Still others, like those described next, have a combination of both.

Christina Stolfa, Nacogdoches, Texas

Christina Stolfa conducted an action research study to determine whether all students in her fourth-grade multiabilty-level inclusive classroom were receiving the writing instruction they needed to be successful writers. She did a case study focusing on three students who represented three ability levels in her classroom: Mark, Pat, and Nicole. Mark was a low-ability student who left class during reading and math for special help in a resource room. Because of the severity of his disability, he had spent the previous year in a self-contained special education classroom. Pat was identified as gifted and talented. Nicole was seen as an average student.

Conclusions

I found that if classes are to be successful, both in state assessments and in the minds of the students, classroom teachers must be given assistance or the class sizes must decrease. I know this is a difficult conclusion, but it is the most appropriate summarization. With a large gap between the levels of abilities in a fourth grade classroom it is difficult to use whole group instruction most of the time and actually reach and make an impact on students. The three children in this study represent the three major ability levels present in my classroom. If I am teaching the whole group, it is common that one of the groups will not be receiving the instruction that is most appropriate for them.

Because of the severity of emotional and social issues, I feel that Mark benefited the least from the instruction given. Much of this was out of our hands; however, there are other children like Mark who suffer from the lack of desperately needed one-on-one instruction. Children like Pat will excel in most situations, but they are also done an injustice when their minds are not stretched to their full capacity. Children like Nicole are often overlooked because they can stay afloat without calling attention to themselves. However, they deserve the attention and assistance that the others receive as well.

Recommendations

My recommendations include continuing writing conferences and structured writing lessons throughout the year. My hope is that all three students will be able to learn more strategies to help them complete and excel on the state-mandated writing tests and proceed successfully to fifth grade.

Also, all children deserve success, and it is important that they achieve it. Classrooms, both teachers and students, greatly benefit from smaller class sizes. It allows more time to communicate and use constructive criticism, which will help students become more involved, more confident writers in the end, no matter what the ability level ranking.

Jo Henriksen, St. Louis Park, Minnesota

Jo Henriksen is a gifted education teacher at Peter Hobart Elementary and Aquila Primary Center in St. Louis Park, Minnesota. Instead of the traditional parent–teacher conference, she studied student-led conferences involving identified gifted students in grades 1 through 3. Before their conferences, students were asked to synthesize and describe in writing their learning during the quarter. This information was shared with parents during the conference.

Jo's goals in this action research were to understand fully the process of student-led conferences and to see whether they were beneficial and worth continuing. To collect data, she created a survey for students (see Figure 11.1). She recorded her thoughts and impressions following each conference. A checklist was created to guide her reflections (see Figure 11.2).

In the checklists in Figures 11.1 and 11.2, Jo Henriksen defined specific behaviors or attributes. The checklist allowed her to focus on these attributes consistently with each student. After presenting the data in her report, Jo wrote the following conclusion.

Name: _____   Grade: _____   Today's Date: _____

HOW DID YOUR CONFERENCE GO?

1. Who came to your conference besides you?   mom   dad   both
2. Were you glad you could come to your conference?   yes   no   not sure
3. Do you think your parents learned more about what you are doing in class?   yes   no   not sure
4. Did you learn more about putting facts into categories?   yes   no   not sure
5. Did you get to talk enough?   yes   no   not sure
6. Was the time long enough for the conference?   yes   no   not sure

7. What is the best part of getting to come to your own conference?

8. Could anything make the conference better next time?

FIGURE 11.1   Student Survey Form

Name: _____   Grade: _____   Today's Date: _____

REFLECTIONS ON THE CHILD-LED CONFERENCE

1. Who came to the conference?	mom	dad	both
2. Was the tone of the conference pleasant?	yes	no	comments:
3. Did parents seem to learn more about what happens in class?	yes	no	comments:
4. Did the child handle the vocabulary of the categorizing exercise?	yes	no	comments:
5. Did the child handle the categorizing exercise?	yes	no	comments:
6. Did the child get to talk enough?	yes	no	comments:
7. Was the time long enough for the conference?	yes	no	comments:

8. Do any points need to be remembered because of this conference?

9. Do you need to schedule another appointment for a conference without the child? Topic?

FIGURE 11.2   Teacher Reflection Form

Conclusions

I came to the following conclusions regarding student-led conferences:

1. They were a wonderful opportunity to meet with children in a pleasant situation.

2. Children learned more about what they have learned, thanks to this form of conferencing.

3. The conferences were energizing as opposed to energy draining.

4. Our district schedules the fall conferences very early. Since my gifted education program doesn't start until the second full week of school, I barely have time to get much work done with the children before it is conference time. I am going to have to do some thinking about the tightness of the schedule.

5. I will do more preconference planning with each child before the big night.

6. I routinely have a family night each spring. This is an opportunity for all to see what students have produced. I am thinking that I will have this night prior to spring conferences. That way, less time will be needed at conferences to explain the projects. More time can be devoted to discussion and assessment of projects.

7. Whereas I can't insist that parents schedule conferences, I am really determined to have conferences with virtually 100% of my students.

8. The conferences will still be only 25 minutes in length. Many of my students, being who they are, love to talk at length. I will have to think about how to reconcile the time allotment to still satisfy the desire of these children, if possible.

9. I absolutely will continue the practice.

Final Thoughts

Overall, I would have to say that my decision to conduct student-led conferences was good. I have worked in gifted education for 9 years, in regular education a lot longer. I know what makes children happy a lot of the time and what helps parents to feel secure some of the time. I also know what helps me to maintain zest for the job that I do. I designed the conferences to meet the needs of my students and families. I also designed the conferences to be a tool to help me to be more effective in my position. Conferences are an inherently difficult time for me; however, I look forward to making this time more positive and productive through the use of student-led conferences.

Cathy Stamps, Fifth Grade, Hopkins Elementary School

Cathy Stamps was interested in finding out if her fifth-grade students learned better when they sat by their friends or when she assigned them seats. She collected data by (a) taking field notes focusing specifically on students' behavior, attitudes, and production; (b) comparing samples of students' work that were completed in both settings; and (c) administering a student survey. She made the following conclusions and recommendations:

Based on my observations and student responses, I would conclude that learning is positively affected when students have a say in where they sit. They feel more ownership in their learning; therefore, they are more excited about learning. I know when I am at conferences or workshops, I would much rather have my choice of people to work with versus being told who to work with. I think the saying, "Treat others the way you would like to be treated" applies to this situation. By giving students a chance to self-assign themselves, I discovered that students wasted less time working out differences that often hinder them when trying to complete a task in a minimal amount of time.

My experience with this investigation has been beneficial. Students knew what was expected and also knew the consequences if they couldn't handle working in self-assigned groups. However, I did assign seats periodically in order to mix up the class and decrease cliques.

Delinda Whitley, Mt. Enterprise, Texas

Delinda Whitley conducted an action research project in a seventh-grade classroom in a rural east Texas school. The purpose of her study was to determine whether working in pairs to discuss reading assignments would improve her students' reading comprehension. The conclusions and recommendations of her study are presented here.

Conclusions

Most students did perform better on vocabulary and comprehension assessments after working together in pairs on reading assignments. The mean for test scores increased 21.4 points from the first week to the sixth week's test. Students who did show improvement were those who seemed to struggle with homework. The ability to complete assignments quicker than by themselves reflected higher test score means. Assessment scores did not improve for the two students with the highest independent reading levels.

I discussed my findings with a colleague who taught math. My findings were consistent with studies that she has conducted in her classroom. I found that the really low and extremely high students did not benefit from paired reading, whereas the average and low average students gained tremendously. When students were given ownership and a voice, their learning became more meaningful and productive. Through the use of conversation and repeated readings, fluency increased, as did comprehension. For students who did not benefit from paired readings, the traditional instructional method is still needed. Students need to hear good literature read and modeled for them. I am grateful for this opportunity and definitely plan to incorporate paired readings in my classroom setting.

Recommendations

No method of reading instruction is the best. Balancing the traditional instructional method with paired students may allow greater gains for all students. Students will be focused and directed toward specific literary elements. They may also continue to benefit from modeled oral reading from the teacher through traditional instruction. Consequently, allowing students to complete some work in pairs should allow for a higher assessment test scores. Allowing students to work in pairs will also give them a voice in their learning and make it more enjoyable. Because some students are more vocal and learn auditorily, the repetition of novel information or vocabulary in a paired working assignment will also help them develop their literacy skills.

Darlene Cempa, Whitney Point, New York

Darlene Cempa was a student teacher when she conducted an action research project to examine the benefits of using cooperative learning in a fifth-grade classroom in which there was a high proportion of students with learning disabilities. Three data sources were used for this study: (a) a field observation checklist to document on-task and off-task behaviors, (b) anecdotal records based on conversations with the classroom teacher and classroom observations, and (c) interviews conducted with the classroom teachers and special education teachers.

Discussion

This action research project provided some interesting insight into ways to educate children with ADHD. First, teachers should try to use cooperative learning techniques if they have students with ADHD. These techniques appear to help keep the students engaged, on-task and encourage peer interaction. The research in the literature review reinforces this concept, and it makes sense.

Second, students need to be properly trained in cooperative learning techniques in order to receive the most benefit from cooperative learning. This point has been shown in studies by Robyn Gillies (Gillies, 2006; Gillies & Ashman, 2000; Gillies & Boyle, 2006) and was shown through my research as well. As the students became more skilled at cooperative learning and better understood their roles, they benefited more and were better able to scaffold for one another.

For me as a pre-service teacher, this project provided insight that will assist me in my development as a teacher. I was able to see the importance of systematically documenting any issue or question that I wish to better understand. With the new requirements of implementing Response to Intervention (RTI) methods in order to determine if a student needs additional services, I will frequently need to systematically and thoroughly gather data. The cornerstone of RTI is that the teacher must thoroughly document the issue that is noticed, and then document specific, research-based interventions that he or she has used with the student over a period of time. If the interventions used do not improve the student's academic performance, the student is referred to the Committee on Special Education (CSE) for services. The RTI documentation is given to the CSE to evaluate for placement, in addition to other testing that may be done by the school psychologist. This approach places more control over referrals in the teacher's hands, but it also requires thorough and systematic documentation.

In addition, I have gained greater appreciation for both the needs of students with disabilities and the diverse ways that I can address these needs as a teacher. Many techniques that are not widely used in many of today's public schools might help different groups of students. It is important that I keep current on research and pedagogy news through reading and following professional journals and joining professional groups.

IMPLICATIONS OR RECOMMENDATIONS FOR FUTURE RESEARCH

Good research of any kind often results in as many new questions as it does answers. That is, you will find areas that need to be explored. Action research reports sometimes include a section describing these possible future research topics.

Morgan Chylinski, Jamesville, New York

Morgan Chylinski conducted an action research project that examined the effectiveness of hands-on learning for science in a third-grade classroom. After discussing her findings and recommendations for practice in her report, she identifies several areas for possible future research.

Recommendations For Research

The research in this study supports hands-on inquiry in the elementary classroom. More research must be done in order to determine the overall effectiveness of this type of science. Research needs to be done at various grade levels, settings and with various methods of hands-on inquiry in order to make the data more accurate. Since the study was only conducted in a third grade classroom, additional grade levels should be looked at to see if these results are accurate for all children in the elementary school. Hands-on inquiry may be effective in the third grade, but not in kindergarten so these various grade levels should be examined. Furthermore, similar studies need to be done in different locations to make sure that hands-on inquiry is not only valuable other places besides rural schools. This study examined a very small sample so students in different areas need to be studied in order to check and see if these results are specific to this certain population.

In this study, the teacher only used the BOCES hands-on buoyancy unit. Further studies would need to try out different types of inquiry in order to see the effectiveness of various methods. One form of hands-on inquiry might be less valuable then another in teaching elementary school children. In addition, research should look at the effectiveness of a completely hands-on science curriculum. Hands-on inquiry was shown to be successful in this study, but it is not known if it should be used in conjunction with other methods. Maybe hands-on inquiry is best used in combination with traditional teaching methods. In order to completely understand the effectiveness of hands-on inquiry, research needs to be done to see how much of the curriculum should be taught through this method or if a variety of methods should be used.

This study found that students' writing improved as they progressed throughout the unit. Further research needs to be done to see how successfully science can be integrated into other areas of study. Schools are extremely focused on test scores in Math and ELA so science needs to be integrated into other subjects so that the curriculum is not lost. We live in a world driven by technology so students need to have problem solving and critical thinking skills in order to be successful. Science cannot be lost in the curriculum therefore more research needs to be done on the effectiveness of integrating other subject areas into writing especially through hands-on inquiry.

Karen Randle, Trumansburg, New York

Karen Randle conducted an action research project in a fourth-grade classroom to examine the effects of using the visual arts and authentic art making to enhance the quality of students' creative writing. Here are her described implications for teaching and future research.

Implications For Teaching And Future Research

The implications for teaching are such that incorporating visual arts specifically and certainly authentic art making should not be viewed as extra-curricular or "icing on the cake" activities but as essential methods in the practice of teaching. By doing so, we avail students to additional modes of understanding, of expressing their thinking and of organizing their thoughts thus freeing cognitive resources to learn more deeply.

The implications for future research point to expanding the current research to different grade levels to ascertain how using visual arts affects writing specifically and academic achievement in general for younger versus older students. In addition, subsequent research should explore how using visual arts and art making in the classroom meet the call for differentiated instruction to address the needs of diverse learners.

EVALUATION OF THE STUDY

There is no such thing as the perfect study. After reporting conclusions and recommendations, some researchers like to evaluate the effectiveness of their study, explain particular aspects of it, or describe how they might do it differently the next time.

Jim Vavreck, St. Peter, Minnesota

Jim Vavreck conducted a study to see how his sixth-grade students perceived intelligence and creativity. Data were collected by using a questionnaire and a self-rating scale (see Figures 11.3 and 11.4). Jim evaluated his study as he reported the data. He did a nice job of letting us inside his head as he wrestled with various parts of his study. You can also see him thinking as a researcher in the way every question answered seemed to result in another question asked. I have included an excerpt:

> The students in this study generally seemed to feel that either creativity or intelligence was a personal strength. Only 13% rated their intelligence and creativity as equal. A follow-up question regarding what evidence each student could give for his or her personal ratings in intelligence and creativity would be helpful in identifying how students are differentiating between creativity and intelligence as they rate themselves in each.
>
> ### Other Implications
> It appears that I should have described the rating scale more clearly. It seems that either this group is exceptionally above average or else the students did not understand the concept of average. On the other hand, perhaps they have a good, albeit unrealistic, self-concept. Or maybe they pictured extremely low students to compare themselves with.
>
> I am also interested in exploring the differences in how the girls rated themselves and how the boys did using a much larger sample. The current indication is that the girls rated themselves higher in intelligence and creativity. A longitudinal study could be done to see if the self-ratings in creativity and intelligence change over time.

Name: _____

1. What is intelligence?
2. What is creativity?
3. How are intelligence and creativity related?
4. Is it possible to be creative without being intelligent?
5. Is it possible to be intelligent without being creative?

FIGURE 11.3   Student Survey

Name: _____

1. How creative are you on a scale of 0–10 where 5 is average?
2. How intelligent are you on a scale of 0–10 where 5 is average?

FIGURE 11.4   Student Self-Rating Scale

Staci Wilson, Irving, Texas

Staci Wilson conducted an action research project in her kindergarten classroom to see what skills her students were learning in the blocks center of her classroom. She wanted to understand why blocks were important to the curriculum and in what ways children benefited from manipulating blocks. In describing the limitations of her study, she describes not only how her study might have been changed, but also future research projects related to this area.

Summary Of Findings And Conclusions

I found that students do learn important and useful skills from manipulating blocks on a daily basis. Students learn physical, cognitive, social/emotional, and language skills from working in the block center either individually or in groups. The kindergarten students also learned important skills in many different areas of the curriculum that will provide a base education to be built on later in their education.

Students developed skills in mathematics, science, language, social studies, the arts, and technology. By the teacher fostering an open environment for construction, the students are able to "build" their way to education. The teacher must facilitate the learning environment for these young students, but the children will be able to perform the necessary tasks that the teacher requests.

These young students do not realize that they are performing such detailed tasks because it comes so naturally to them. This is learning at its best because children are learning from doing. The teacher must facilitate these experiences because the children don't know how to do this on their own. Once the required objectives are explained or set out for the students, the development of many different skills can and will occur.

Recommendations

When utilizing a block center in my own classroom, I will make sure to foster experiences that cater to all areas of development. Keeping in mind the many different materials that can be placed in this center I will be able to achieve a fully rounded curriculum in my block center. Based on my observations I would recommend to other teachers to utilize blocks in their classrooms on a daily basis. My research indicates many positive benefits from using blocks in this way. Teachers could also benefit from working with their students and making observations on their own. I learned many different things about my students when interacting with them during this study. I feel it would give teachers an insight to students' thinking and creativity.

Limitations Of The Study

The students in this study were allowed only 20 minutes each day to work in the blocks center. I feel that the depth of development would have been deeper and the results of this study more meaningful if more time were given to centers. I feel that children at this age level need more time for free movement and construction of their education.

If I could continue this study, I would observe the same block center in other classrooms in different areas of Texas. I would want to see the impact of development in many different economic areas of the state. I feel that the impact of the center for students might be different from that of my study. Also, students in different socioeconomic strata in the state would probably interact with one another differently. It would be interesting to make these observations and set up the same center in different schools to see the changes and differences across the board.

I would also like to extend this study even broader by examining older students in different subject areas. I would want to observe and question them on the importance of blocks and see whether playing here had a role in their understanding of their current curriculum. I feel that it would give a closing gap to what I and research indicate are great developmental measures started in kindergarten. Knowing the development over time would show how the basic fundamentals that research and my observations indicate are actually being used and extended.

DESIGNING A NEW PLAN OR PROGRAM

Designing a new plan or program puts the action in action research. That means you have to do something or make a plan to do something. In some rare instances the results of an action research project will indicate that everything is just fine, in which case your action research plan is a plan to do nothing. However, most action research projects result in one of five possible outcomes.

1. *Greater understanding of the situation, child, or students in general.* In this case, you should describe how your interactions or instruction will change to reflect this greater understanding.

2. *The discovery of a problem.* Finding and defining a problem are the initial elements of the problem-solving process. If your action research project results in the discovery of a problem, use the problem-solving strategies described in Chapter 4 to create a plan of action. Once a plan has been created, it can be implemented and evaluated. This calls for another action research project, and thus action research becomes a vehicle for the continued growth and evolution of a classroom or school.

3. *A plan, program, or pedagogical method is found to be effective.* An action research report would describe why and how it is effective and allow you to make a case for its continued use. Also, even in an effective plan, program, or pedagogical method, some elements can be made more effective. Your research report should identify these.

4. *A plan, program, or pedagogical method is found to need modification.* Any new plan on paper rarely results in its perfect functioning in reality. Having to adjust and adapt is a normal part of doing anything new or innovative. An action research report is used in this situation to identify the elements that need to be modified and to describe how they will be changed.

5. *A plan, program, or pedagogical method is found to be ineffective.* Action research can be used to document the ineffectiveness of a program. Your research report can be used to support the change or elimination of the plan, program, or pedagogical method.

Creating a New Plan or Program

Sometimes as a result of your action research, you need to design or create a new plan or program. You will likely be more successful if the new plan or program contains the following three elements: (a) a school philosophy or mission statement, (b) goals, and (c) a rationale.

School Philosophy or Mission Statement.   Each school or school district should have a school philosophy, a mission statement, or both. Putting this at the top of any new plan helps you align your objectives with the school's and provides support and justification for the ideas that follow.

A school philosophy is the general belief, policy, or set of ideas formulated by the educational system that reflects the values of the school and community. This may describe the nature of learning or how education and learning fit in a broader scheme of human endeavors. Consider the following example:

> The Anytown School District is a cooperative, democratic venture between students, parents, teachers, and community. It shall be the policy of this district to maintain the highest academic standards, to engage in the best practices in education, and to enable every child to reach his or her full potential.

Thus stated, the school philosophy can be used to support plans that would help maintain high academic standards, such as smaller class sizes, increased teacher development activities, and more books and computers in the classrooms. It can be used to justify change when current practices do not reflect what research describes as the best practices in teaching, such as when schools engage in an over-reliance on standardized tests to describe learning or educational progress. It also can be used to support new programs or the reallocation of resources when certain students are not able to reach their full potential, such as those with special learning needs, the intellectually gifted and highly creative, students with physical disabilities, and those from minority cultures. Thus, a school's philosophy can be used as an agent of change and continued growth.

A mission statement states what the school is trying to accomplish in a general sense. Consider the following example:

> The purpose of our education system is to help learners acquire the knowledge and skills necessary to become constructive world citizens, informed decision makers, and lifelong learners.

The mission statement is sometimes combined with or incorporated into the school philosophy. If your proposed plan or program meets resistance by colleagues, a building principal, or a school board, a mission statement can be used to justify or support what you want to implement.

Goals.   Goals define what you hope to accomplish with your new plan or program. They also help you in evaluation. That is, to determine success, you judge whether you have met some or all of your goals. Goals also help keep your plan focused and prevent you from wandering into unrelated areas. Again, you can create a better case for your new plan or program if your goals are aligned with the school philosophy and mission statement.

Rationale.   The rationale explains why the goals are important. You describe the benefit to the learner, the school, or society in general. Sometimes it helps to put your goals in a theoretical context.

A Less Formal Plan of Action

Depending on the nature and purpose of your action research project, sometimes it is appropriate to have an informal plan of action. This may be a simple description of your intentions or a list of specific steps that you plan to take. Action research is built on the premise that some type of action will result from your research. The final measure of your action research is the degree to which it clearly asks and answers your question, communicates your ideas, and serves to promote positive change.

A final word: I want to reiterate that the items described in this chapter should be adapted to your particular situation to meet the needs of your research project.

SUMMARY

- The final part of an action research report is making conclusions and recommendations, evaluating the study, and making a plan of action.
- Research projects often illuminate other areas for future research.
- A conclusion is a reasoned deduction based on your findings.
- A recommendation is a general suggestion for change based on your findings.
- An evaluation assesses the general effectiveness of your study and explains any interesting or important elements of it.

- A plan of action describes exactly what you intend to do as a result of your action research.
- Action research should result in some form of written document or report, which varies in length and formality.
- A new plan or program is more apt to be successfully implemented if it includes a philosophy or mission statement, goals, and a rationale.

QUESTIONS AND ACTIVITIES

1. Read your school district's philosophy or mission statement or use that of another school district. Do you agree with it? What would you include or eliminate? Can you find an instance in which practice does not align with this philosophy or mission statement?
2. Create your own philosophy or mission statement for your school district and for your classroom.
3. Find a plan, program, or piece of curriculum. Identify the goals. Do the goals align with the mission statement and rationale?
4. Describe a change you would like to see. Use your district's philosophy or mission statement to support your ideas.
5. Describe a class or a particular subject area. List three to eight general goals for that class or subject area. Provide a rationale for their importance.
6. Use the excerpts of one of the studies presented in this chapter to create a plan of action.

POSSIBLE RESEARCH QUESTIONS FOR ACTION RESEARCH PROJECTS

1. What types of interactions occur at parent–teacher conferences? Are parents generally satisfied? How might the interactions be improved?
2. Do report cards do a good job of describing learning? Are parents satisfied with the form currently used? Are teachers satisfied with the form currently used? Do students feel that this form describes their learning? What would students wish to include? What do parents wish were included?
3. Is learning affected in any way if students are allowed to work together?
4. Does being able to work in small groups to complete homework assignments increase understanding or learning?
5. Do advanced organizers used before a lecture or class session improve student learning? Used as a prereading activity, does it seem to improve comprehension? What do students think?
6. What happens if students are asked to create concept maps as postreading experiences or homework assignments instead of the traditional comprehension worksheets or other types of homework? Does learning improve? Do students' attitudes change? What do students think?
7. What adaptations or accommodations are made for English language learners in your classroom, school, and district?

8. In the pause technique, you pause in the middle of a lecture or class session and ask students to work in pairs to highlight important ideas and to review notes. What effect might this have on students learning in elementary, middle, and high school? How do students perceive this? Are there differences related to gender or ability?

9. What would students like to include in a learning portfolio to demonstrate their learning? What happens if students are allowed to make some or all choices in this regard?

10. What note-taking skills do students seem to lack? What are the results of instruction in this area? Does instruction here transfer to other academic areas?

11. The two-column note-taking system is one in which students draw a vertical line down their note-taking page that leaves about a two- to three-inch column on the right for their ideas, observations, or associations (Figure 11.5). Do students benefit from this type of note taking? Are they able to make personal connections? Do they seem better able to apply or extend concepts? Do they seem better able to transfer skills or concepts to real-life situations?

Notes	Ideas, observations, or associations

FIGURE 11.5 Two-Column Note-Taking System

CHAPTER TWELVE

WRITING AN ACTION RESEARCH REPORT

Unless you are making an oral presentation or conducting action research only for your own edification, you need to create some sort of written document describing your observations and findings. This chapter contains suggestions for writing an action research report.

An action research report is written using an academic writing style. Academic writing enhances the credibility of your report and increases the likelihood that it will be read. It is not within the scope of this book to describe at length the many parts of academic writing; however, the tips offered in this chapter should get you through most academic writing situations. For further information and tips about academic writing, visit my website at: www.AR-Johnson.com.

TONE AND STYLE

Academic writing is different from creative writing in that it is more concise and written as objectively as possible. The prime directive in academic writing is clear communication; thus, ideas are presented in a logical, orderly manner so that the reader is able to gain a maximum amount of understanding with a minimum amount of time and effort.

Traditionally, experimental research is written in an objective style. You will not find any I, you, or me pronouns—only the facts described in third person. Personal observations are saved for a special section at the end of the report and are also written in third person. The goal in experimental research reports is to eliminate any bias or subjectivity on the part of the researcher and allow only the data to speak.

Action research, however, is written in a more subjective style. It is recognized that you are part of the research; thus, your thoughts and observations are valued and are recorded along the way. (You can see this personal, reflective writing style in the sample research reports in the Appendix A.) But keep in mind that an action research report is not a letter to the editor. Pronounced biases or hidden agendas are fairly easy to spot and detract from your accuracy and credibility.

In your action research report, you must demonstrate that your descriptions are fair and honest if your research is to be given credence. Consider the following examples:

Less effective: I really believe that schools should throw away those disgusting state standards that require that certain things be taught in a certain way. These outrageous mandates are an insult to our hard-working, knowledgeable teachers who know best how to meet the needs of students. It also sucks all the joy and creativity out of teaching.

More effective: Teachers can become more effective when they have a certain amount of freedom in determining what is taught, and also when they are able to design learning experiences in a way that best matches their teaching style and the needs of their students. State mandates do not always allow teachers to make the best choices or to utilize their creativity.

Avoid using highly charged language and emotional buzzwords:

Less effective: I strongly believe that using invented spelling is the best strategy I have ever seen for helping young children learn to write. I really like the way that students in this study thought about the message instead of worrying about correct spelling. And don't forget all the excitement that was generated as students eagerly shared their wonderful new creations with each other. And of course, there was the pride of taking home a finished product to share with parents. Using invented spelling helped to produce elaborate and imaginative ideas, helped children organize their writing, and created an environment that is very productive and enjoyable. Invented spelling is a must for primary students.

More effective: Invented spelling seems to have been effective in helping young children learn to write. Children in my classroom were able to concentrate on communicating their ideas rather than worrying about spelling. They seemed to create writing that was more elaborate and better organized than when they were using conventional spelling. They also seemed to enjoy sharing their ideas in these settings. It seems that invented spelling is an effective technique to use in moving children toward mature writing.

Avoid Value Statements

A value statement is where you say what you believe to be true based on a personal value without offering support. That is, you tell your readers what they must, should, or ought to do, think, or believe. Even if a sentence does reflect your values, it can be made stronger by taking out value words such as *must, should,* and *needs to be.* Instead, state the idea and support it.

Less effective: Teachers really should use reading workshop.

Why? Why should teachers use reading workshop? Is it just because you say so? Sorry, but that is not reason enough. Instead, the more effective writer below makes a statement and then supports it with a reason.

More effective: Using reading workshop enables teachers to provide multi-level instruction that meets the needs of all students.

Less effective: All educators need to use a holistic approach to literacy instruction.

More effective: Using a holistic approach to literacy instruction enables teachers to meet the needs of all their students.

Extremely Objective

Removing all personal pronouns from your writing (*I, me, you,* and *yours*) creates a different effect. Compare the two paragraphs that follow. What do you notice?

It is more effective to create sentences that state an idea and then support it. This will help avoid the use of value statements. A value statement is where the writer describes a belief without offering support. That is, the reader is told what must, should, or ought to be done. Even if a sentence does reflect the writer's values, it can be made stronger by taking out value words such as *must, should,* and *needs to be.* Instead, the idea should be stated and supported.

It is more effective to create sentences that state an idea and then support it. This will help you avoid the use of value statements. A value statement is where you say what you believe without offering support. That is, you tell your readers what they must, should, or ought to do. Even if a sentence does reflect your values, it can be made stronger by taking out value words such as *must, should,* and *needs to be.* Instead, state the idea and support it.

Including second-person and third-person pronouns creates writing that seems more connected with your reader. One is no more correct than the other; however, some find it easier to read writing that has some personal connection.

Again, the subjective stance is appropriate for your action research reports. Personal pronouns such *I, me,* and *my* may be used; however, from a purely stylistic point of view I would recommend that you limit their use. This enables the ideas and information to make your case and creates a stronger presentation.

Pronouns

A pronoun is any word that takes the place of a noun.

Example: The dogs were in the back yard. They were chasing each other.

In the sentence above they takes the place of the noun *dogs*.

Personal Pronouns

A personal pronoun takes the place of specific nouns (names of people, places, or things). They are used instead of the specific name to avoid repetition and to make the sentence flow more smoothly.

Example: Tony eats cherries. He also likes apples.

In the preceding sentence *he* takes the place of *Tony*.

Types of Person Pronouns

	Singular	Plural
First Person: The person or people who are writing.	I, me	we, us
Second Person: The person or people who are being written to.	you	you
Third Person: The person, people, or things that are being written about.	she, he, her, him, it	they, them

FIGURE 12.1 Grammar Mini-Lesson: Pronouns

PRECISION AND CLARITY

This section describes tips for making your academic writing more clear and precise.

Writing and Speech

Your academic writing is distinctly different from speech in that it is more precise and formal. As such, it should not sound like two people talking.

Avoid Speech-isms

Avoid colloquialisms or *speech-isms*. A colloquialism or a colloquial expression is when a word or phrase that is acceptable for informal conversation is used in a formal writing or speaking situation. Examples:

Colloquial: A lack of classroom support really started to *get to* the teacher.

Noncolloquial: A lack of classroom supported really started to frustrate the teacher.

Colloquial: This will *as likely as not* enhance achievement test scores.

Noncolloquial: This will likely enhance achievement test scores.

Colloquial: This is *without a doubt,* the most effective comprehension strategy.

Noncolloquial: This is the most effective comprehension strategy.

Colloquial: This just shows that teachers need quality classroom literature to be successful.

Noncolloquial: Teachers need quality classroom literature to be successful.

Avoid Nonwords

A nonword is a word that does not need to be there. If a word is not needed, do not use it. Too many words get in the way of your message.

Less effective: Basically, what they needed was more time.

Less effective: In essence, what they needed was more time.

Most effective: They needed more time.

From versus Than

Which is correct? (a) Writing is different from speech, or (b) Writing is different than speech. (Obviously it is the first one because that is the one used above.)

Different from. "Different from" means not the same. In most cases, this is the correct form when you are comparing two nouns.

Hint. A way to remember is to make short sentences and see which one sounds right: (a) Writing differs from speech, or (b) Writing differs than speech.

Different than. Different than means you are comparing a noun to a clause. A clause is a group of words that are part of a sentence that contain a subject and verb.

The campus is different than it was 30 years ago.

In the sentence above "it was 30 years ago" is the clause. "The campus is different" is the main sentence with the noun in it.

Hint. Again, a way to remember is to make short sentences and see which one sounds right: (a) Buildings are different than they were or (b) Buildings are different from they were.

FIGURE 12.2 Grammar Mini-Lesson: From versus Than

Use Adverbs with Caution

An adverb is a word that modifies or expands on a verb, an adjective, or another adverb. Its sole purpose is to alter or enhance what you have already written. The best advice is to avoid them when you can as they tend to clutter or confuse. If your language is precise and concise there is no need for adverbs.

Sometimes adverbs are used to enhance the degree to which something is or is not. They are sometimes used to add subtle editorial comment to what should be an objective sentence. Examples of degree-enhancing adverbs are words like: *very, extremely, incredibly, really, super, amazingly, sadly, amazingly, unbelievably,* and *remarkably* . Do not use these!

Not academic writing: Incredibly, *the students did not make any academic gains.*

Simply present the information and let the reader decide what is or is not incredible, amazing, or sad.

Academic writing: The student did not make any academic gains.

The more degree-enhance adverbs you use, the farther you travel from concise, objective, academic writing.

Adverbs

Verb. The dog runs fast.

In this sentence *runs* is the verb.

Verb with an adverb: The dog runs really fast.

In this sentence *really* is the adverb because it modifies or tells us more about the verb *run*. Not only does the dog run fast, but the dog runs really fast.

———————————

Adjective: My dog Emmet is energetic.

In this sentence the word *energetic* is the adjective.

Adjective with an adverb: My dog Emmet is extremely energetic.

The word *extremely* tells us more about Emmet's energy and, thus, is the adverb.

———————————

Adverb: My dog Mickey is always hungry.

In this sentence *always* is the adverb.

Adverb with an adverb: My dog Mickey is almost always hungry.

In this sentence *almost* is the adverb as it modifies *always*. It could be avoided by simply writing, "My dog Mickey is often hungry."

FIGURE 12.3   Grammar Mini-Lesson: Adverbs

The sentence: He was unprepared for the exam.

The sentence with a degree-enhancing adverb: He was really unprepared for the exam.

The sentence with two degree-enhancing adverbs: Amazingly, he was really unprepared for the exam.

The sentence with three degree-enhancing adverbs: Amazingly, he was really, very unprepared for the exam.

As you begin to become more aware of academic writing and compare it to the spoken language that you hear around you, you will begin to notice the degree to which spoken language is laced with degree-enhancing adverbs.

Example: He is really, really, super excited to begin using academic writing in all his projects.

REDUCING BIAS

One of the goals of academic writing is to present your ideas as clearly as possible. Bias of any kind gets in the way of your message and diminishes your credibility. Freeing your writing of bias will increase the chance that your message will be received accurately.

Person-First Language

Person-first language is used to portray people as people and not as labels or categories. The goal of person-first language is to preserve the integrity of the humans about whom you are writing. For example, using the term, *learning disabled students* would reduce this to a category. Instead, person-first language would use terms such as, *people who are learning disabled* or *students with learning disabilities.* They are people first who have a condition, trait, or characteristic; they are not their condition, trait, or characteristic. You would not refer to *redheads* as if they were a separate category of humans; rather, you would say *people with red hair.*

Exceptionalities

Sometimes the word *disabilities* is used here. Do not use the words *handicap* or *handicapped.* Again, the general rule of thumb is to refer to people who have specific conditions; do not refer to conditions as if they were specific people.

Incorrect: mentally retarded, mental retardation, intellectually challenged, intellectually disabled

Correct: students with developmental cognitive disability, people with cognitive disabilities, students with developmental disabilities

Incorrect: slow learner, retarded, learning disabled people

Correct: a person with learning disabilities

Incorrect: brain-injured, brain-damaged

Correct: people with traumatic brain injury

Incorrect: cripple, invalid, handicapped, physically challenged, confined to a wheelchair, disabled people

Correct: people with Alzheimer's, a person who uses a wheelchair, people with disabilities

Incorrect: mental patient, the mentally ill, the insane, neurotics, a neurotic person, psychotics, autistic children

Correct: People with mental illness, people with psychiatric illness, people with neurosis, children with autism

Incorrect: blind person, blind people

Correct: person who is blind, visually impaired people

Incorrect: deaf person, deaf-and-dumb, deaf-mute

Correct: a person who is deaf, persons who are deaf or hard of hearing

Incorrect: emotionally disturbed, emotionally or behaviorally disturbed people

Correct: students with emotional/behavioral disorders, people with emotional disabilities

Incorrect: an epileptic, a paraplegic, a hemophiliac

Correct: a person with epilepsy, a woman who is paraplegic, a boy who is hemophiliac

Incorrect: normal classroom, normal people, normal family

Correct: general education classroom, people without a disability, traditional families

Normal People.   Do not use the term, *normal* under any circumstances when you are referring to people. There are no such things as normal people, normal classrooms, or normal families. Normal is statistical term. Although there are statistical norms and a normal range of test scores, there is no such thing as a normal person. To indicate such would be to say others are abnormal. Instead, use the term, *persons without a disability* or it is acceptable in this case to use a double negative such as *people who are nondisabled*. In education, use the term *general education classroom* instead of normal classroom.

LEP.   English language learner (ELL) is preferred over the term, *limited-English-proficient* (LEP; even though this term is used by federal government). LEP describes a group of people in terms of what they cannot do. Other terms to use include *people who are nonnative speakers* or *students who are ELL*. The term *English-second-language (ESL) learners* has been used, but this is not always accurate because for many students who are nonnative speakers, English might be their third or fourth language.

Gender

Gender is different from sex. Sex refers strictly to the biological dimensions of being male or female; gender includes the sociocultural and psychological dimensions as well. In other words, one's gender identity refers to sexual differences that include the general parameters for acceptable behavior as established by society, peers, and one's family and the sociocultural context that describes what it means to be male or female.

Three Rules.   Here are three rules to follow in creating writing that is free of gender bias:

1. Whenever possible, use *man* to refer to a single male human and use *human* to refer to all humanity. It is humankind versus mankind. It is one small step for humans versus one small step for man. All humans are created equal versus all men are created equal.

2. Eliminate *man* as a designator of roles or categories whenever possible. Example: congressperson, chair or chairperson, news anchor, and firefighter. These have been accepted forms for many years.

3. Never use the male pronoun *he* when referring to both genders. This almost does not need to be addressed; however, it is mentioned here as a reminder because occasionally writers forget. To get a sense of how accustomed we have become to gender-neutral language, go to your library and look for a textbook written in the '70s or before. The male pronouns leap out at you.

Following are three tricks to use in avoiding gender bias in your writing:

Trick #1. Use plurals whenever possible.

 Incorrect: A reader must decide which comprehension strategy he will use.

 Correct: Readers must decide which comprehension strategy they will use. (Notice that *writers* is plural so *they* must also be plural.)

 Better yet: Readers must decide which comprehension strategy to use.

Trick #2. Do not use pronouns.

Incorrect: When a student is reading a textbook he should use a comprehension strategy.

Correct: When reading a textbook a comprehension strategy should be used.

Better yet: Comprehension strategies should be used when reading a textbook.

Trick #3. Use that or that person.

Incorrect: When a student has trouble understanding a textbook he should use a comprehension strategy.

When a writer gets writers' block he should use a prewriting strategy to generate ideas.

Correct: When a student has trouble understanding a textbook that student should use a comprehension strategy.

When a writer gets writers' block that person should use a prewriting strategy to generate ideas.

Better yet: Using a comprehension strategy will enhance understanding.

Note. Using *s/he* or *he or she* should be avoided if possible. These are messy and cumbersome.

Sexual Orientation

Reference to sexual orientation should be included in your writing only when pertinent. "*Sexual orientation* refers to an enduring pattern of attraction, behavior, emotion, identity and social contacts" (APA, 2009, p. 74). The term, *sexual orientation* should be used instead of *sexual preference*. The latter infers choice, and this is not the case in the majority of situations. Other terms to eliminate include *gender orientation* or *gender preference*. As well, do not use obtrusive labels such terms as *the gays* or *the lesbians* or *LGBT people* or *the homosexuals*. This infers that there is a monolithic block of people who all think and act the same way. The terms preferred are *gay men, bisexual men, lesbians,* and *bisexual women*. These are more accurate and preferred over the broader term *homosexual*.

LGBT and Transgender

LGBT (or *GLBT*) is a term that stands collectively for people who are lesbian, gay, bisexual, and transgendered. Transgender refers to persons whom identify or express a gender that is different from their sex at birth. The term, *transsexual* sometimes gets confused with *transgender*. *Transsexual* refers to somebody who had gone through or is going through a medical procedure to change sex.

There is still much debate about whether the correct term is *transgendered* or *transgender*. When referring to a specific person the *-ed* form should be used. "*The* *person who is transgendered,"* makes more sense when using person-first language than *"a person who is transgender."* When referring to groups or nonperson entities the term, *transgender* makes sense, such as *transgender community, transgender studies, transgender groups,* or *transgender laws.*

Race and Ethnicity

These terms are often used interchangeably in describing groups of people. Race refers to the classification of people according to specific physiological features or characteristics such as hair or skin color. Ethnicity refers to a shared sense of identity or a pattern of characteristics based on nationality, race, religion, or language. Oftentimes you will see these categories designated as "Race/Ethnicity" or "Race-Ethnicity."

We want to use the correct term; however, this is still confusing as acceptable terms, groups, and perceptions continue to evolve. For example, Table 12.1 contains the U.S. population data related to race/ethnicity from the 2000 census (U.S. Census Bureau, 2005).

The 2010 Census first asked respondents if they were of Hispanic, Latino, or Spanish origin. These terms refer to ethnicity or origin, as Latinos can be of various races. Respondents were then asked to identify race using the following categories: White, Black or African American, American Indian or Alaska Native, Asian Indian, Chinese, Filipino, Other Asian, Japanese, Korean, Vietnamese, Native Hawaiian, Guamanian or Chamorro, Samoan, or Other Pacific Islander.

This is what I can say for certain in regard to using the correct racial and ethnic terms:

1. Categories related to race/ethnicity are proper nouns so they should be capitalized.
2. These categories are highly dependent on social perception and, thus, are continually evolving.

TABLE 12.1   U.S. Population Data from 2000 Census

RACE/ETHNICITY	TOTAL NUMBER	% OF TOTAL POPULATION
White	211,460,626	75.1%
Hispanic or Latino	35,305,818	12.5%
Black or African American	34,658, 190	12.3%
Asian	10,242,998	3.6%
American Indian or Alaska Native	2,475,956	0.9%
Native Hawaiian and Other Pacific Islander	398,835	0.1%
TOTAL	**281,421,906**	**100%**

LENGTH

How long should your action report be? Long enough to say what needs to be said; short enough so as not to bore or confuse the reader. This means using as few words as possible. There is nothing more frustrating than having to sort through a thick forest of words to try to find an author's point. If you use too many words, your ideas are obscured and you lose the reader. Using fewer words increases the likelihood of your report being read and understood. In your action research reports, always consider what does not need to be there. Good writers know how to state their ideas using a minimum number of words.

> *Less effective:* I believe that writing is extremely important because it helps my students organize their thinking. This is helpful. All people, students as well as adults, should try to develop their writing skills. This will help in their school lives as well as in their careers. Writing forces you to think through your ideas before you begin writing. You have to record your ideas to see what it is you believe about a thing. Also, the very act of generating ideas helps you to see the relationships between more things. This is what creativity is. Creativity has to do with seeing connections, associations, and relationships. Thinking also shapes our writing. Sometimes you do not know exactly what it is you are going to say. When you write, you see your thoughts hung out in space, frozen in time. The advantage of writing is that you can go back and tweak it to get it just right before you deliver the message.

> *More effective:* Writing shapes thinking by helping the writer to generate ideas, see relationships, and put ideas in an organized form. However, thinking also shapes writing. With writing, we can see our thoughts, organize them, and edit them to get them just right before we deliver them.

CLARITY

The clarity of your final report should be such that another person could read it and duplicate your steps. As stated previously, clarity can be enhanced by using as few words as possible. It can also be enhanced by entering a teaching mode. That is, you assume that the reader knows nothing and you must explain to them what you did and what you saw. Clarity can also be enhanced by the organization of your report. To organize your thoughts, first create an outline so that you are able to see the logical structure of your report. Then use headings and subheadings to let the reader see the structure and to show when you move from one major idea to the next.

HEADINGS

Following is an example of a short section I wrote that enters into a teaching mode but does not use headings.

Consciousness

Consciousness is that which we choose to be aware of, both internally and externally. Consciousness is a composite of those thoughts and images that we attend to. Jungian theory describes four levels of consciousness.

Collective consciousness is the outer world of values and perceptions that a society shares. Here every stimulus has a response. Machines have gears, springs, and levers, all operating according to the laws of physics. All physical effects spring from physical causes, and time is conceived of in strictly linear terms. This is the objective outer world where reality is determined by repeatability and the laws of cause and effect.

The collective unconscious is a part of the human psyche that is shared by all. An illustrative metaphor might be to think of it as psychic cyberspace to which every human is connected. Here, every thought, action, and emotion ever experienced by humanity is embedded and available to us in the form of archetypal images. Archetypal images are those images formed around patterns within the collective unconscious and birthed into human consciousness as symbols and motifs.

Personal consciousness or ego is the thinking with which we are consciously aware. This can include logical reasoning as well as emotions and intuition. To expand personal consciousness, one becomes aware of a wider variety of stimuli, both internal and external. This can be done through meditation or simply slowing the mind and concentrating on being aware.

The personal unconscious is the layer of thinking not readily accessible to our conscious mind. Contained here is material that has reached consciousness and been forgotten, such as repressed memories, emotions, and personal experiences. It also contains material that has not yet reached consciousness, such as archetypal images. This is the subjective inner world where reality is determined by meaning. That is, the images perceived here are real insofar as they have some meaning or significance for us.

Now here is the same piece of writing with the headings inserted. Notice the difference in the clarity and understanding.

Consciousness

Consciousness is that which we choose to be aware of, both internally and externally. Consciousness is a composite of those thoughts and images that we attend to. Jungian theory describes four levels of consciousness.

Collective Consciousness

Collective consciousness is the outer world of values and perceptions that a society shares. Here every stimulus has a response. Machines have gears, springs, and levers, all operating according to the laws of physics. All physical effects spring from physical causes, and time is conceived of in strictly linear terms. This is the objective outer world where reality is determined by repeatability and the laws of cause and effect.

The Collective Unconscious

The collective unconscious is a part of the human psyche that is shared by all. An illustrative metaphor might be to think of it as psychic cyberspace to which every human is connected. Here, every thought, action, and emotion ever experienced by humanity is embedded and available to us in the form of archetypal images. Archetypal images are those images formed around patterns within the collective unconscious and birthed into human consciousness as symbols and motifs.

Personal Consciousness

Personal consciousness or ego is the thinking with which we are consciously aware. This can include logical reasoning as well as emotions and intuition. To expand personal consciousness, one becomes aware of a wider variety of stimuli, both internal and external. This can be done through meditation or simply slowing the mind and concentrating on being aware.

Personal Unconscious

The personal unconscious is the layer of thinking not readily accessible to our conscious mind. Contained here is material that has reached consciousness and been forgotten, such as repressed memories, emotions, and personal experiences. It also contains material that has not yet reached consciousness, such as archetypal images. This is the subjective inner world where reality is determined by meaning. That is, the images perceived here are real insofar as they have some meaning or significance for us.

THE BASIC ELEMENTS OF STYLE

The *Publication Manual of the American Psychological Association* (2009) is the final word on all issues related to elements of writing style in the social sciences. However, the information included next should enable you to be successful in most of academic writing situations. For a more complete description of the process and product related to academic writing see *A Short Guide to Academic Writing* (Johnson, 2003a).

1. *Font.* Use 12 point font, Times or Times New Roman.
2. *Margins.* Use one inch margins on the top, bottom, and sides. Margins should be aligned flush left only. Do not use full alignment where margins are aligned on the right and left side. This creates uneven spacing between words
3. *Spacing.* Use double spacing between all text lines of the manuscript. Do not include any extra spaces between sections or headings.
4. *Indentation.* The beginning sentence of all new paragraphs should be indented 5 to 7 spaces. Be consistent throughout. Do not use block paragraphs in your paper. These are paragraphs that are single spaced, flush left, with a space between them.
5. *Useless adjectives.* Do not use useless adjectives. Adjectives can add life and vitality to a piece of creative writing; however, there is a fine line between vitality and subjective insight. If there are too many adjectives in a piece of academic writing, we begin to see the writer more than the writing.
6. *Contractions.* Do not use contractions.

The Basics of Grammar

Correct grammar usage helps to create precision in writing and speaking. Although you do not have to be a grammarian to write well, it is helpful to learn a few basic grammar rules and develop an intuitive sound for the language. Six grammar tips are described here:

1. *Stay consistent with tense.* You may not switch tense on a whim. If you use the past tense in the first part of a sentence or paragraph, you must use it throughout.

Incorrect: After Sam hit the ball he ran. He stumbles on the way to first (past tense and present tense).

Correct: After Sam hit the ball he ran. He stumbled on the way to first (both use past tense).

Correct: Sam hits the ball and runs. He stumbles on the way to first base (both use present tense).

Incorrect: The accident happened because people drive too fast (past and present tense).

Correct: The accident happened because people were driving too fast (past tense).

Correct: Accidents happen because people drive too fast (present tense).

Incorrect: Tony is dirty because he was (past) out working and his dog keeps (present) knocking him down.

Correct: Tony is dirty because his dog keeps knocking him down when he is working.

Correct: Tony is dirty because he was out working and his dog kept knocking him down.

2. *Stay consistent with plurality.* You also may not switch plurality on a whim. If you use the singular in the first part of a sentence or paragraph, you must use it throughout.

Incorrect: A person (singular) should always have their (plural) notebooks.

Correct: A person should always have a notebook.

Correct: People should always have their notebooks.

Incorrect: The class (singular) improved their (plural) scores 30%.

Correct: The class improved its score by 30%.

Correct: People in the class improved their scores by 30%.

Incorrect: A child (singular) often worries about their (plural) first day of school.

Correct: Children often worry about their first day of school.

Correct: A child often worries about the first day of school.

3. *Double pronouns should make sense when one is missing.* This means that if you read the sentence with just one of either pronouns, that sentence should still make sense.

Incorrect: Me and her will go to the dance. (Me will go to the dance. Her will go to the dance.)

Correct: She and I will go to the dance. (She will go to the dance. I will go to the dance.)

Incorrect: Sally and her discussed the plan. (Sally discussed the plan. Her discussed the plan.)

Correct: Sally and she discussed the plan. (Sally discussed the plan. She discussed the plan.)

Incorrect: The prize went to he and I. (The prize went to he. The prize went to I.)

Correct: The prize went to him and me. (The prize went to him. The prize went to me.)

Incorrect: Him and me went to the movie. (Him went to the movie. Me went to the movie.)

Incorrect: Him and I went to the movie. (Him went to the movie. I went to the movie.)

Correct: He and I went to the movie. (He went to the movie. I went to the movie.)

4. *Avoid repetition and redundancy within a sentence.*

Incorrect: Stewart often comes to school tired so we must try to get Stewart to bed on time.

Correct: Stewart often comes to school tired. We must try to get him to bed on time.

Correct: Stewart often comes to school tired; therefore, we must try to get him to bed on time.

5. *Use that for restrictive clauses and which for nonrestrictive clauses.* A restrictive clause is one in which the clause or point is essential to the meaning of the sentence. Use *that* in these instances.

Example: The class that used Andy's book produced excellent writers.

This sentence indicates that there was a class that used Andy's book and there was also at least one other class that did not. The class that used Andy's book produced excellent writers. Thus, the clause is essential to the point of the sentence, as we are clearly identifying a particular class.

A nonrestrictive clause is like a theatrical aside. It adds dimension to the idea; however, the meaning is still largely intact if the clause were not there. Use *which* in these instances.

Example: The class, *which used Andy's book*, produced excellent writers.

In this sentence, the main idea is that the class produced excellent writers. They just happened to have used Andy's book. It does not indicate that there was another class.

6. *Use* that *for restrictive clauses and* who *for nonrestrictive clauses.*

Restrictive clause: Those students that are done with their work may go to recess.
Nonrestrictive clause: Those students, who are done with their work, may go to recess.

The first one indicates that only those students finished with their work are to be allowed to go recess. The second one indicates that these students are allowed to go to recess and also, they just happen to be done with their work.

The Basics of Punctuation: Commas, Semicolons, and Colons

This section describes the punctuation information you will need to get you through the majority of your writing projects.

Comma.   *A comma* is used in the following situations:

1. *Between elements.* Use a comma to separate items in a series. A comma should be used before the last *and* or *or* in the sentence.

> *Incorrect:* The cherries oranges and apples fell to the ground.

> *Incorrect:* The cherries, oranges and apples fell to the ground.

> *Correct:* The cherries, oranges, and apples fell to the ground.

2. *To separate a nonessential clause.* A nonessential clause, like the nonrestrictive clause described earlier, is like a theatrical aside. Here, the message is still intact without its inclusion.

> *Nonessential clause:*   The orange, which had been handled by George, fell to the ground.

The preceding sentence indicates that an orange fell to the floor and it just happened to have been handled by George. This is an example of a nonessential clause. The "George" part of the sentence is an interesting but not essential part of this sentence.

An essential clause means that the information in the middle of the sentence is vital to the stuff at the end and should not be separated by a comma. In the following sentence, there was more than one orange, but only the one handled by George fell to the floor. This is an essential clause, thus *that* is used instead of *which*.

> *Essential clause:* The orange that had been handled by George fell to the floor.

3. *To separate two independent clauses joined by a conjunction.* If you have a compound sentence where both sides of the sentence would be complete sentences by themselves, use a comma.

> *Two independent clauses:* Cherries are better than oranges, and apples are often used for pie.

Both parts of this sentence would work as sentences by themselves: Cherries are better than oranges. Apples are often used for pie. A comma is used here to separate them. In the following sentence, a comma is not used. "Cherries are better than oranges" is a complete sentence; however, "they are often used for pie" depends on the first part of the sentence for it to make sense, thus, it is a dependent clause.

> *A compound sentence with one dependent clause:* Cherries are better than oranges and they are often used for pie.

Do not use a comma to separate two parts of a compound predicate.

> *Incorrect:* Margaret Hamilton played the Wicked Witch, and later starred in coffee commercials.

> *Correct:* Margaret Hamilton played the Wicked Witch and later starred in coffee commercials.

Semicolon. A *semicolon* is used in the following situations:

1. *To separate two independent clauses that are not joined by a conjunction.* This means the semicolon takes the place of *and, but,* and *or.*

No semicolon: The winners were happy but the losers were sad.

Semicolon: The winners were happy; the losers were sad.

2. *To separate elements in a series that already contain commas.* If I wanted to list a series of things in different groups (some fruit things, some vegetable things, and some dairy things), I would use the commas to separate the things within the groups and semicolons to separate the groups. This way the reader knows when the groups end and begin.

Incorrect: For breakfast there was cherries, oranges, and pears, carrots, peas, and beans, and yogurt, cottage cheese, and milk.

Correct: For breakfast there was cherries, oranges, and pears; carrots, peas, and beans; and yogurt, cottage cheese, and milk.

Colon. The rule of thumb for the *colon* is that everything that follows the colon should directly relate to what preceded it. This is done two ways:

1. *A complete introductory clause followed by a final clause to illustrate the point.*

Example: There were three kinds of fruit: cherries, oranges, and pears.

2. *A complete introductory clause followed by a complete sentence that illustrates the point.*

Example: All three agree: Fruit is best for breakfast.

The illustrating sentence that follows the colon above is a complete sentence, thus, it begins with a capital letter.

ADDITIONAL RESOURCES

Figure 12.4 contains a checklist that can be used for your action research reports. This checklist can be downloaded at my website: www.AR-Johnson.com.

Key: 4 = Outstanding, 3 = very good, 2 = average, 1 = below average

Rating	Criteria
_____	1. **Topic:** The research investigates an interesting, relevant, or important topic.
_____	2. **Asks a question:** The researcher puts the topic in the form of a question. The question can be answered by collecting data. The question is clear and answerable.

(Continued)

FIGURE 12.4 Criteria for an Action Research Report

Rating	Criteria
_____	3. **Systematic plan for collecting data:** The researcher describes a systematic plan for collecting data under the Methods section (see Chapter 15). The descriptions of the methods for collecting data are clear, understandable, and easy to follow. (The rule of thumb is that somebody should be able to replicate your action research study by reading your Methods section.) The plan for collecting data is sufficient to answer the question.
_____	4. **Data-based conclusions:** The researcher uses data to answer the question.
_____	5. **Credibility:** The research demonstrates credibility by providing multiple data sources. The researcher demonstrates an unbiased approach. The language used is as objective and value free as possible.
_____	6. **Sentences:** The research uses complete sentences. The sentences (a) are concise yet descriptive, (b) are consistent with tense and plurality, (c) avoid repetition, and (d) make sense and are easy to read.
_____	7. **Paragraphs:** The researcher uses paragraphs to break up and organize larger ideas. The paragraphs (a) make sense, (b) avoid conceptual leaps, and (c) are used to explore or support an idea.
_____	8. **Word choice:** The researcher (a) uses an academic style, (b) avoids speechisms or colloquialisms, and (c) makes pragmatic choices about the quantity and quality of words.
_____	9. **Headings:** The researcher uses headings to organize the paper and make it reader-friendly. All the information under a particular heading is germane to that section.
_____	10. **Quotes and citations:** The researcher uses APA form as described here. The quotes and citations are used intelligently to support the writer's ideas.
_____	11. **Fluency:** The piece flows and is easy to read. Ideas are described and supported.
_____	12. **Structure/Organization:** Structure is used to help carry the ideas.
_____	13. **Form/Mechanics:** The piece looks presentable. The spacing, margins, font, and headings are correct. Spelling, grammar, and punctuation have been attended to.
_____	14. **Strengths of this research report:**
_____	15. **Questions or areas to reconsider:**

FIGURE 12.4   (Continued)

SUMMARY

- Using an academic style of writing in your action research report enhances its credibility and makes it more likely to be read.
- Academic writing is an objective style of writing in which as few words as possible are used in describing data and ideas.

- The clarity of your action research report is enhanced by entering a teaching mode, by using headings and subheadings, and by avoiding colloquialisms.
- Academic writing should be as free from bias as possible.
- Academic writing in the social sciences should be written according the APA *Publication Manual*, sixth edition.

QUESTIONS AND ACTIVITIES

1. Select a letter to the editor from a newspaper. First, list the facts presented, then report the author's ideas using a purely subjective tone.

2. Find a paragraph in a textbook, newspaper, or magazine. Lengthen it by adding words to it while retaining the original meaning. Then, trade your paragraph with a partner and take out all the words that do not need to be there.

3. Go on a treasure hunt. Find the following: (a) a concise, well-written paragraph, (b) a confusing paragraph, (c) a paragraph with a lot of extra words and sentences, and (d) a paragraph that seems overly biased or subjective.

CHAPTER THIRTEEN

PRESENTING YOUR ACTION RESEARCH

If a teacher has a good idea in the middle of the forest but nobody is there to hear it, does that idea make a noise? This chapter talks about venues for sharing your action research and ends with some tips for making effective presentations.

THE EDUCATIONAL ENVIRONMENT

Your Colleagues

The most appreciative audience for presentations of your action research might be your colleagues. These presentations can take the form of a formal staff development inservice, a short talk at a regular faculty meeting, or simply a continued dialogue with colleagues. Whatever the form, these presentations promote conversation among teachers about the dynamics of their classrooms and various pedagogical methods and are essential for promoting reflection and growth in our profession.

When presenting action research projects, your findings are more apt to be attended to by your audience if you keep the presentation short and focused and include only those ideas that other teachers might use in their classroom. Presentations are also enhanced by including some kind of visual aid in the form of a poster, overhead, PowerPoint presentation, or handout. Always leave time for discussion at the end. Important elements for short presentation includ the following:

1. *Your purpose.* Why did you choose to study what you did? Did a particular problem, special interest, or question lead you to your research? Describe your reasons for engaging in the action research project.

2. *Theoretical background.* Keep this short. If available, include some research or basic theoretical ideas related to your question, then link this to classroom practice.

3. *Data collection.* Describe the various forms of data and tell how you collected them.

4. *Findings.* Tell what you found. If your findings lend themselves to visual display, create a poster or handouts with the information in the form of a list, graph, or table.

5. *Conclusions.* What do your findings mean? What do they imply? What might be some of the reasons you came up with your findings? Again, keep this short.

6. *Your plan of action.* Tell what you plan to do or what you might do as a result of your findings. You might also ask teachers to brainstorm ideas for possible actions or possible solutions. This creates dialogue and allows teachers to share their ideas.

7. *Time for questions and discussion.* Finally, always leave time at the end of a presentation for questions and discussion. (More specific presentation tips follow.)

Your Students

Your students will be interested to know what you found. After all, they have a vested interest in what goes on in your classroom. Also, action research mirrors the inquiry process, a powerful learning technique that you might consider using in your class. Inquiry is the process of designing learning activities that incorporate methods of science (Johnson, 2010). In doing inquiry, students are taught to ask a question and then to collect data to answer that question. In sharing your action research with your students you will be modeling the inquiry process as well as demonstrating methods for collecting and presenting data. Just as with teachers, allow and encourage questions and discussion. Students' thoughts and observations at the end of an action research study are often apt and might even be included as a form of data in your final report.

School Boards, Principals, and Administrators: Making a Case

Decisions in education are sometimes made apart from a theoretical context or without considering any of the research related to learning and education. This can result in bad educational practice or educational malpractice. Action research can be used to enable your school or district to make informed decisions. It can also be used to make a case for employing a particular methodology or program. However, when doing action research to make a case, the onus is on you to keep an objective perspective during all phases of your research. That is, you must allow for the possibility that the literature or the data collected might disprove your original thesis.

Your Classroom: Evaluating New Programs

If you are piloting a new program, action research can be used as formative evaluation to see how things are going and what needs to be changed and as summative evaluation to judge the program's effectiveness. The key in using action research for evaluation is to keep the data collection simple and manageable. Do not let data collection get in the way of implementing the new program.

To illustrate how action research might be used in program evaluation, at Minnesota State University, Mankato, I piloted a new approach to my undergraduate literacy methods course. Students spent less time in my class listening to me speak (1 day a week) and more time in an elementary classroom practicing their teaching skills (3 days a week). Before I implemented the program, I made a plan to collect four types of data: (a) a pre- and post-study survey of the undergraduate students, (b) a post-study survey of teachers, (c) observations recorded using field notes, and (d) an analysis of students' reflections collected at eight points during the course of the semester. My goal was to see what was happening with this new approach, what was working, and what needed to be changed.

When the study was completed and the data compiled, I found that overall the new plan was fairly successful in helping to create knowledgeable, skillful teachers. My students could see how the ideas I presented in my methods classes applied to a classroom setting. But like any new program, it needed some tweaks and changes. The data collected were extremely useful in helping to pinpoint the changes that needed to be made. As a final step, I made a short presentation to the dean and to my colleagues at a faculty meeting. There I was able to make recommendations about future programs based on some solid data.

Parent Conferences

I remember as a beginning teacher feeling that I never had enough to say to parents at parent conferences. I was able to describe the child in terms of numbers using scores on standardized tests and homework assignments, but that was about it. As stated previously, many of the data collection methods described in Chapter 6 are forms of authentic assessment. The individual data related to each child can be used to provide a much clearer picture of who that child is as well as his or her strengths and interests.

Also, parents like to know what is happening in your classroom. Sharing your action research in a short newsletter gives them a sense of what is happening. It lets them know that your classroom is an intellectually vibrant place, and it shows that you are always looking for the best methods to use in helping their children grow and learn.

As Part of a Master's Thesis

In the Special Education Department at Minnesota State University, Mankato, one of the options we have used as part of our master's thesis in Cross Disciplinary Studies is to require that students present their research project to an audience. After all, why should they do all the work for a thesis and have it read only by the members of their graduate committee? We want this new knowledge to move out into the teaching field where it can be used and applied.

Presentation venues may include a district or school inservice as described previously, a professional conference (described in the next section), a parent organization, a graduate class, or a university-sponsored conference consisting of action research projects by other graduate students. General guidelines for the research presentation are in Figure 13.1.

The Presentation Response Form in Figure 13.2 is used to assess and give feedback to presenters. This form can be downloaded from my website (www. AR-johnson.com). If action researchers make their presentations in their districts, at a conference, or in some other off-campus location, I give them self-addressed stamped envelopes and ask that three people present evaluate their presentation. We also ask that they turn in an audiotape of their presentation so that we can listen and evaluate.

THE PROFESSIONAL ENVIRONMENT

Professional Conferences and Conventions

These days most researchers in education recognize the importance of including teachers' voices in the conversation. Professional conferences and teachers' conventions are a good place to create this conversation. I would recommend contacting local or state organizations that hold conventions and ask them to send you a proposal form. The proposal form you receive describes exactly what you need to include and usually needs to be returned 4 to 6 months before the conference date.

Academic Journals

You might consider sending your study to an academic journal. This is a good way to get your ideas out there for others to see and use. Start with state journals

1. The presentation should be between 30 and 45 minutes in duration.
2. Enter a teacher mode. Remember, the audience knows nothing about your topic.
3. Describe the problem, topic, research question, or area of investigation as well as what brought you to it.
4. Include a short synthesis of related research or the theoretical background (review of the literature).
5. Briefly describe how you collected your data.
6. Describe your results or what you found. Along with your recommendations, this should be the heart of your presentation.
7. Include your recommendations, practical application, or plan of action. Make sure there is a strong connection between your results and your recommendations, application, or plan of action.
8. Be clear and concise. Include only what will be of interest to your audience. What you choose not to include is as important as what you choose to include in a presentation.
9. Use a visual aid of some kind (overhead, poster, PowerPoint, video clip, or handouts).
10. Include 5 to 10 minutes for questions at the end.

FIGURE 13.1   Guidelines for an Action Research Presentation

Action Research Project

Presentation Response Form

Presenter: _____ Date: _____

Session title or topic: _____

Name and position of person completing this form: _____

Directions: This is a presentation of his/her Master's Thesis. Please rate this presenter's session on the following items using this scale: 5 = excellent, 4 = good, 3 = average, 2 = fair, 1 = poor

Content
  1. Relevance of action research project to its intended application: ____
  2. Importance of this action research project: ____
  3. Connection of action research project to practice: ____
  4. Ground in the literature: _____
  5. Appropriately rigorous, sheds new light in an area/application: ____

Scholarship
  6. Action research project enhanced professionalism of presenter: ____
  7. Demonstrated knowledge directly linked to research literature: ____
  8. Quality of content and methods reflects graduate level work: ____
  9. Limitations acknowledged: ____
 10. Credible work, lacking in bias: ____
 11. Used data to answer a question: _____
 12. Made recommendations based on data collected: _____

Communication and Presentation
 13. Ability to convey ideas/meaning: ____
 14. Familiarity/ease with topic/study: ____
 15. Clarity of presentation: ____
 16. Ability to respond to questions and address concerns: ____
 17. Professional quality of handouts/materials/visual aids: ____
 18. Overall professional quality of presentation: ____

Specific comments regarding strengths and weaknesses of this presentation
(use the back side if necessary):

FIGURE 13.2   **Presentation Response Form**

or smaller publications that are focused on areas related to your study. You can get addresses and submission requirements for these as well as other important information at the following websites (see Figure 5.1 for a more complete list):

  1. National Science Teachers Association Journals and Publications: www.nsta.org/journals
  2. National Council for the Social Studies: www.socialstudies.org
  3. International Reading Association: www.reading.org
  4. National Council of Teachers of Mathematics: www.nctm.org
  5. National Council of Teachers of English: www.ncte.org

To find other possible academic journals to submit your action research studies, do an Internet search using terms such as *education, teachers, publishing, academic journals,* or some variations of these.

Academic journals are peer-reviewed, which means that two or more people look over your writing, make comments and suggestions (not always pleasant), and recommend whether to publish. Do not get discouraged, however, if you get your action research report back with a rejection or many suggestions for improvement. It is quite common for writers to have to revise several times before an article is finally accepted for publication. Although this process may seem a little intimidating at first, getting feedback and specific comments is one of the best ways to improve your writing.

ERIC

As described in Chapter 5, ERIC stands for the Educational Resources Information Center. Sponsored by the National Library of Education at the U.S. Department of Education, it is a massive database containing information on all imaginable subjects related to education. ERIC has evolved since the second edition of this book. It now accepts fewer types of material but of higher quality. Accepted types include research reports, dissertations, and conference papers and presentations. You can submit your action research projects online at www.eric.ed.gov.

LOCAL COMMUNITY ORGANIZATIONS

In most communities people outside education appreciate hearing about the latest teaching trends and ideas. Often, the perceptions these people have of school and education are based on their own experiences (which can be 20 to 40 years old) and what they read about in newspapers and magazines. Neither of these are very accurate sources. Presenting your action research at functions such as Rotary lunches, social and professional groups, religious organizations, parent organizations, or other types of gatherings provides people in your community with an updated version of the latest trends in education and, at the same time, generates good public relations for your school.

MAKING EFFECTIVE PRESENTATIONS

This section describes some more specific tips for making effective presentations. You can find four video presentations related to making video presentations at my action research website (www.AR-Johnson.com).

Planning the Presentation

1. *Know your audience.* Present only what you think your audience needs to know or what is of interest to them. For example, what is of interest to a teacher will be different from what is of interest to a parent, student, administrator, or community group.

2. *Say only what needs to be said.* Presenting every facet of your topic does not mean you have communicated effectively. Information dumping is different from making an informative presentation. What you do not include is just as important as what you do include. As well, not all aspects of your report are of equal importance. Focus on the important stuff. The majority of your time and attention should be given to your data and implications or recommendations based on that data.

3. *Use structure to carry your ideas.* Structure is the skeleton used to support and carry your big ideas. Create structure by identifying sections and subsections related to your purpose statement. Some people do this by using an outline to design an initial draft of their presentation. Others use a web or semantic map. Structure enables you to create a more organized and coherent presentation.

4. *Include questions and discussion prompts.* These can be used at the end of your presentation to get your audience to interact with the material. Questions and discussion prompts can also be used to get audience members to share important experiences of information that might enhance your presentation. As well, they can be inserted at planned points during the presentation. Questions and discussion prompts should be planned and purposeful. And finally, make sure you leave time at the end for these (see below). How many should you include? A few more than you think you will use.

General Platform Skills

1. *Be mindful of time parameters.* You have a limited amount of time when giving a presentation of any type. These limits may be defined by the time allotted to you or by the amount of attention your audience is willing to give you. The onus is on you to be aware of and stay comfortably within these parameters. You lose credibility if you become one of those speakers who suddenly realize they have 3 minutes of allotted time left with 10 or more minutes of material. They suddenly start talking like an overcaffeinated chipmunk while flipping quickly through their PowerPoint slides.

A couple of tips to avoid chipmunk syndrome: First, remember that the goal of presentation is not to fill time but to say something. Make sure you are only saying what needs to be said (see above). Second, practice your presentation a couple of times before you speak so that you have a general sense of time. Third, have a watch or some sort of time device lying next to your notes so you can easily see how much time you have (looking at your watch can be distracting). Fourth, know that less is usually better than more. Err on the side of too little rather than too much. And finally, use questions and discussion prompts at the end to provide a cushion and adjust for time.

2. *Be mindful of pacing.* You do not want to go too fast or too slow. However, a slower more conversational style is usually more effective. This allows you to make natural pauses at important junctures for emphasis and enables your audience to fully process the information you are providing. However, it is common to

go too fast if you feel tense or nervous. This is another reason why it is important to practice your presentation ahead of time.

3. *Use vocal inflection and pauses.*   You communicate with the tone and inflection of your voice as well as your words. A well-modulated voice with comfortable pauses and inflection creates a presentation that is easier to listen to and understand and also enables you to highlight points of emphasis. Also, avoid using a lifeless, monotone speaking voice.

4. *Use a public speaking voice.*   No one will hear you if you cannot be heard. In your presentation use a slightly louder voice than you think necessary. Speak to the very last person in the very last row. Nobody should have to strain to hear you. A public speaking voice should be louder, clearer, more precise, and slower than your private speaking voice.

5. *Use your face and body to communicate.*   You communicate with your facial expressions and body as well as your words. Communicate confidence and credibility by standing up straight. Do not lean on or hide behind a podium. Keep both feet on the floor, use hand gestures appropriately, and fully face your audience. Use facial expressions and hand gestures for points of emphasis.

6. *Maintain eye contact.*   Look at your audience to the greatest extent possible. Make sure you look at all members of the audience instead of focusing on a few. This enables you to make a more personal connection and provides immediate feedback. (You will be surprised at how much the body language of your audience tells you about your presentation.)

7. *Do not read your report.*   Standing at a podium and reading your report creates a very dull presentation. Do not do this. Also, communication that is effective in written form is different from that communication that is effective in oral form. Writing is visual and allows the reader to see the structure and move back and forth to check for understanding. Oral language is purely auditory and is presented in linear form. Thus, your oral presentation should be shorter and more condensed than your written report.

8. *Use an advanced organizer.*   An advanced organizer is anything that shows the structure of what is to be learned or presented up front. It could be in visual form such as an outline, web, chart, or diagram. It could be in verbal form. For example, *"The purpose of this presentation is to . . ."* or *"Today I will examine four ideas related to . . ."*

PowerPoint Specifics

1. *Use an advanced organizer.*   If you do not use a verbal advanced organizer (see preceding discussion), insert a visual advanced organizer right after the title of your presentation. This lets the audience know the structure of what is to come and enhances their ability to understand and encode new information.

2. *Use words or short phrases to hold ideas.*   You are the information transmission device, not the PowerPoint. PowerPoints (and handouts) are merely transmission enhancement devices. Thus, you should look to use a minimal number of words to hold and organize ideas. Use complete sentences only when you are presenting specific recommendations, applications, or rules. Use paragraphs only when you are showing an exact quote or the phrasing of a law or regulation. These instances should be very rare.

3. *Use two to four ideas per slide.* Again, words and phrases should be used to hold and organize bigger ideas. Slides with two to four ideas enable your audience to focus on a few points without being overwhelmed. It also creates a more engaging presentation as you move to new slides more frequently.

4. *Use 24 to 28 point font.* This allows you to put a space between your idea holders and provides enough room for you to insert pictures or diagrams on each slide.

5. *Capitalize on the multimodal nature of PowerPoint.* PowerPoint is a visual medium. Enhance this by finding appropriate pictures or other graphics to illustrate the points made. You can find images online, use a scanner, or create your own images with a digital camera.

6. *Do not read from your PowerPoint.* It is highly likely that your audience can read. They can probably read silently faster than you can read to them orally. Again, do not rely on a PowerPoint as an information transmission device. It is an organizing device used to hold bigger ideas. Where you have complete sentences or in those rare instances where you have more than a sentence, pause and let your audience read. (Nothing is more irritating than having somebody read to you what you just finished reading.)

7. *Show transition points.* If you are transitioning from one topic to another, use a heading or some other device to indicate this. You do not want to move to a new topic and leave the audience wondering how the previous ideas related to the new. Headings that are centered, boldfaced, and underlined can be used to indicate transition points. You can also tell your audience, *"New topic here."*

8. *Differentiate using font, size, color, and underlining.* These can all be used to denote transition points as well as headings, subheadings, and supporting ideas. The differentiation also makes your slides easier to comprehend and more visual pleasing.

Effective Handouts

A well-designed handout can be effective in enhancing your PowerPoint presentation, or, although not as effective, they can be used in place of a PowerPoint. Some basics here:

1. *Show the structure of what is to be covered.* A handout should contain an outline, web, chart, or diagram that shows the major ideas and how they are related to each other. The structure should be readily apparent.

2. *The handout is not a written document.* Again, avoid paragraphs. Use words and short phrases to hold your ideas. Like the PowerPoint, the handout is not an information transmission device.

3. *The handout should be single-sided and use one sheet of paper.* This will enable the structure to be very visible. As well, try to leave enough space on it for your audience to record notes.

Online Video Presentations

YouTube and other types of online streaming videos can be an effective way to record and present your ideas. This, for the most part, is a new medium that we are still learning how to use most effectively. I have included several video presentations on my website and have over 250 instructional videos on my YouTube account (Andyaxe, 1976). These are worth looking at, not because they are perfectly produced; rather, because they provide a sense of what works and what does not, and they reinforce and illustrate some of the ideas from this chapter. These are not highly technical video productions. You will see that I have some more-effective and some less-effective presentations. You will see also that my presentations continually evolve from earliest to latest productions. Two points: First, it takes time and practice to feel comfortable with this new medium. Take baby steps. You cannot take big steps if you are not first willing to take little steps. And second, it takes time. A 5-minute video sometimes takes two or more hours to put together and record. Some of the videos you see are second, third, and even fourth takes.

With this background information, a couple of tips are offered here:

1. *Understand the medium.* An effective online presentation is different from an oral presentation. You cannot simply record and post an oral presentation and expect it to be effective online. The online presentation is given to a different audience, in a different form, and in a different setting. In an online presentation, people's attention spans are shorter than they are for an in-person presentation. Thus, the video presentations should be used with PowerPoint or some other visual medium and need to be quickly paced.

2. *Do not create another talking head.* Spend some time looking at instructional videos online. Do a search under videos using education terms such as: *reading-instruction-phonics.* You will find a variety of instructional videos along with a lot of good examples of bad presentations. Some of these bad presentations include people simply talking into a camera. Ugh! Remember, this is a visual medium not an auditory medium. An effective video presentation is very visual. This means having pictures or diagrams on every slide and changing slides fairly often. Again, use only two to four ideas on a slide. The onus is on you to hold your audience's attention.

3. *Communicate with your face, hands, and voice.* Because most video presentations focus on the upper part of your body, your facial expressions and hand gestures become more important. Use these to highlight points of emphasis and hold your audience's attention. As well, vary your speaking rate, timbre, and inflection, and use pauses to good effect (see earlier discussion).

4. *Try to create video presentations that are three to eight minutes in duration.* Anything over 10 minutes becomes hard to watch. Again, this is much different from an in-person oral presentation. It is harder to stay engaged when watching. I have found that three to eight minutes tends to be the optimum length. This means that longer presentations need to be broken into two or more shorter segments. Remember, your audience does not have to see your complete presentation all in one sitting. Video presentations that are broken up into manageable parts can be seen over time and digested more easily.

5. *Use your video image most times.* It is generally more effective to have your image appear on the screen as you are talking with a PowerPoint in the background. This creates a more personal connection and enables you to communicate with more than just your words. However, you can use just a PowerPoint with a voice-over for a different effect. There may be times when you do not want to become a distraction, when you want the audience to focus overtly on the images and ideas. Also, I have found it effective to use a voice-over when I had a tightly scripted presentation or when the specific words and word order were so important that I read directly from a script. In these cases, a voice-over narrative was more effective.

6. *Speak from an outline.* Just like an in-person presentation, your video presentation should be planned with a coherent structure. Speak with your notes in front of you just below camera level. Look at the camera as much as possible and your notes as little as possible.

SUMMARY

- Your colleagues and students are often interested in hearing about the findings of your action research project.
- Action research can be used to make a case for a particular methodology or program or for evaluating new programs.
- The data collected in action research can be used to provide a more complete picture of your students.
- Professional conferences, academic journals, and the Education Resources Information Center are all viable venues for sharing your action research projects.
- Local community organizations are often interested in hearing of the latest trends in education and may also be a good place to present your action research findings.
- Effective presentations take planning and preparation.
- Attending to a few platform skills enhances the quality and effectiveness of your presentation.
- PowerPoints and handouts should be used to hold and organize bigger ideas and not as information transmission devices.
- Online video presentations can be used as venues to present and share your action research projects.
- Presentation is an online medium should look different in form and substance than in-person presentations.

QUESTIONS AND ACTIVITIES

1. Visit the ERIC website. Find five articles or reports related to an area of interest.
2. Do an Internet search to find possible journals to submit an action research report. List three journals you might consider.
3. List three other places besides a journal where you might present your action research report.
4. Identify two or three effective lectures or presentations you have experienced. What were the common elements or characteristics here? Share your ideas in small group. What common ideas did you discover? How might these be used to inform your own presentations?
5. Do a search for online video presentations or lectures. Find two that you feel to be effective and informative. What were the common traits or elements? Find two that you feel to be ineffective and hard to watch. What were the common traits or elements? Share your ideas in small group. What common ideas did you discover? How might these be used to inform your own presentations?

POSSIBLE RESEARCH QUESTIONS FOR ACTION RESEARCH PROJECTS

1. How do students use the Internet?
2. How are teachers using the Internet and other technology to enhance learning?
3. What are some technologies that might be used in the near future to enhance learning?
4. What do students find to be an effective class lesson or presentation?

CHAPTER FOURTEEN

ACTION RESEARCH AS MASTER'S THESIS

I would encourage those of you who are in graduate programs in education to consider doing an action research project for your master's thesis. In advising graduate students over the years, I have found that writers tend to find these projects more interesting and enjoyable to do. Action research projects are also more likely to affect their classroom practice. Not coincidentally, these projects usually seem to be more interesting to read and of better quality.

BEFORE YOU START

The graduate thesis represents the culminating experience of a graduate program. In it you must demonstrate that you are able to utilize academic sources to come to a conclusion in a way that will move the field forward. Following are nine tips and a flexible guide to use in structuring your action research thesis. Note, however, that colleges and universities have varying requirements for the master's thesis.

Nine Tips for Writing Your Master's Thesis

1. *See your advisor before beginning your graduate paper.* It is recommended that the first consultation occur at least 1 year and not less than 6 months before the projected completion. It takes a great deal of time to comprehend and synthesize all the ideas necessary for a graduate thesis. Your goal is to create a professional paper that contributes to the field, and this cannot be done in a few weeks.

2. *Decide on a topic or area of research first, then put it in the form of a question or questions.* A clear focus saves you much time in your research and results in a tighter and more coherent paper.

3. *Keep your thesis proposal short and flexible.* Most graduate programs ask students to write a thesis proposal. This is a very short description of your research project with 5 to 10 literature sources used to put your research question into a theoretical context. Proposals usually have to be preapproved by a graduate committee and the department of graduate studies at your school before you begin. Your initial proposal is a flexible guideline of your intended research project. It is common for the final product to look somewhat different from the proposal. Figure 14.1 contains an action research proposal form. This form can be downloaded at my website, www.AR-Johnson.com.

Action Research Proposal

Name: _____   Date: _____

I. Topic or Problem
What are you interested in? What problem do you see in your school or classroom? What do you want to investigate? Your topic should not describe what you wish to find; rather, it should simply indicate an area of interest to you. Example: Meeting the needs of gifted elementary readers in a general education setting.

My topic is _____.

II. Question
Put your topic in the form of one to three questions. The question or questions are used to help guide your search for data or articles. Do not start with the answer, as this will make your research much more difficult. Example: (a) What special needs do gifted readers have in the elementary grades? (b) How can general education teachers best meet these needs within the confines of reading instruction?

My question/s is/are:

1.

2.

3.

III. Methodology
Briefly describe your initial plan for collecting data. For a qualitative study you should use at least two sources. This should be considered a flexible plan at this point.

IV. Advisor's Signature
Check with your advisor and get his or her signature before continuing.

_____   _____
Advisor's Signature   Date

V. Sources
You will need a minimum of 15 sources for the literature review. These sources could be journal articles or chapters in academic textbooks. For the purpose of the proposal, you will need to see whether there is enough written on your proposed topic. Therefore, list at least eight possible journal articles or book chapters that may be of use to you (use correct APA form here).

(Continued)

FIGURE 14.1 Action Research Proposal Form

VI. One Empirical Study

For your proposal, find one empirical study related to your topic. *Empirical* means that it uses data or systematic observation. In the proposal, use one or two sentences to describe each of the following:

1. Purpose:
2. Subjects or participants:
3. Treatment or conditions:
4. Measures, instruments, or ways of collecting data:
5. Results (data collected):
6. Conclusions (what do the data mean or imply?):

VII. Initial Literature Review

Using correct APA form, write an initial review of the literature using three of the book/article sources and the one empirical study source described earlier. This initial literature review should be between four and eight pages in length and should contain an introductory paragraph and a reference page, all in correct APA style (sixth edition).

FIGURE 14.1 (Continued)

4. *Do not expect your advisor to be an editor.*   The onus is ultimately on you to write in a logical, coherent, objective style that can be easily understood by all who read your paper. An advising professor will provide feedback and some editorial comments, but this is much different from taking on the role of an editor.

5. *Start collecting journal articles for your literature review as soon as possible.* All master's papers contain a review of the literature related to the topic or research question. A number of sources are needed. (I tell my graduate students that a minimum of 25 is needed, but there are a wide variety of opinions here.) These sources must be from current texts or juried academic journals (see your advisor if you have questions here). It takes time to read, take notes, and synthesize all the material you read; thus, allow plenty of time for this stage. Some graduate students try to take shortcuts at this stage; however, I have found that these shortcuts always end up being "long cuts."

6. *Create a preliminary outline for your literature review.*   An outline is used to help you find a logical structure. This structure is like the frame of a house and is used to hold your ideas together. Some like to use an inverted triangle that goes from most general to most specific. For example, if I were writing a paper on gifted learners and reading in the elementary school, I would use the following sections: (a) gifted learners, (b) reading in the elementary school, and (c) gifted learners and reading in the elementary school.

7. *Begin to plan how you will collect data.*   Teachers often use a pilot study in their class to experiment with and refine several data collection methods before selecting those they will use. Keep in mind that your data collection must be well planned and systematic.

8. *Plan on revising each chapter at least four times.*   Revision is what separates good writing from average writing. Revision is at the heart of writing of any kind.

9. *Assume the reader knows nothing.* Adopt a teaching, describing mode. The reader should know exactly what you are doing and why, and be able to replicate your procedures.

THE ACTION RESEARCH THESIS

Described next are the parts that might make up a master's thesis using action research. This is not meant to be a recipe; rather, it is a flexible guideline. The order and parts to be included may vary depending on your research topic and the requirements of your college or university. Your advisor may also ask for slight variations of this form; thus, it is imperative that you meet with your advisor before you begin. This will save you both a great deal of time and help you avoid frustration.

Abstract

The abstract is a brief summary of the thesis, study, or journal article. Its purpose is to give readers a very concise overview. For a thesis you should include (a) the purpose or problem; (b) pertinent information about participants; (c) pertinent information about the methodology; and (d) basic findings, conclusions, and recommendations. You have a limited number of words here. Most abstracts are between 150 and 250 words. Use as few words as possible. Sample abstracts are included in the next section.

CHAPTER I
INTRODUCTION

1. Introduction to the Topic (no heading for this section)
   A. Identify the problem or area of interest.
   B. Provide background information.
2. Purpose Statement (heading, centered, boldface)
   A. State purpose of paper/study. Example: *The purpose of this paper was to examine the writing workshop in my second grade and to describe effective implementation practices.*
   B. Put the purpose in the form of one or more questions. Example: *The specific research questions are . . .*
      1. *What is happening during my writing workshop?*
      2. *Is the writing workshop effective in developing my students' writing skills?*
      3. *If so, how should the writing workshop be implemented in a primary grade setting?*
3. Importance of the Study (heading, centered, boldface)
   A. Tell why this study is important.
   B. Example: *The information here will be of value to . . . It will also provide elementary teachers with a plan to . . .*

4. Definition of Terms (heading, centered, boldface)
   A. List important terms.
   B. Briefly describe each term using one or two complete sentences.

CHAPTER II
REVIEW OF THE LITERATURE

1. This builds the foundation for your thesis. Here you provide background information to support your question or to put your research topic in a theoretical context. Also, you want to see what others have found related to your topic that may be of use in your action research.
2. Gather material. Consider using 25 to 40 sources. Use current, peer-reviewed journal articles whenever possible.
3. After reading each piece, take notes listing the citation at the top and only those items of importance below. Use headings whenever possible. This will make it easier to organize your notes.
4. Begin thinking about the structure. Some people like to web or outline to find structure initially. As data in the form of your notes are gathered, begin to look for categories. Your initial structures should be very flexible because they most likely will change.
5. As you write this chapter, use headings and subheadings to break up the text. It is very hard to read several pages of text without headings.
6. Describe empirical research related to your topic. When describing research studies, try to use one or two sentences to describe each of the following: (a) the question or purpose of the study, (b) the number and type of participants, (c) the treatment or conditions involved, (d) the type of measures, and (e) the results and conclusions.
7. This chapter ends with a brief summary of the major points covered that is generally about one paragraph in length. Sometimes the summary is put in list form with each point cited.

CHAPTER III
METHODOLOGY

1. Participants (heading, centered, boldface)
   A. Describe the people involved. The reader should know ages, number, gender, ethnic makeup, and anything else you feel is pertinent to your research.
   B. Describe the environment: classroom, school, or community.

2. Materials (heading, centered, boldface)
   A. Describe any materials used in your research. If you are using a particular curriculum, product, or procedure, describe it fully. Include relevant examples in an appendix. Remember that the reader knows nothing.
   B. Describe all types of measuring devices. If surveys, checklists, rubrics, or rating charts are used, describe them briefly, then include a sample in the appendix.
3. Procedures (heading, centered, boldface)
   A. Describe the length of the study.
   B. Describe how you collected the data, how much, and how often.
   C. Use past tense in describing all aspects of your methodology and findings. Research always exists in the past, in a specific time and place.
   D. If you use a special curriculum, technique, or procedure, let the reader know exactly what it is. This section should be described in such a way that one could pick up this chapter and replicate your procedures.
4. Analysis (heading, centered, boldface)
   A. Describe how you will organize and analyze your data. Inductive analysis will most likely be used for your field notes and other qualitative data.
   B. Quantitative data will generally be analyzed using totals and mean scores. Here a simple comparative analysis will be made. It is outside the scope of this book to talk about statistical methods; however, statistical analysis is also an option.

CHAPTER IV
FINDINGS

1. Restate your research questions.
2. Describe the data that answer that question (this chapter is often the longest chapter in an action research thesis).
3. Describe the themes, categories, and patterns.
4. Use illustrative examples for each category.
5. Use tables, graphs, figures, and artwork as necessary.
6. Use headings and subheadings to make the structure readily apparent.

CHAPTER V
DISCUSSION

1. Overview of the Study (heading, centered, boldface)
   A. Restate the general purpose of the study.
   B. Briefly describe how the results were obtained.

2. Summary of Findings (heading, centered)
   A. Provide a brief summary of the findings.
   B. This may be one to two paragraphs.
3. Conclusions (heading, centered, boldface)
   A. Move beyond the data. Tell what these results mean.
   B. Describe possible implications of the results.
4. Recommendations (heading, centered, boldface)
   A. Describe how the results might be used in your classroom.
   B. Describe how the results may be used to bring understanding to other classrooms or situations.
   C Sometimes the conclusions and recommendations merge.
5. Limitations of the Study (heading, centered, boldface)
   A. Describe things that may have hindered or affected your findings.
   B. Describe things that you needed to change during the study, or things that did not go as expected. Remember, a good study is not one that proves your particular point; rather, a good study is one that looks carefully, reports accurately, and fairly represents the bit of reality that you experienced.
   C. Describe the limitations or applicability of the findings. For example, your recommendations might be applied only to a certain segment of the population. Also, were you able to look at all facets of the problem?
   D. Describe ideas for future research related to your research.

EXAMPLES OF ABSTRACTS

Following are some examples of abstracts used for master's theses. Other examples of action research abstracts can be found at my website: www.AR-Johnson.com.

Tina Williams, Osconda, Michigan

Abstract

The purpose of this qualitative study was to understand the factors influencing families to choose homeschooling as the primary method of education for their children. This research was conducted with 42 families who participated in homeschooling and resided within the Jefferson County Public School district located in Louisville, Kentucky. Data was collected through 16 parent questionnaires, nine parent interviews, and 26 on-line group forum discussion boards. Data was gathered to determine the participants' views and experiences with homeschooling including their decision making processes, the perceived benefits and challenges associated with homeschooling, and student attitudes towards their education. The results indicated that the participants perceived the benefits of homeschooling outweigh the challenges, students attitudes towards their education are more positive when schooling was done at home, and a majority of the participants experienced dissatisfaction with some aspect of school as one reason they initiated homeschooling. These findings are some of the factors influencing parents to homeschool. Public school teachers, principals, and administrators should examine why parents are choosing home-schooling in place of public schooling and adjust their policies, teaching methods, and procedures to best fit the needs of the public they serve.

Michaelene M. Archer, Spring Arbor, Michigan

Abstract

This action research study investigated the effects of targeted interventions on the performance of students in first grade in math at Warner Elementary School in Spring Arbor, Michigan. The participants were twenty-two first grade students in a general education classroom. The targeted interventions occurred as a result of assessments that were administered each week to determine the needs of the students. Students who scored at a remedial or intermediate level were placed in a small group for targeted interventions. Besides occurring in small groups, for differentiated instruction, the students received support from lessons that incorporated Multiple Intelligences and used manipulative materials. The results of this study suggested that students felt as though the targeted interventions helped them gain a better understanding of the concepts that had been taught. The results of this study also suggest targeted interventions helped students to perform more successfully in academics.

Kari Ervans, Reading, Michigan

Abstract

This study describes the effects of the use of e-mail, word processing and Moodle in my Creative Writing class. This class was comprised of seven juniors and seniors who were first and second year creative writing students. The community is suffering economically along with the rest of the state and because of this the school is struggling. The use of technology has become a big issue in the district. Current research shows that technology can be used to motivate students; technology also has its pitfalls. The teacher-researcher used student surveys, quick writes, student self-assessments and teacher assessments to collect the data. The study found that students enjoyed the use of e-mail and word-processing but had mixed feelings about the use of Moodle. The findings were mixed in regards to how well the students' writing seemed to improve with the use of technology but overall technology was well received as an educational tool.

EXAMPLES OF FULL MASTER'S THESES

Readers have asked that I share some examples of full-length master's theses. Space precludes me from doing that here; however, I have included three examples of complete master's theses at my website, www.AR-Johnson.com. Brief descriptions of these theses are provided here.

Darlene Cempa, Whitney Point, New York

Darlene Cempa conducted an action research project to examine the use of cooperative learning techniques in a fifth-grade classroom in which there was a high proportion of students with learning disabilities. This research focused on students' on-task and off-task behavior. Observations were made during typical instruction, which included instructional input followed by cooperative learning activities. She found that there was a higher degree of on-task behavior during these cooperative learning activities.

Karen Randle, Trumansburg, New York

Karen Randle conducted a study to examine the effects of integrating visual art and the writing process. She wanted to see if these had any effect on the quality of students' creative writing. Her study used three writing conditions: (a) open-ended textual story prompts, (b) fine art images as story prompts, and (c) student-created artwork as story prompts. Data were collected using students interviews, field observations, and artifact analysis. The findings indicated that open-ended prompts, both textual and visual, led to more imaginative storylines, more complex sentence structure, and more elaborate character development when compared to a highly scripted writing prompt. As well, using visual art and art production in the prewriting process led to greater student engagement in the writing process and heightened student investment in the end product.

Morgan Chylinski, Jamesville, New York

Morgan Chylinski conducted an action research project to examine the effectiveness of hands-on learning in an elementary science class. Participants in this study were a third-grade class in Central New York. The study focused on a hands-on bouncy unit that was taught over the course of one week. The findings indicated that students enjoyed learning using hands-on techniques and that students' learning increased.

THE LAST WORD

I have found that graduate students like to have some idea of what goes into a thesis; however, I once again reiterate: The structure described in this chapter is a flexible guideline that should be adapted to meet the needs of your particular research question.

CHAPTER FIFTEEN

STRATEGIES FOR PROFESSIONAL GROWTH AND DEVELOPMENT

ACTION RESEARCH AND THE PROFESSIONAL DEVELOPMENT OF TEACHERS

It is not possible, in 2 years of preservice teacher education, to create a finished teaching product. (My undergraduate students are always surprised when I tell them this.) To think otherwise demonstrates a lack of understanding related to the complexities and multiple dimensions of teaching. Master teachers spend years learning, developing, and refining their teaching craft. At best, teacher preparatory institutions can get preservice teachers ready to begin their teaching journey by helping them (a) construct a body of knowledge related to teaching and learning, (b) identify a philosophy and cultivate certain dispositions, and (c) acquire some basic pedagogical skills. These are all necessary and important things to get one started in education, but they in no way indicate that a new teacher has reached his or her full potential as a teacher.

Once in the field, professional development is up to each teacher and to the school district that employs him or her. But is professional development really necessary? Must we always be changing? Yes and yes. As our society and our students change, so too must our educational institutions change to address their varying needs. And as new educational research gives us more insight into teaching and learning, our teaching practices need to continue to evolve to reflect these new findings. Change is the only constant in the universe. To stay the same in the midst of change is to devolve (which is a form of change).

There are a variety of other ways to develop professionally. Following are some strategies for professional development. Of course, action research can be a powerful tool to help with each of these.

More Knowledge Please

One of the major differences between experts and novices in any field is their amount of knowledge (Sternberg & Williams, 2009). Experts have more of it; novices have less of it. Thus, one effective form of professional development is to expand one's knowledge base related to teaching and learning, pedagogy, or a particular subject area. This can be done most simply by developing a plan for reading books and educational journals. If you have not taken an educational psychology course in a while, I would recommend starting with a basic text in this area. This will reacquaint you with some of the basic theories of learning. You will most likely find that having been in a classroom for a couple of years, the information found here now seems much more relevant and interesting than when you first encountered these ideas as an undergraduate preservice teacher. After that, the following steps can be used to guide you.

Step 1: Identify a Topic of Interest or Importance.   What is it that you want to know more about? Is there some area of your teaching in which you want to develop expertise? If you are unsure of where to start, it may be helpful to quickly list things that are of interest to you. The process of writing quickly (without thinking or analyzing) allows your unconscious mind to kick in a few ideas. Also, conversation with other teachers is another way to generate possible professional development ideas. Looking to your own professional practice to identify topics creates a much more powerful professional development experience than having somebody else decide what you should learn (like in the typical after-school workshop or teacher inservice).

> *Example:* Ms. Vinatieri was interested in helping her second-grade students enhance their reading fluency. The school district in which she was working had recently bought an expensive new commercial reading program that had tutors working individually with low-ability readers, drilling them in letter sounds and word lists that were read outside any meaningful context. Although the commercial program cited research that claimed success, this approach did not seem efficient or effective to Ms. Vinatieri. Further, the meaningless drill and practice was dreary and seemed to reinforce the negative attitudes her low-ability readers already had toward reading. She wondered whether the curriculum director and the superintendent had done any research before investing so much time and money into this commercial program. Thus, her topic was reading fluency.

Step 2: Identify a Goal or Goals.   Why is this topic of interest to you? What is the end result? What do you hope to do with this knowledge? Do you want to develop content area knowledge? Are you looking for activities related to a subject or unit of study? Are you looking for new pedagogical strategies? Do you want to align your teaching with best practice? Do you want to make sure your teaching methods reflect the latest research and theories in the field? Identifying a possible goal will enable you to be more focused as you search.

> *Example:* Ms. Vinatieri had three goals: First, she wanted to see whether there was any objective research that supported the methods used in the new program. She was looking for research conducted by qualified researchers who were not affiliated with the company producing the commercial program and that was published in peer-reviewed journals. Second, she wanted to find a variety of practical, research-based strategies that could be used to help develop reading fluency. She was looking for methods that were effective and aligned with the way students naturally learn. Her third goal may seem a bit subversive, but she wanted to know if those responsible for making these decisions in her district were responsible decision makers. Did they spend a little time up front reviewing the research literature before reaching a conclusion that would affect so many? Did they take a broad, unbiased look? Or did they instead start with the answer and look only for bits of data that supported their preconceived ideas? In a sense, she wanted to hold those in administration accountable.

Step 3: Put Your Topic in the Form of a Question or Questions. There is a tremendous amount of information published on most topics in education. Having a specific question in mind before reviewing the literature will help you focus only on that information that is of direct relevance to your goals.

> *Example:* Ms. Vinatieri's specific questions were, What research-based strategies or practices can be used to enhance students' reading fluency? How should these strategies be used?

Step 4: Find Peer-Reviewed Books and Academic Journal Articles. Just because it is in a book does not mean it is a credible source. What books are credible? First, look to see who publishes it. You can generally put more trust in those that are published by major publishing companies in education such as Allyn and Bacon, Sage Publications, Merrill/Prentice Hall, Heinemann, McGraw-Hill, Association for Supervision and Curriculum Development, Houghton-Mifflin, and Harcourt Brace. These can be considered peer-reviewed publications. To publish with these companies, authors must write a prospectus in which they provide a research-based perspective and justification for their book. Authors must also include an outline describing the content and sample chapters. These prospecti are then sent out for a blind review by various experts in the field who either recommend them for publication or for rejection. Once accepted, publishing companies usually send out each chapter for further peer review. This process allows one to be fairly certain that the information found in these texts has some theoretical context or research-based support. A second way to check the credibility of books is to scan the chapters to see if the authors cite their sources. Avoid books that make broad undocumented claims without citing their sources such as, "Research reports that . . ." or "Scientists say that . . ." or "It has long been documented that . . ." or "It is well known that . . ." Also, if sources are cited, check the reference section at the end of the book to see if they are from peer-reviewed academic journals.

Also look for peer-reviewed academic journals. It is not likely that these would be available at most public libraries. If it is possible, find a college library or look for them on the Internet. Also, many public schools now have access to data-bases such as ERIC (Educational Resource Information Center) that contain peer-reviewed research and journal articles. You can go directly to the ERIC database at www.eric.ed.gov, although most peer-reviewed journal articles found there are not available without paying a subscription fee. There are, however, many websites that provide free access to peer-reviewed journals. Doing a quick Internet search brought me to the websites in Figure 15.1. And there are many more to be found.

As mentioned earlier in this book, magazine articles should not be used when looking for credible information in education for two reasons: First, magazines, as well as newspaper articles, are written by reporters who usually have little exper-tise in the field; therefore they are not likely to be able to put information in any sort of meaningful context. Also, reporters tend not to be familiar with relevant research and related theory; thus, they are not able to distinguish between con-jecture and theory-based ideas. And second, magazines and newspapers do not have peer review. They are instead reviewed by an editor or editors who have little expertise in the field of education.

Council for Exceptional Children provides access to two journals, *Exceptional Children* and *Teaching Exceptional Children:* http://journals.sped.org

The Allan Review (journal related to adolescent literacy): http://scholar.lib.vt.edu/ejournals/ALAN/alan-review.html

Early Childhood Research and Practice: www.ecrp.uiuc.edu

Electronic Journal of Science Education: www.unr.edu/homepage/jcannon/ejse/ejse.html

International Journal of Special Education: www.internationaljournalofspecialeducation.com

Issues in Educational Research: www.education.curtin.edu.au/iier/iier.html

The Reading Matrix: An International Online Journal: www.readingmatrix.com/journal.html

The International Journal of Wholeschooling: http://education.wayne.edu/wholeschooling/Journal_ of_Whole_Schooling/IJWSIndex.html

Directory of Open Access Scholarly Journals in Education (many peer-reviewed academic journals can be found here): http://www.ergobservatory.info/ejdirectory.html

Academic Journal Exchange (many peer-reviewed academic journals can be found here): www.rapid intellect.com/AEQweb

FIGURE 15.1   Free Online Peer-Reviewed Journals

The Internet provides a tremendous amount of knowledge literally at our fingertips. Internet websites can be invaluable tools for getting information very quickly; however, they should never be the sole authority on anything. Although they can contain a great deal of useful information, the vast majority of websites cannot be considered credible sources. Anybody can put things up on a website. (Even I have a website: www.OPDT-Johnson.com.) Thus, things found on Internet websites should be taken with a grain of salt (or perhaps the whole salt shaker). (Note that websites are different from peer-reviewed journals and journal articles that are found online. These can be used with a fair amount of confidence.) The best way to use Internet websites is to look for information or ideas after you have done some initial reading from academic books and journals.

> *Example:* Ms. Vinatieri first did a search for peer-reviewed articles on her school's ERIC database. Using the advanced search engine, she put in the key words *reading*, *fluency*, and *research*. For the types of publications, she narrowed her search to journal articles and research reports. Her search came up with 456 publications. She skimmed titles and abstracts and selected the eight in Figure 15.2 to examine more thoroughly.
>
> She also found a couple of books related to literacy instruction in her school's professional development library. In each she located the sections that described fluency and strategies to promote fluency (Figure 15.3).

Ferrara, S. L. (2005). Reading fluency and self-efficacy: A case study. *International Journal of Disability Development and Education, 52,* 215–231.

Hudson, R. F., Lane, H. B., & Pullen, P. C. (2005). Reading fluency assessment and instruction: What, why, and how? *Reading Teacher, 58,* 702–714.

Kubina, R. M. (2005). Developing reading fluency through a systematic practice procedure. *Reading and Writing Quarterly, 21,* 185–192.

Kuhn, M. R. (2005). Comparative study of small group fluency instruction. *Reading Psychology, 2,* 127–146.

Martin-Change, S. L., & Levy, B. A. (2005). Fluency transfer: Differential gains in reading speed and accuracy following isolated word and context training. *Reading and Writing, 18,* 343–376.

Mastropieri, M. A., Leinart, A., & Scruggs, T. E. (1999). Strategies to increase reading fluency. *Intervention in School and Clinic, 34,* 278–283, 292.

Richards, M. (2000). Be a good detective: Solve the case of oral reading fluency. *The Reading Teacher, 53,* 534–539.

Stahl, S. A. & Kuhn, M. R. (2002). Making it sound like language: Developing fluency. *The Reading Teacher, 55*(6), 582–584.

FIGURE 15.2   Journal Articles Related to Reading Fluency

Allington, R. L. (2005). *What really matters for struggling readers: Designing research-based programs* (2nd ed.). Boston: Allyn & Bacon.

Gipe, J. P. (2006). *Multiple paths to literacy: Assessment and differentiated instruction for diverse learners, K–12* (6th ed.). Upper Saddle River, NJ: Merrill/Prentice Hall.

Johnson, A. P. (2008). *Teaching reading and writing: A guidebook for tutoring and remediating students*. Lanham, MD: Rowman and Littlefield.

FIGURE 15.3   Books Related to Literacy Instruction

Step 5: Read, Take Notes, and Look for Applications.   As you skim your articles and chapters, record only information that is directly related to your question.

> *Example:* Having her questions identified made it easier for Ms. Vinatieri to quickly read and comprehend her articles and chapters. She skimmed until she found the specific information she was looking for. Then she recorded only the necessary information in her notes.

Step 6: Look for Internet Ideas and Applications That Are Supported by Research-Based Theory.   Because of the abundance of information found there, an Internet search is most effectively done with some degree of relevant background knowledge. This knowledge enables you to quickly evaluate websites.

> *Example:* Ms. Vinatieri first gained background knowledge by reading journal articles and books. She then used this knowledge-based context to search the Internet and look for additional fluency strategies that could be supported by research-based theory (Figure 15.4).

Step 7: Apply and Take Action.   Examine your notes carefully. What trends or patterns do you notice? What do they suggest? The last step is to create an application and plan of action based on the information you find.

> *Example:* Ms. Vinatieri found nine fairly simple research-based strategies that could be used to help students develop their reading fluency. She realized that many of the strategies she found were superior to the ones described in the

---

www.auburn.edu/~murraba/fluency.html

www.jimwrightonline.com/pdfdocs/prtutor/prtutor_lesson3.pdf

www.balancedreading.com/fluency.html

http://www.ldonline.org/article/6354

FIGURE 15.4   Websites Related to Reading Fluency

expensive commercial program. Also, her students seemed to be more inclined to want to do her activities. She wrote the steps to each of the strategies she found (Figures 15.5 and 15.6) and gave a quick after-school inservice to the teachers in her building.

Process and Empowerment

The steps described in the previous section are similar to those used to conduct an action research project (described in the next chapter). In fact, this sort of literature review is a form of action research as the same basic process is used: Ask a question

PPPP (Preview, Pause, Prompt, Praise)

1. Preview: Tutor engages students in brief preview of the story/section: title, pictures, headings, predictions ("What do you think this story is about?").
2. Tutor/student read aloud together until the student wishes to read alone.
3. Pause: If student stumbles, tutor will pause.
   a. Provides opportunity to self-correct.
   b. Student uses context clues, words parts, rereads sentence.
4. Prompt: At the end of the sentence, if the student has not figured out the word, the tutor will prompt, "Let's read that again."
   a. Give semantic clues ("What makes sense here?")
   b. Give pronunciation if needed.
5. Praise: Praise for self-correction.
6. Continue reading with the student, then drop out.
7. At the end: "What was your favorite part?" There are no wrong answers.

Reread to Meet Standard

1. Find a piece of reading at a particular grade level.
2. Count off 100 words.
3. Set a goal for time.
4. Students reread until they meet the WPM standard.
5. Use zone of proximal development (get a little outside and a little ahead of the student).

Tape, Check, Chart

1. Distribute photocopy of reading selection.
2. Using audiotape, have students read selection out loud.
3. Replay tape and check mispronounced words (put a check on copy for mispronounced words).
   a. Listening gives them a sense of what makes sense.
4. Reread and audiotape again.
5. Replay and draw an X through mispronounced words.
6. Reread and audiotape.
7. Replay and circle mispronounced words.
8. Record the number of errors each time: Students see the number of errors go down.
   a. Record in portfolio— 8—3—1

Older Peer Tutor

1. Pair older students with younger ones to help "tutor."
2. The tutoring is designed to help older students read easier text and develop fluency.

Time Chart

1. Read passage out loud.
2. Time with stopwatch and record.
3. Repeat twice more.
4. Record times in portfolio.

Johnson, A. P. (2008). *Teaching reading and writing: A guidebook for tutoring and remediating sudents.* Lanham, MD: Rowman and Littlefield.

FIGURE 15.5   One-on-One Tutorial Approaches for Fluency Development

Choral Reading for Fluency
1. Have students read together.
2. Find short stories, picture books, segments of longer books, poems, or even song lyrics.
3. Read together, picking individuals and small groups to read parts.

Reader's Theater
1. Students work in groups.
2. Create a play out of a story or create their own.
3. Use narrators and characters.
4. Can use sound effects and music.

Echo Reading
1. Teacher reads a sentence in book or board.
2. Students read it back.

Repeated Reading
(large group or small group)
1. Find a piece of text.
2. Divide students into pairs.
3. One student reads as fast as s/he can for one minute. Buddy checks to make sure no words were skipped.
4. Stop and record number of words read (have prenumbered pieces of text).
5. Repeat the process with the same buddy. Record the number of words read in one minute.
6. Put scores on a graph in a portfolio and switch (other buddy reads).

Johnson, A. P. (2008). *Teaching reading and writing: A guidebook for tutoring and remediating students*. Lanham, MD: Rowman and Littlefield.

FIGURE 15.6   Small-Group and Whole-Class Activities to Develop Fluency

and then look for data to answer that question. The only difference here is that the data are found in academic books and peer-reviewed journals instead of in your classroom or school. Again, I stress the importance of not starting any sort of research project with an answer. This bias limits what you might see and makes the process much harder. In research, as in life, let the data speak.

Understanding this process enables you to construct knowledge and become an expert in any area. This can be empowering. One of the big ideas that I hope you will take from this book is that knowledge is power. Having a body of research-based and theory-based knowledge related to teaching and learning allows you to take control of your profession. You no longer need to rely on or believe the top-down recommendations that are given to you by school districts or government agencies. Neither do you have to depend on administrators, publishers, or college professors to tell you what "the research" says about a particular subject or what the appropriate method or approach is. Instead, a body of knowledge related to teaching and learning enables you to offer research-based alternatives, and with a highly informed teaching population we can all begin to say "no" in a loud and united voice when a principal, superintendent, college dean, or government agency asks us to do something that is not in the best interest of our students. Knowledge is power.

Online Professional Development

The classroom teacher is the most significant variable in determining the quality of education students receive (Darling-Hammond, 1999). Four types of knowledge are needed to be an effective classroom teacher: (a) content knowledge or knowledge of subject matter; (b) pedagogical knowledge or knowledge of teaching strategies, skills, and techniques; (c) pedagogical content knowledge or knowledge of how to teach specific content or skills; and (d) knowledge of learners and learning or knowledge of human development and how people learn (Bruer, 1999; Eggen & Kauchak, 2010). Thus, the most effective, efficient, and economical ways to improve the quality of education in schools is to make sure teachers continue to have the research-based skills or strategies (pedagogical knowledge and pedagogical content knowledge) they need to be successful. To this end, see the online professional development sites for teachers listed in Chapter 1, Figure 1.5, and also listed on my own website (www.AR-Johnson.com).

Other Professional Development Opportunities

A more generalized approach to professional development is wide reading. This also serves to enhance your ability to plan, teach, and make sound decisions. A subscription to a peer-reviewed academic journal will keep you up to date on the latest developments in a particular field. Figure 15.7 contains a list of some of the major journals and national organizations in various educational disciplines. Some books and other sources that may be of interest and serve to enhance your professional development are listed on my website (www.AR-Johnson.com). Other professional development strategies include conferences and workshops, college courses, professional discussions with colleagues, experimentation with reflection in regard to trying new strategies in your classroom, and of course, deep reflection.

OBSERVING YOUR OWN PRACTICE

Observation, reflection, and analysis of one's own teaching practice are simple yet effective ways to approach one's professional development. Action research, a systematic observation of your own teaching practice, can become a vehicle to help with this. Following are described some simple ways to enhance your own teaching practice through this process. As is the case throughout this book, the stress should be on the concept of simplicity. Rigor and effectiveness are much different from complexity. The best and most useful action research projects are usually the simplest ones.

Best Practice

In their book *Best Practice: New Standards for Teaching and Learning in America's Schools,* Zemelman, Daniels, and Hyde (2006) described was has come to be known as best practice. These are the teaching strategies and educational practices that a body of research has shown to be effective in keeping all students engaged in appropriate learning activities and enhancing learning. Figure 15.8 contains a chart that summarizes some general best practice recommendations that go across all curriculum areas. A simple way to use Zemelman, Daniels, and Hyde's chart for professional development is to record instances of each best practice recommendation in a weekly planner. At the end of each day use a red tally mark to indicate

Gifted Education
Gifted Child Today, Journal for the Education of the Gifted, and *Journal of Secondary Gifted Education,* published by Prufrock Press. Website: www.prufrock.com

Roeper Review. Website: www.roeperreview.org

National Association for Gifted Children is the most recognized national organization. They do not have a journal that I can recommend for teachers. Website: www.nagc.org

Literacy
The Reading Teacher and *Journal of Adolescent and Adult Literacy,* published by the International Reading Association. Website: www.reading.org

Language Arts, Voices from the Middle, and *English Journal,* published by National Council of Teachers of English. Website: www.ncte.org

Social Studies
Social Education and *Social Studies and the Young Learner,* published by the National Council for the Social Studies. Website: www.ncss.org

Mathematics
Teaching Children Mathematics, Mathematics Teaching in the Middle School, Mathematics Teacher, and *Online Journal for School Mathematics,* published by the National Council of Teachers of Mathematics. Website: www.nctm.org

Science
Science and Children, Science Scope, and *The Science Teacher,* published by National Science Teachers Association. Website: www.nsta.org

Holistic Education or Progressive Education
Encounter: Education for Meaning and Social Justice, published by Great Ideas in Education. Website: www.great-ideas.org

Young Children
Young Children, published by National Association for the Education of Young Children. Website: www.naeyc.org

Special Education
Exceptional Children and *Teaching Exceptional Children,* published by the Council for Exceptional Children. Website: www.cec.sped.org

Journal of Whole Schooling, a free online journal published by the Whole School Consortium. Website: www.wholeschooling.net

---

FIGURE 15.7   Academic Journals

---

when something from the Provide Less list occurred in your classroom and black marks to indicate when something from the Provide More list occurred. At the end of each week, count the number of red and black tally marks and record these on a graph or chart. This sort of tallying helps you become aware of your own teaching practice as it relates to best practice. As the year goes on, you should see an increase in black tally marks and a decrease in red tally marks. To get more specific, you can number the items in each list so that you have a sense of the types of the specific practices that occur in your classroom each week.

PROVIDE LESS

- Whole-class, teacher-directed instruction (e.g., lecturing); student passivity (sitting, listening, receiving, and absorbing information)
- Presentational, one-way transmission of information from teacher to student
- Prizing and rewarding of silence in the classroom
- Classroom time devoted to fill-in-the-blank worksheets, dittos, workbooks, and other seatwork
- Student time spent reading textbooks and basal readers
- Rote memorization of facts and details
- Emphasis on competition and grades in school
- Use of pull-out special programs
- Use of and reliance on standardized tests

PROVIDE MORE

- Experiential, inductive, hands-on learning
- Active learning in the classroom, with students doing, talking, and collaborating
- Diverse roles for teachers, including coaching, demonstrating, and modeling
- Emphasis on higher-order thinking; learning a field's key concepts and principles
- Reading of real tests, whole books, primary sources, and nonfiction materials
- Responsibility transferred to students for their work (goal setting, record keeping, monitoring, sharing, exhibiting, and evaluating)
- Choice for students (e.g., choosing their own books, writing topics, team partners, and research perfects)
- Enacting and modeling of the principles of democracy in school
- Attention to affective needs and the varying cognitive styles of individual students
- Cooperative, collaborative activity, developing the classroom as an interdependent community
- Heterogeneously grouped classrooms where individual needs are met through inherently individualized activities, not segregation of bodies
- Delivery of special help to students in regular classrooms
- Reliance on teachers' descriptive evaluation of student growth, including observational/anecdotal records, conference notes, and performance assessment rubrics

FIGURE 15.8   **Best Practices for Enhancing Learning**

I highly recommend Zemelman, Daniels, and Hyde's book for every school's professional library. It could become the basis of a weekly book club for teachers. There are chapters related to best practice in each of the subject areas: reading, writing, mathematics, science, social studies, and the arts. And at the end of every chapter, charts like those in Figure 15.9 are included that list things to increase and decrease for effective learning. If you are an elementary or middle school teacher who teaches more than one subject area, one subject area could be the focus for a month with the same sort of tally system used as previously described. This book also includes a chapter devoted to the seven structures of best teaching practice: small-group activities, reading as thinking, representing to learn, classroom workshop, authentic experiences, reflective assessment, and integrative units.

Audiotaping Lessons

For teachers involved in the complex act of teaching, observation, reflection, and analysis during a teaching episode is not always possible or pragmatic. However, audiotape can be effectively used to record teaching episodes for later analysis. I prefer audiotape over videotape because it is much easier and far less intrusive to use. It is easy to turn on a tape recorder, set it on the front table, and begin teaching. It is much more difficult to set up a camera, adjust the view, and get students acclimated to it. Except for student movement and certain nonverbal behaviors, I find that almost as much information is collected with audiotape as with videotape.

1. *Types of questions.* Use tally marks to indicate the number of times a particular type of question is asked (see Figure 15.9).

2. *Level of questions and activities.* Use tally marks and Bloom's Taxonomy to determine the level and frequency of your questions or activities (Figure 15.10).

3. *Students responding.* Do you call on the same students during discussions? Are all students involved? Record the students called on to answer questions during a lesson. Use a table or graph to show this information.

4. *Wait time.* Do you pause to allow students to fully process the question before calling on them? Use a stopwatch to determine the length of time between when you ask a question and when you call on a student. Record these time intervals. Use a bar graph to show the number of times at each interval level, or use a line graph to show how the average time interval changes over time.

5. *Management statements.* Are you proactive in preventing management issues? Or do you react to a problem situation that has already happened? Figure 15.11 can be used to record the types of statements made related to classroom management.

6. *T-chart for observation and analysis.* Many times researchers do not know exactly what they are looking for until they see it. The T-chart in Figure 15.12 can be used to record interesting or important parts of your lesson and your analysis of those parts. This is an open-ended inquiry. Record your objective observations or what you noticed in the left column and your subjective thoughts, applications, or analysis of the idea in the right column. On the bottom, jot down any big ideas or conclusions made based on this observation and analysis. Focus on a class or subject area that seems to be more troublesome for you than others. Also, the T-chart is useful for trying a new strategy, methodology, or activity where you simply want to find out how it is working. Doing a series of T-chart observations over time will provide you valuable information you would not have otherwise noticed.

Open-ended question	
Closed-ended question	

FIGURE 15.9   Types of Questions

Level or Type of Thinking	Times Used
1. Knowledge. Recalls facts or remembers previously learned material *Knowledge level operations:* define, describe, identify, list, match, name, tell, describe, show, label, collect, examine, tabulate, quote, duplicate, memorize, recognize, relate, recall, repeat, reproduce, or state	
2. Comprehension. Grasps the meaning of material *Comprehension level operations:* interpret, explain, summarize, convert, defend, distinguish, estimate, generalize, rewrite, contrast, predict, associate, differentiate, discuss, extend, classify, express, indicate, locate, recognize, report, restate, review, select, or translate	
3. Application. Uses learned material in a new situation *Application level operations:* apply, change, compute, demonstrate, operate, show, use, solve, calculate, complete, illustrate, examine, modify, relate, change, classify, experiment, dramatize, employ, interpret, operate, practice, schedule, sketch, or write	
4. Analysis. Breaks things down into parts in order to understand, organize, or clarify *Analysis level operations:* identify parts, distinguish, diagram, outline, relate or associate, break down, discriminate, subdivide, analyze, separate, order, explain, connect, classify, arrange, divide, select, infer, appraise, calculate, categorize, compare, contrast, criticize, differentiate, examine, experiment, question, or test	
5. Synthesis. Puts parts together to form a new whole *Synthesis level operations:* combine, compose, create, design, rearrange, integrate, modify, substitute, plan, invent, formulate, prepare, generalize, or rewrite	
6. Evaluation. Uses a given criterion to determine the value of a thing or quality of a product or performance *Evaluation level operations:* appraise, criticize, compare and contrast, support, conclude, discriminate, find main points, explain, infer, deduce, assess, decide, rank, grade, test, measure, recommend, convince, select, judge, argue, choose, compare, defend, estimate, judge, predict, rate, select, value, or evaluate	

FIGURE 15.10   Bloom's Taxonomy

| Proactive management statements: | |
| Reactive management statements: | |

FIGURE 15.11   **Management Statements**

7. *Analysis of time.*   We can increase learning in our classroom by making better use of our time. There are four concepts of time: First, *allotted time* is the time allotted to teach a specific subject. If math class lasts from 1:00 to 2:05, the allotted time is 65 minutes. Second, *instructional time* is the time you are actually engaged in instruction. This is the allotted time minus the transition time and time getting settled and organized to teach. Third, *time-on-task* (TOT) is the time students are actively engaged in relevant learning tasks. Rather than sitting passively, students are doing something. They are actively engaged in discussion, small-group activities, practice, note taking, or something else. However, students may be struggling with tasks that are too difficult for them or too easy. And fourth, *academic learning time* (ALT) is the time students are successfully engaged in tasks that are relevant to the purpose of the lesson. Academic learning time is different for each student.

By the way, a simple, effective, and inexpensive way to increase learning is to increase TOT and ALT. The DRC in Figure 15.13 can be used to collect data here.

8. *Use of multilevel differentiation strategies.*   With RTI and an increased emphasis on inclusive classroom strategies, it may be help to document what strategies you are using, when, and how often. Multilevel strategies include such items as tiered activities, agendas, literature circles, group investigations, cooperative learning activities, or learning contracts (Tomlinson, 1995). Other multilevel strategies include modified assignments, cluster grouping, learning stations, learning centers, reading workshop, and writing workshop (Johnson, 2009). You can record these in a weekly planner, collect lesson plans along with reflective analysis of each lesson, or design some sort of DRC (see Figure 15.14).

Descriptive, Not Prescriptive

A word of caution in regard to research on effective teaching: Educational research was never meant to prescribe a standard teaching experience; rather, when used

Things Noted	My Analysis
Ideas or conclusions:	

FIGURE 15.12   **T-Chart for Observation and Analysis**

Class Period or Lesson:

Date: **Time:**

Allotted time:	
Instructional time:	
Time-on-task:	
Academic learning time:	

Ideas or conclusions:

FIGURE 15.13   Data Retrieval Chart for Analyzing Time

---

appropriately it describes effective practices that can be used to enhance learning. Not understanding this important concept, some have chosen selectively from the vast array of educational research in an attempt to break the complex act of teaching into a series of mechanical behaviors. Choosing only research studies that measure isolated teaching behaviors as they affect standardized scores, some have created and prescribed standardized lists of teaching behaviors. The implication here is that such lists represent what effective teachers must do. Such is the case with Danielson's *Framework for Teaching* (1996), and Hunter's *Mastery Teaching* (1982). Both of these texts reduce teaching to simply performing a standardized series of subskills (Johnson, 2000b). Teaching becomes a contrived, lifeless act. And

Multilevel Strategy	Date	Class or Subject	Reflective Analysis

---

FIGURE 15.14   Data Retrieval Chart for Multilevel Differentiation Strategies

having this concrete list of "research-based" practices, administrators and university student teaching supervisors (who should know better) have used these as evaluative devices, insisting that all teachers must have these prescribed elements in all lessons. This view demonstrates a severe misunderstanding of educational research and a limited exposure to research and theories related to teaching and learning.

Research-based teaching practice and other theory-based strategies are meant to describe general principles and practices that are to be adopted and adapted to fit the particular teaching and learning situation. This is the case with Zemelman, Daniels, and Hyde's (2006) description of best teaching practices in Figure 15.8. These do not prescribe what must be; rather, they describe what might be—general principles and practices that can be used to enhance learning.

A FINAL WORD

Action research is perhaps the most efficient and effective way to address the professional development of teachers. As stated at the beginning of this book, action research allows teachers to connect education theory and research to their classroom practice and helps them to become more reflective and analytical in their teaching practice. Action research is also economical in terms of the time and money invested and the returns garnered in the form of increased learning by students and improved practice by teachers.

SUMMARY

- A knowledge base related to subject areas, learning theory, classroom management, and pedagogical methods is important in teaching and learning to teach.
- Action research is an efficient and effective method of attending to the professional development of teachers.
- Experts in any field have a body of knowledge from which to draw to help in solving problems.
- You can develop a knowledge base and become an expert in any area by following these seven steps: (a) identify a topic of interest or importance; (b) identify a goal or goals; (c) put your topic in the form of a question or questions; (d) find peer-reviewed books and academic journal articles; (e) read, take notes, and look for applications; (f) look for Internet ideas and applications that are supported by research-based theory; and (g) apply and take action.
- A literature review is a form of action research as you ask a question and answer it with data.
- Understanding how to acquire knowledge and become an expert empowers teachers and makes them less dependent.

- Having a body of knowledge related to teaching and learning enables you to effectively evaluate new programs and offer research-based alternatives when necessary.
- Other professional development opportunities include wide reading, conferences, workshops, college courses, professional discussions, and experimentation with reflection.
- Systematically observing your own teaching practice is one form of professional development.
- Zemelman, Daniels, and Hyde's (2006) recommendations for best teaching practices can be used to help you chart and increase instances of best practice occurring in your classroom.
- Individual lessons can be audiotaped for later analysis to examine (a) types of questions asked, (b) level of questions and activities, (c) student responses to questions and classroom discussions, (d) wait time, (e) management statements, (f) general observation and analysis, (g) time-on-task and academic learning time, and (h) multilevel differentiation strategies.
- Education research describes effective teaching practices; it should never be used to prescribe the experience.

QUESTIONS AND ACTIVITIES

1. Describe the knowledge you think is important for teaching. What do teachers need to know?
2. What skills are important for teaching? What do teachers need to be able to do?
3. Describe your philosophy of learning. How do students learn?
4. Practice using one of the techniques for observing your own practice described in this chapter. Share your results and any insights you have about the process.
5. What do you think is the best way for classroom teachers to continue their professional growth and development?
6. What are some topics or areas of interest you would like to investigate as part of a professional development project? Put your inquiry in the form of a question or questions.
7. Visit one or more of the free online journals. Look for three to five interesting or important articles.
8. Knowledge is a form of empowerment. What is an area in your classroom, school, or district that you would like to change? Find and list the titles of three articles or book chapters that might provide you with credible information related to this area.
9. List five professional development activities in which you would be mostly likely to engage. Put them in order from most useful to least useful in terms of your professional growth.
10. Examine Zemelman, Daniels, and Hyde's list of best practice recommendations. Describe five areas you want to focus on for your own classroom.

11. Examine the recommended journals. If you do not already subscribe to one, which journal seems to be of most interest to you? Visit the websites to get more information.

POSSIBLE RESEARCH QUESTIONS FOR ACTION RESEARCH PROJECTS

1. Find three to five inspiring teachers. Ask them to describe a beautiful teaching experience that they've had. Look for commonalities among their descriptions.
2. What is your philosophy of teaching? What traits and practices do you value? Keep track of which practices, strategies, and reactions reflect what you believe to be true about teaching and learning.
3. Find an area or situation that interests you. How might you look at it from many angles?
4. What instances of best practice occur in your classroom each week?
5. How much time do your students spend each day engaged in authentic reading experiences (reading silently for pleasure or to get information that is of interest to them)?
6. What types and levels of questions do you usually ask in a whole-class teaching situation? How do your questions compare to research related to teacher effectiveness?
7. What taxonomical level do most of your activities and assignments represent? What would happen if you gave your students choices, providing a low-level and a high-level activity for an assignment (a tiered activity)?
8. What type of management statements do you use? How does this compare to research related to teacher effectiveness?
9. Pick a class or subject area. Examine this class for two or more weeks using an audiotape recorder. What is the average TOT and ALT? What are strategies that can be used to increase these?
10. How do you differentiate the curriculum to meet the varied needs of learners? What different strategies do teachers in your school or district use to differentiate the curriculum?
11. Read Tomlinson's book, *How to Differentiate Instruction in a Mixed-Ability Classroom* (2001). Pick one or two strategies to try. Use a T-chart or field notes to record what happens.
12. Use one of the reading fluency strategies described in this chapter. Use timed reading to record students' progress in reading fluency. Are there differences among students? Do you notice an effect?

APPENDIX: SAMPLE ACTION RESEARCH PROJECTS

This appendix contains several short action research projects along with my comments. Most of these action research projects do not contain a literature review. Although the literature review adds an important dimension that connects your ideas to the literature, it is not always a necessary element.

Sample A.1 Alison Reynolds, Minneapolis, Minnesota

Few action research projects have touched me as much as the one written by Alison Reynolds. She demonstrated how the domains of art and science might sometimes overlap. Indeed, both are ways of seeing and representing reality. Alison examined a small part of her world and brought it to life. She used words as an artist uses paint to create a picture on the canvas of our minds.

When Alison started this action research project, she was overwhelmed by the large quantity of data. She wanted us to understand the environment in which she worked but did not know where to start. She solved her dilemma by focusing on one student. You can see in her poignant picture a portrayal of the human spirit and an understanding of her teaching environment.

THE PAINTER

Sammy

There is a way that he comes into the classroom that is similar to the way that a storm blows into town. It is something akin to a little breeze that follows him through the doorway. By the end of class the furniture often lies toppled from his winds. At 12 years of age his anger is profound. He is verbally confrontational and is often "up in your face." Everyone is a "bitch" to him; he uses "fat ass" for men, "whore" and "slut" for women, and "fish" for girls his age.

Sammy has been at Greenwood Treatment School for 2 years. Greenwood School is one step above residential treatment. It is populated by students who have been unable to benefit from a slew of public schools throughout the Twin Cities area.

Sammy is a large boy weighing about 175 pounds. He possesses an artistic nature. Although he uses profanity for his daily interactions now, the rhythm of his speech often sounds a little delayed and awkward. It is as if he is not quite comfortable with this new persona of his. He acts like a tough guy who still has to think about his lines before saying them. His rage is real though. The expression of that rage is awkward and violent, but there is water in that well.

At School

When Sammy started at Greenwood School 2 years ago he was rambunctious, followed the classroom jokers, and did more fooling around than anything else. He was not verbally confrontational. He was not assaultive. He was not violent. Naturally, he did have conflicts with other students, but these conflicts had a different tone to them. They were conflicts about small student disputes such as taking someone else's chair, grabbing someone's pencil, or having a little too much fun at the expense of another.

Sammy was in the fifth grade when he started at Greenwood School, but his academic level was in the third to fourth grade range. I first met him because he started coming to my classroom to get his academic skills caught up. I had suggested to his fifth grade teacher that because of Sammy's academic delays, he might be better served in a lower level classroom. I was working in a third/fourth grade classroom at the time.

I worked with Sammy for a year and a half to try to get him caught up with his peers. He applied himself to learning addition, subtraction, and multiplication. He completed simple writing assignments. He read as many second and third grade–level books as possible in a given class period. At the end of each class, Sammy could see the math that he did, the writing that he completed, and the stack of books that he had read.

The purpose of all this work was not only to help him catch up academically with his peers but also to provide him with a visual pile at the end of every class that he could look at and say, "I did this much today." Helping Sammy to build his confidence relating to his academics was as important as his acquisition of academic skills. He became very focused on completing his work, often ignoring other classroom disruptions. He also became less vulnerable to the criticism of his fifth grade peers.

Painting

It was during this period that Sammy started painting watercolor pictures. He would title each one the same: "A Sunny Day." Because he would give these pictures to me, I acquired a large collection of Sammy's artwork.

I learned much about Sammy because he talked a great deal to me. He told me about his impoverished home life. He spoke about the violence in his neighborhood. He described the struggles of his family members. His father had come to "the States" from Mexico. His mother was African American. He had a 20-year-old brother in prison. He had an 18-year-old brother who was getting ready to marry his pregnant girlfriend. Sammy understood that his life and the lives of those in his family had troubles, but the troubles had not possessed his spirit and heart.

The Zoo

One day our school went to the Minnesota Zoo. Many of the students were doing tough guy clowning with each other while walking around the grounds. I broke off from the main group with a smaller group of these students. Sammy was with us. As we were walking, running, and bumping into each other, there on a grassy knoll was a flock of baby ducklings with their mother.

Sammy stood and watched the ducks for a long moment. Then he spotted an older duck approaching the group of ducklings. Sammy took off running after that duck. He chased it all over the grassy lawn, around trees and bushes. He never caught the duck, but if he had I am sure that it would have been safe in his care. He was still at that child's age where he would chase and capture something because of its freedom, and then tenderly care for what he had caught.

Life

On the Tuesday following the school's trip to the zoo, Sammy came to school, but I did not see him the entire day. The following day the same thing happened. I spoke with the school's therapy staff to ask why Sammy had come to school but was not participating in class or other activities.

Sammy's brother, the one who had been preparing to marry his pregnant girlfriend, had been killed. Sammy was at home on a Sunday evening and heard somebody knocking at the door. Sammy opened the door and saw his brother lying on his stomach with a trail of blood behind him. His brother had been shot and had crawled on his stomach up to his home. He died at the doorway.

Sammy's heart turned that night. He became the embodiment of his family's troubles. It is common to hear him banging against the lockers in the hall, yelling at the top of his lungs. The therapy staff working with him stated that they were trying to help Sammy find more appropriate ways of dealing with his anger.

Surprisingly, about 2 months after the murder of Sammy's brother, students at school started to use that tragedy and loss as a means of getting to Sammy. They made fun of him for having a brother who had been murdered.

Life At School

I don't see Sammy as much as I used to. He mostly stays with his sixth grade classmates. When I do see him, it is only to talk. We speak about how someone who has "passed" lives on in the hearts of those who were close to him. We speak about how to use the death of someone close to you to make you a stronger person on this earth. Periodically we speak about education and opportunity. When someone interrupts these conversations, Sammy immediately switches back into his aggressive and proving new self. I, along with everyone else, become the "bitch."

I don't expect to receive "A Sunny Day" picture ever again. Summer has passed for him. Yet, I know that he still holds a paintbrush in a hand behind his back. I don't know what his new pictures will look like. I don't know what will happen to him. I do know that if a student loses faith and strength in his soul, you lose the ability to teach him.

The desired action in the case of Sammy is a call for understanding. Alison enables us to see a human face and real-life problems behind the statistics and test scores.

Sample A.2 Kay Dicke, Eden Prairie, Minnesota

Kay Dicke created a nice, crisp introduction that draws the reader right into the paper. Her descriptions are precise, allowing us to see exactly what is happening at each stage.

MOTIVATING STUDENTS TO READ

Reading is an important part of a child's education. All subjects at any grade level include reading in many forms, whether it's nonfiction or a classic piece of fictional literature. There are many children who enjoy reading, but there are also many who do not. The benefits of reading are limitless, but what can be done to motivate all students to increase their time spent reading?

Action Research Question: How can I motivate my sixth grade students to increase their time spent reading?

Methods Of Collecting Data

Collecting data was the first step of the action research process. The first method utilized was a general reading survey given to 27 sixth grade students.

Questions asked pertained to the amount of free time out of school students spent reading and the types of books they read. Results of the survey showed that the majority of students like to read but most spent very little time outside of school doing it, usually 1 to 3 hours each week. Of the books read, adventure and humorous books were by far the most popular genres selected. The survey results supported a need for increased reading by these sixth grade students.

The next step of the research process was to begin observing and taking daily field notes during a 1-week period. These observations took place throughout the day during a variety of different subjects. Many questions from the student survey were considered as these observations were made, including, How often did students read during the school day? What types of reading did they do? What kinds of books do they select to read during their free reading time? What can be done to promote more reading by all students? Are students choosing books that are appropriate for their reading abilities?

Observations led to some general conclusions: Several students were observed reading and making great progress by completing one or more books throughout the week. At least seven students really did not seem to take an interest in the books they selected and spent more time looking around the classroom. Others had a different book each day, not actually reading one book completely. Students interested in reading often chose to read after completing assignments in class. There was definitely a wide variety of readers in this group.

From my field notes a checklist was created (see Figure A.1). Each day for 1 week during silent reading time a small group of four or five students was observed. The checklist was used to look for the following behaviors: being on task, progress completing the same book, and the type of book being read. The checklist was an easy and useful method of collecting specific data.

After 2 weeks of collecting field notes and using my checklist, I asked students to begin using a log sheet to record the number of minutes and the genre of books read over a 2-week period both at home and at school. The number of minutes was totaled and written on a chart to track their progress.

Findings

Students responded positively to the reading log at school. They were very dedicated about tracking their minutes. As the study progressed, they took on more responsibility with their reading and began to make sure to track minutes spent reading their social studies book and other expository reading material encountered throughout the day.

STUDENT	DATE	TIME	TYPE OF BOOK	ON TASK	COMMENTS

FIGURE A.1   Independent Reading Checklist

At first, the number of minutes read at home was not as high as at school. Many students had very poor results here and quite a few did not return the log sheet from home. However, the minutes read at school and home were documented and would be used as a baseline to measure progress.

A high percentage of sixth grade students seemed to pick up on the importance of reading through their logs. A chart was posted in the classroom on which their minutes of reading were tracked. Many students compared their minutes to others' and seemed pleased with their results. They were always eager to get a new reading log sheet. Also, positive comments were made by parents at conferences. Here, goals were set to improve the time spent reading at home in order to increase students' total minutes.

The next log sheets were given for an additional 2 weeks. Again, these students took real initiative in tracking their reading minutes at school. However, the results of the home log were just as poor as the last time. Many still did not turn them in or if they did, they did little reading. However, 80% of the students in this class did improve their total minutes of reading (in school and at home) from the first reading log.

I realized that I needed to take more time discussing my expectations for the home logs. I talked with students and found that they read a lot of things at home such as web pages on the Internet, magazines, and even cereal boxes. I encouraged them to log those minutes and helped them to realize that they were reading more than they thought.

The results of the third reading log were improved again: 92% of the home logs were returned this time and the number of total minutes read (in school and at home) was increased.

Conclusions

Students took pride in their accomplishments here, and at the same time, they found that reading can be something enjoyable to do every day. Small gains were made in the amount of reading time. By the end of the school year my ultimate goal would be to get all students reading more and reading more independently without instruction.

Sample A.3 LouAnn Strachota

LouAnn Strachota, a paraprofessional working in a classroom, was in the process of getting her teacher certification. I included her work to show how preservice teachers might use action research to analyze and reflect on their learning environments. LouAnn wanted to study the behavior of students in one of her classes; however, she did not know where to start. This is a common predicament among beginning action researchers. To provide more focus, she did a short pilot study to see what behaviors students were displaying. She used this initial observation to create a checklist (see Figure A.2). Then, instead of trying to chart every student's behavior, she decided to look at one student each day. This made the task more manageable and helped her focus on specific behaviors over a predetermined time.

ON- AND OFF-TASK BEHAVIOR
IN A HIGH SCHOOL HEALTH CLASS

This study was undertaken in order to examine the relationship between on- and off-task behavior in an Emotional Behavior Disorder (EBD) level 4 resource room in a high school health class. I work as a paraprofessional here and am in the process of getting my teaching certification. I was interested in finding out why there were differences in students' on- and off-task behaviors.

Collecting Data

Data were collected from observations using a checklist that indicated on- and off-task behavior at 5-minute intervals (Figures A.2 and A.3).

This health class was taught from 10:17 a.m. to 11:12 a.m. 5 days a week. I chose to study students' behavior in this particular class because there were only four students here: three boys and one girl. One of these

Student's Name: <u>Don N</u>   Date: _____

Recorded at 5-minute intervals.

ON-TASK BEHAVIOR. THE STUDENT IS:	10:30	10:35	10:40	10:45	10:50	10:55	11:00
—Working							
—Listening to directions		x		x	x		
—Reading			x				
—Engaged in listening	x						
—Working with somebody else							
—Responding to the teacher							
—Other							

FIGURE A.2   On-Task Behavior Checklist

students was observed each day over the course of 17 school days. The behavior of each student was noted at 5-minute intervals.

The first few times that students were told that they were going to be observed they kept watching to see what marks they were being given. After a few days, however, the stigma of being observed wore off and they acted in their usual manner.

The Classroom Setting

This EBD classroom contained 10 chair-desks placed in a half-circle surrounding a kidney-shaped table in front of the room. There were three study carrels in the back of the room and a teacher's desk in the front of the room on the far left side. Rules regarding behavior were posted on a chart in front of the room. The study carrels were used for students who displayed disruptive or inappropriate behaviors. If there were additional infractions, students were sent to an independent study room.

Other behavior management techniques included three forms of classroom contracts: limited, expected, and privileged. Each contract had varying levels of student privileges.

Recorded at 5-minute intervals.

ON-TASK BEHAVIOR. THE STUDENT IS:	10:30	10:35	10:40	10:45	10:50	10:55	11:00
—Talking to somebody						x	x
—Doodling							
—Listening to another student							
—Looking in his/her desk							
—In a study carrel							
—Working on something else						.	
—Making noises							
—Walking around							
—Other							

OBSERVATIONS:
Don has not been to class for a few days—but while here he was working very well until the last 10 minutes of class. He then walked around the room and talked to other students in the room.

FIGURE A.3 Off-Task Behavior Checklist

Findings

One noticeable observation was that students had a hard time staying focused around 11:00 a.m. because they were hungry. Students started watching the clock around this time, waiting for the bell to ring. Included here are the observations for each student (see Table A.1).

Don

Don was observed only twice due to low attendance. When others were working on assignments, Don seemed to work well and stay on task. During the last 10 minutes of class he usually talked to other students.

Sally

Sally was observed four times. She seemed to spend most of her time working with an aide. She missed 3 days of class during this observation. When she returned, she worked hard to catch up on her assignments.

TABLE A.1   Total On-Task and Off-Task Behaviors

STUDENT	ON-TASK BEHAVIOR	OFF-TASK BEHAVIOR
Don	85%	15%
Sally	90%	10%
Tom	80%	20%
Harry	83%	17%
Total Average	84.5%	15.5%

Tom

Tom was observed four times. He came every day but sometimes had to leave early to prepare for a choir concert that he was in. One day he was the only student in class and was able to work without distraction and stay on task. However, if somebody else was talking, Tom became easily distracted. When Sally was in the room, he often wanted to talk with her. He told another student that he had a crush on her. He was asked several times by the teacher or aide to stop talking. When Sally was not in class Tom's on-task behavior improved by 15%. Tom is a good student and can work very well in class when he wants to. However, it appears that he is easily distracted by Sally.

Harry

Harry was observed six times. His lowest percentage for on-task behavior was 40% and his highest was 100%. On his low day, Harry complained about being extremely tired and said he was not going to do any work. My observations also showed that he did not stay on task very well when he was tired. When he was tired, he complained that he was not feeling well and said he wanted to lie on the floor. If Harry appeared to be in a good mood, he worked very well and stayed on task. Harry also stayed on task much better if there was only one other student in class.

Conclusions

The high percentage of on-task behavior could be contributed to the small class size. My observations showed that when fewer students were in class they spent more time working. Also, students completed all assignments and stayed on task when they were working directly with the teacher or with me.

Off-task behavior resulted most often when (1) students were moody or tired, (2) students finished their assignments early and disrupted others, (3) there were more students in the class, and (4) one student liked another and preferred talking to work.

Recommendations

Based on these observations, I recommend the following:

1. Students should have something else to work on or read when they are finished with their work. They need preplanned assignments and other things to do to keep them occupied.
2. Students should be separated from other students if they keep talking.
3. Assignments should involve opportunities for hands-on experiences and allow students to interact. This would keep them involved and prevent boredom.
4. The units should be made more interesting by using content enrichment activities that keep students involved.

Things That Worked

These are some of the things that seemed to work in this health class:

1. Students recorded their ideas of what was interesting or important in each chapter (instead of using a study guide or worksheet).
2. A bingo game was created with the vocabulary words from each chapter.
3. Teams were used and a quiz game was created that used questions from the assigned chapters.
4. A visual organizer that showed the content covered during the unit seemed to help students understand.

Final Thought

Overall, I feel that a variety of methods should be incorporated into the curriculum to keep EBD students on task and interested in the subjects being taught.

Sample A.4 Georgina L. Pete

Georgina's action research project reads much like a staffing report (which it was). At the end of this report she outlines four things that she will try to implement to improve the situation.

HELPING BRANDON

Being the new talented and gifted (TAG) teacher in a suburban school district in the Twin Cities metro area, I had high hopes of starting the year off with a bang. However, I was approached not long after the school year started by a fourth grade teacher who had threatened one of her students with being taken out of the TAG program because of his low grades in her classroom. I decided this was an issue I needed to become involved with.

This is a summary of the information I collected and the recommendations made for this student.

Data Collection

Information collected for this research was in the form of conferencing, observations with field notes, and interviewing. All data were collected over a 4-week period during the months of October and November.

The Conference

The first step was to set up a conference with the classroom teacher (Ms. Lee) and the principal (Ms. Kelly). Ms. Kelly was very familiar with this student, who I will refer to as Brandon, as she had him in her office several times to deal with discipline problems. In fact, she said that he had the most discipline offenses in the school. Ms. Kelly printed out a list of his infractions. These had to do mostly with being disrespectful and physical aggression.

The conference was very informative. Brandon's behavior in class, on the bus, and during recess was not what I saw when he was in my TAG classroom. I knew him to be polite, excited about learning, humorous, and well liked by his peers. Ms. Lee painted quite a different picture. She thought of him as very disrespectful and said he was not cutting it with his classroom assignments (he was not turning them in). Since he was not showing her his giftedness she felt he should not have the privilege of leaving the regular education classroom to go to the TAG classroom.

Ms. Kelly played a key role in this conference. She was very concerned about Brandon's future, as was I. She felt that the TAG classroom was something very important to him. Here he felt like he had some power and importance. She cautioned that taking away his TAG classes might make this troubled boy's situation more disastrous. I agreed.

We all agreed that something needed to be done to help Brandon steer his school career in a positive direction. His test scores indicated that he should have been operating at a much higher level; however, he was getting Cs and Ds in his classes. I agreed to make observations of him in the classroom and on the playground to see what might be done. The teacher and principal were going to stay in close contact with Brandon's mother (the father did not seem to play an active role in his son's education). All agreed that the mother needed to play a more active role in Brandon's education and help out with any action plan.

Observations

Brandon could be very sneaky and dishonest. He would look you in the eye and tell you he had all his work done when he did not. When I observed him in the classroom, he seemed to have a high level of on-task behavior if he was working with a partner in a situation in which both needed to cooperate in order to get the assignment done. However, when working by himself, he did not use his time very efficiently and became a distraction to others with his silliness. He also did not seem to put a great deal of effort into his assignments. Ms. Lee said that in the past, Brandon had claimed to have lost missing assignments or left them at home.

I also observed Ms. Lee to be very negative. In every discussion that I had with her, she never made one positive comment about him, whereas Ms. Kelly had made several positive comments and expressed concern for his future and seemed to have a real interest in turning his situation around.

Interviews

I interviewed Brandon and three of his peers in his TAG group. This gave me the impression that he has a history of being unorganized and irresponsible. They all agreed that they would not like to have Brandon in charge of getting something done for a group activity because "he never gets anything done." However, all looked favorably at him as a friend and seemed to enjoy working with him in TAG classes. They especially liked listening to him discuss and tell stories.

Brandon agreed that he needed to work hard in school at being more focused on his responsibilities. His attempts to be better organized and more responsible with his assignments usually lasted only a day at the most.

Recommendations

Based on the information collected here, I recommend the following:

1. Brandon should be placed in a different classroom. His mother also made this request, which Ms. Kelly granted. I believe that both the mother and Ms. Kelly felt as I did, that Ms. Lee was not a positive influence on Brandon and that he would be better matched with another teacher.
2. I will check in with Brandon on a regular basis. He is a very social person and likes an audience. I think that given an opportunity to express himself in an appropriate manner with somebody who is not continually pushing him to complete his homework with a higher quality, Brandon might feel less of an urge to act out by being silly in class and causing distraction. My goal here will be to encourage quality effort.
3. Communication with Brandon's mother must improve. He should get some positive calls home when he makes progress. His mother is used to getting calls home about discipline and late assignments, but not for positive behavior. I will be responsible for contacting her when Brandon and I have made some breakthroughs.

4. Brandon and his family should work on his organizational skills. I will recommend some reading for him and his family along this line.

Conclusions

I am hopeful that Brandon will benefit from these recommendations. I find him to be a very pleasant boy, but also someone who could end up being a leader in a negative way. I feel confident that he will enjoy having my interest in him so that he can express himself freely. He will be helped in all areas by a strong commitment at home to quality and organization.

Sample A.5 Teresa Van Batavia, Eisenhower Elementary, Hopkins, Minnesota

Teresa Van Batavia's research shows the work of a master teacher carefully observing her students and making decisions based on students' needs. In this report she is able to create a good sense of being there. As you read the notes from her writing conferences, this classroom comes to life. Suddenly you can see exactly where her students are as writers. She also takes us inside her head, letting us overhear her thinking as she processes the information and makes decisions based on that information.

WRITING WORKSHOP

My first grade students at Eisenhower Elementary are involved in a writer's workshop setting at least three times a week. My concern is that children may be slipping through the cracks—doing little or no writing and not being noticed.

Data Collection

The first form of data collection that I used was that of a weekly checklist. As I circulated among students during the 2-week period from November 15 through December 3, 1999, I carried a clipboard and checked off each type of writing activity that I observed (see Figure A.4). This checklist became an effective tool for helping me to choose mini-lesson topics for the children. I will continue to use this on an informal basis throughout the year.

In addition to the checklists, I met individually with each student and also collected their writing folders for further study of their writing habits. Following are my notes of these conferences.

Conference Notes—Individual Students

Joni is most comfortable starting with an illustration and then writing one or two sentences to accompany the picture. Her latest effort, however,

Writer's Workshop Checklist, Week of November 15–19, 1999

Generating/prewriting	ℍℍℍℍ I
Drawing/sketching	ℍℍ III
Drafting	ℍℍ ℍℍ ℍℍ ℍℍ ℍℍ ℍℍ I
Revising	ℍℍ I
Editing	III
Conference/talking	I
Reading	I
Other	ℍℍ II

FIGURE A.4   Writer's Workshop Checklist

is a story inspired by her neighbor's car accident. She is struggling with understanding how to expand it beyond two sentences.

Lynn and Valerie have regularly referred to their topic list and have created two to three stories each. Their writings have a solid beginning, middle, and end.

Tony, Walter, Jason, William, and Sonjia have accomplished very little over the past 2 months. Their folders contain very primitive drawings. All five students described frustration in choosing an idea and drawing or writing about it. Brainstorming ideas together failed to elicit a solid topic any of the five were willing to write about.

Tim has worked feverishly for the past five writing sessions on a story about his broken arm. He has included a great deal of detail on his surroundings as well as his emotions at the time.

Publishing has become Ryan's frantic goal. He worked diligently on a story titled "My World," a hodgepodge of facts and opinions about the world around him. We revised and edited together and now he is ready for publication.

Becky and Cassandra, two highly able students, have made little progress. The contents of their folders are simple drawings with little depth in writing.

Brian, Nancy, and Kirsten have successfully used the Five W's Web (who, what, where, why, and when) to generate ideas for their stories. They made a smooth transition from web to rough draft. All three found the web to be a useful tool and plan to use it again.

Picture books are the focus for Heather and Alicia as they sketch and then add the text to their drawings.

Unable to fathom the fact that he may choose topics for himself, Mitchell fluctuates between drawing and finding me to ask if his topic choice is acceptable. He is able to construct a very creative, oral story. These stories lose a lot in the recording process, which is difficult for Mitchell.

Conference Notes—Writing Difficulties

Two boys in my class are plagued by a need to spell each and every word perfectly. They are reluctant to put anything in writing without first verifying with an adult. This has had an adverse effect on the quality of their thoughts.

Another child has very poor fine-motor skills and several speech difficulties. He has been unable to function in this setting without an adult close by his side.

Conclusions

The two forms of data collection that I used supported each other in pointing out that I have a wide variety of stages of the writing process occurring on a daily basis. First of all, as I feared, five of my struggling students were frequently off task, frustrated by writer's block, unable to come up with a topic (even from their personal topic lists), and unable to sustain a 15–20 minute work period. As a result, I will begin a series of short mini-lessons with this small group. These lessons will begin with topic selection. This group of students seems to need a detailed step-by-step introduction and guided tour through the stages of the writing process. It will be necessary to bring them from start to finish through the entire process in a more structured setting.

I found the majority of my students to be in the drafting stage of their writing. These students varied widely in ability, but were similar in the fact that they could remain focused on their writing for a longer period than the three struggling writers mentioned previously. Seven of my students created a Five W's Web to generate ideas for their topic (a mini-lesson that was taught 2 weeks earlier). Of these seven, five were able to make the progression from the web to a piece of writing that had a beginning, middle, and end.

Given the results of the data I have collected, it seems sensible to proceed in the following manner: First, I need to address the needs of the struggling readers and writers by breaking the writing process down into more manageable steps. I plan to do this in the form of mini-lessons at the beginning of each writing period for this small group. We will choose a topic, brainstorm or generate ideas, and create rough drafts together. Students will be taught to work with a peer for revising and editing.

Second, I have a large group of children who are spending the majority of their time in the drafting and illustrating stages. I plan to revisit prewriting strategies regularly for a few weeks until I see a greater number of students applying these strategies. I believe that I have moved too quickly in expecting these children to pick up on brainstorming and webbing. I will need to do a great deal more modeling for it to transfer to their writing. When I am satisfied that this is a tool that the students understand and are able to use, I will move on to creating a first draft or sloppy copy of the web and brainstorming sessions that I have created as examples. I think that spending more time on each phase will lead to more children reaching the revising and editing stages.

Final Thoughts

This research has provided me valuable information in assessing the productivity and value of the writer's workshop model as it exists in my classroom. Although I found weak areas that need to be addressed, I also found children who greatly enjoy the freedom of choice. These children cannot wait to bring out their red folders and write about topics of utmost importance to them: broken arms, mothers with cancer, favorite pets, vacation trips, cherished holidays, and many others. One child recently reveled in the discovery that the red folder could be pulled out at any time during the day when he had a few extra minutes. The motivation to write exists. I now need to find the right combination of lessons to channel this desire through the stages of the writing process to publication.

Sample A.6 Linda Roth, St. Peter School District, St. Peter, Minnesota

This study was conducted by Linda Roth, a gifted education coordinator in St. Peter, Minnesota. She has included a short review of the literature at the beginning of her study. Notice how this serves to connect her observations with the ideas of others.

THE SOCIAL, EMOTIONAL, AND ACADEMIC ADJUSTMENT OF AN ACCELERATED ELEMENTARY STUDENT

This action research study investigated the social, emotional, and writing development of a student who moved directly from a fourth to a sixth grade classroom.

Background

Grade acceleration can have a positive effect on the achievement of gifted students (Davis & Rimm, 1998). This strategy allows students to advance at an appropriate pace in order to meet their education needs.

Researchers studying acceleration find that there are very few problems with social adjustment, academic achievement, or other effects (Colangelo & Davis, 1991). Advantages included improved task commitment, confidence, and academic advances.

On average, gifted students who are accelerated do as well as or better than older students in the same classroom, their social and emotional development is normally quite high, and they are more inclined to choose older students as companions (Clark, 1983). Therefore, the issue of age and maturity does not seem to be of consequence here.

Those who are apprehensive about the practice of grade skipping are concerned that skill gaps may surface in basic areas. Barbara Clark (1983) recommends that accelerated students be monitored and continually assessed. When considering a student for acceleration, it is important to have a thorough knowledge of the needs and abilities of that student with support from administration and staff at all stages (Gallagher & Gallagher, 1994).

Identification Of The Action Research Problem

I work as a gifted and talented coordinator in the St. Peter, Minnesota, school district. A student in one of the elementary schools was accelerated from a fourth to sixth grade classroom. In this action research project I examined the social, emotional, and academic effects of this acceleration.

The Student

Bill was an 11-year-old male student. At the end of fourth grade he was going above and beyond the fourth grade tasks assigned to him. His fourth grade teacher described him as a good student, a nice person to talk to, and knowledgeable in many areas. He grasped concepts easily, finished assignments with time to spare, and completed extra assignments quickly. Other teachers who had worked with him gave him high praise for motivation, task commitment, and advanced knowledge. The hope was that by grade skipping, his enthusiasm would continue.

Behavior checklists completed by four teachers who had worked with him showed that he displayed many positive behaviors that might enable him to get along with his peers, function independently, and be successful academically.

On an academic achievement test Bill scored in the 95th percentile in reading and the 97th percentile in math. On a standardized ability test, he had an IQ score of 128, ranking him at the 97th percentile and classifying him in the superior range. On a standardized writing test it was found that his writing score was low because of the lack of sentence detail. Comments were made by the test facilitator and his fourth grade teacher that although his sentence structure, legibility, spelling, capitalization, punctuation, and sentence structure were good, Bill did not go into a great deal of detail in his writing.

Implementation of the Action Research

This study was begun during the fall of Bill's sixth grade year. The objective here was to find out how he was adjusting to skipping a grade, specifically in the area of writing. The social/emotional area was not a great concern to parents and teachers; however, for the well-being of Bill, I felt it important to also monitor this area of adjustment as it could have a bearing on the success of his acceleration.

Writing

Creative writing and expository writing samples were taken from Bill's sixth grade classroom portfolio. Other writing samples were taken from short answer tests and e-mail between Bill and me. These samples were evaluated using a writing rubric for middle school level performance. Format, mechanics, word choice, and organization were evaluated. In the creative writing samples, Bill's spelling, punctuation, and capitalization were of good quality. Words were used correctly and clearly; however, special or advanced vocabulary was not noted. In his expository writing, the introduction, paragraphs, and conclusions were present, but they were very brief and had little detail. No attempt was made to elaborate beyond what was being asked.

After an e-mail conversation with me and an interview with his classroom teacher regarding the importance of detail and elaboration, Bill was asked to write a creative story about a turkey. For this story, he was able to use his interest in technology and science. He wrote a four-page handwritten story about a turkey who lived in a space age city and visited a robot factory to obtain robot armor to protect himself from hunters of endangered species. This story ended with the explanation that it was all a dream sequence. This time more detail was evident, showing that Bill was capable of using detail and elaboration when writing about something that was of interest to him.

Social and Emotional Adjustment

Interviews with Bill were held weekly. In each of these he expressed great satisfaction with his new surroundings. Bill said that in sixth grade he was able to do whatever he wanted. He seemed to enjoy the freedom to make his own choices when assignments were completed. He also liked the responsibility of getting assignments done and turning them in on time.

Bill expressed concern about missing concepts in math; however, he felt that he generally got the ideas easily. His test results showed that he was not experiencing problems in this area. Bill also expressed concern about his art class. He felt he could put more effort into his drawings.

A goal Bill set at the beginning of the year was to get assignments in on time. He felt that he had met this goal. He also set a goal related to behavior, which was to not push people or interfere with their personal space. He felt this too had been met. Generally, Bill was pleased with his time management style and prided himself in completing his homework quickly.

Bill's sixth grade teacher was interviewed regarding his social and emotional adjustment as well as his academic performance. His teacher was pleased with all areas of adjustment. Bill had made friends in the class and had found others with similar interests. He had made two close friendships and was spending time with one of them outside of school. This teacher said that Bill was highly respected for his intellect and was sought after by classmates for information and help in academic areas. Academically, Bill was doing well. The teacher reiterated that he grasped new concepts in math quickly and needed little repetition to master them.

Conclusions

Overall, grade acceleration seems to have been successful here. Positive social interactions and academic achievement have been noted. Extra attention to his writing needs to be continued during the remainder of the year. Support from the classroom teacher and me will be important to the success of this student. Monitoring the support of Bill should continue throughout the year to ensure that problem areas do not develop.

References

Clark, B. (1983). *Growing up gifted*. Columbus, OH: Merrill.

Colangelo, N., & Davis, G. (1991). *Handbook of gifted education*. Boston: Allyn and Bacon.

Davis, G. A., & Rimm, S. B. (1998). *Education of the gifted and talented* (4th ed.). Boston: Allyn and Bacon.

Gallagher, J. J., & Gallagher, S. A. (1994). *Teaching the gifted child* (4th ed.). Boston: Allyn and Bacon.

Sample A.7 Angela Hassett Brunelle Getty, Martinez, California

This study by Angela Hassett Brunelle Getty looks at gender and special education referrals. She does a nice job of connecting her findings to the research literature. Notice how she keeps things as simple as possible to create a report that is easy to read. Also, she uses tables to display her findings. This creates a visual action research report that also enhances the readability. A simple, well-written report like this is much more apt to be read than one that is long and unorganized.

GENDER IMBALANCE IN SPECIAL EDUCATION

Purpose

This action research project was conducted to examine the relationship between gender and teacher referrals for special education services in our school. Do teachers possess certain biases toward males because of their behavior? Are males referred to student study teams (SST) more often than females? How many of the students referred actually qualify for special education services?

Participants

Participants in this study were students from kindergarten through fifth grade in an elementary school with high state academic achievements. The student population at this school consisted of 66% White, 19% Asian, 6% Hispanic, 4% Other, 3% Black, and 2% Filipino. Instructional staff provided support to students through special programs such as reading specialist, counseling, special education, library, vocal and instrumental music, gifted and talented education, physical education, and science and computer education.

Procedures

In our school, teachers refer students who they suspect have special needs to an SST. The SST then looks at various classroom data and that from psychoeducational assessment. This study examined the files of students who had been referred by their teacher to the SST during the 2002–2003 school year. There were 35 total files; 23 of them were active SST files, and 12 had been resolved or were in process of a psychoeducational assessment. Figure A.5 shows the grade and gender breakdown.

After obtaining the permission of the vice principal, who is in charge of the SST process, student SST files and cumulative files were collected for those students whose teacher had initiated the SST process during some part of the 2002–2003 school year. Each student's file was then reviewed. Data were collected using a student data sheet. This was a data sheet designed to collect the following information: grade level, gender, month they were referred, reason for referral to the student study team, and whether they qualified for special education services.

Files were reviewed to see if students were referred for behavior, academics, or both. In order to be consistent throughout the data collection

GRADE	TOTAL	MALE	FEMALE
Kindergarten	3	1	2
1st	8	4	4
2nd	8	4	4
3rd	5	3	2
4th	9	5	4
5th	2	2	0
Total	35	19	16

FIGURE A.5   **Files Examined for SST**

process, *behavior* was the term used to indicate those instances in which classroom teachers described a student using the terms "difficulty staying focused," "lacks motivation," "off task," "not independent," or "easily distracted." *Academics* was the term used to indicate when a student was below grade level in specific academic areas.

Analysis

Data were analyzed by noting the referral totals and separating them by gender into the following three categories: behavior only, academics only, and behavior and academics. Also noted were the number of students referred to special education versus those who qualified for special education services. This too was broken down into gender categories.

Findings And Conclusions

Reasons for Referral

In our school, slightly more males than females were referred (see Figure A.6). Slightly more males were referred for both behavior-only reasons as well as behavior and academics. Slightly more females were referred for academics-only.

Because of the limited numbers in this action research project, no strong conclusions can be made; however, the results seem to reflect the results of Phipps's (1982) study of 165 special education students. Phipps examined the differences between males and females in academic achievement and behavior

	TOTAL	MALE	FEMALE
Behavior Only	11	7	4
Academics Only	11	4	7
Behavior and Academics	13	8	5
Total Number of Students	35	19	16

FIGURE A.6   **Reasons for Referral to Student Study Teams**

and looked at how this affected the referral process. In her study, behavior was the reason for referral in 83% of the cases for boys, but in only 45% of the cases for girls. She concluded that boys might be over-placed in special education classes to relieve the pressures of behavior management in the regular education classroom. Further, she posited that girls may be excluded from referral to special education programs because of their passive and more manageable behaviors. Lloyd, Kauffman, Landrum, and Roe (1991) have also reported that boys outnumber girls in special education referrals by a ratio of more than 2:1. Higher referral rates have also been reported by Anderson (1997), Flynn and Rahbar (1994), MacMilliam, Gresham, Lopez, and Bocian (1996), McIntyre (1988), Shinn, Tindal, and Spira (1987), and Ysseldyke, Vanderwood, and Shriner (1997).

Qualifying for Special Education Services

This study found that of the students referred, there were slightly more females than males who actually qualified for the special education services (see Figure A.7). Of these, one female qualified was for academics only and two females for behavior and academics. One male qualified for academics and behaviors. This may reflect the study by Flynn and Rahbar (1994), who found that girls seemed to be less likely to be referred and thus, under-identified for remedial services.

Plan Of Action

Based on the information found in this study, I will be making the following suggestions to our school principal:

1. Teachers should be made aware of the general tendency to over-identify boys for referral to special education programs. I will recommend teacher

	TOTAL	MALE	FEMALE
Number of Students Referred for Special Ed. Services	14	7	7
Number of Students Who Qualified for Special Ed. Services	4	1	3

FIGURE A.7   Students Referred Versus the Number Qualified for Special Education Services

inservices be conducted to inform teachers of this and provide instruction on behavior management techniques that would work specifically with the male population. Also, we may want to provide inservices on teaching practices that are less likely to cause behavior problems.

2. Because there are often fewer behavior problems, girls may be under-identified for referral. This is something that needs attention in the coming year. Again, teacher inservice and training should be made available to inform teachers of female learning styles.

3. Our school needs to have more pre-referral interventions that are documented before students are referred for psychoeducational assessments. We should probably set up some procedures for this, with a variety of intervention strategies that could be used by classroom teachers.

4. We need to keep our eye on this issue. A study like this should be conducted every year.

References

Anderson, K. G. (1997). Gender bias and special education referrals. *Annals of Dyslexia, 47*, 151–162.

Flynn, J. M., & Rahbar, M. H. (1994). Prevalence of reading failure in boys compared with girls. *Psychology in Schools, 31*, 66–71.

Lloyd, J. W., Kauffman, J. M., Landrum, T. J., & Roe, D. L. (1991). Why do teachers refer pupils for Special Education? An analysis of referral records. *Exceptionality, 2*, 115–126.

MacMillian, D. L., Gresham, F. M., Lopez, M. F., & Bocian, K. (1996). Comparison of students nominated for prereferral interventions by ethnicity and gender. *Journal of Special Education, 30*, 133–151.

McIntyre, L. (1988). Teacher gender: A predictor of special education referral? *Journal of Learning Disabilities, 21,* 382–383.

Phipps, P. A. (1982). The LD learner is often a boy—Why? *Academic Therapy, 17,* 425–430.

Shinn, M. R., Tindal, G. A., & Spira, D. A. (1987). Special Education referrals as an index of teacher tolerance: Are teachers imperfect tests? *Exceptional Children, 54,* 32–40.

Ysseldyke, J. E., Vanderwood, M. L., & Shriner, J. (1997). Changes over the past decade in special education referral to placement probability: An incredibly reliable practice. *Diagnostique, 23,* 193–201.

Sample A.8 Michelle Bahr, Shakopee, Minnesota

As part of my Literacy Methods graduate course that I teach at Minnesota State University, Mankato, I have my students conduct short action research projects related to literacy. I have found that these often serve to reinforce many of the ideas that I try to get across during class (the importance of choice and holistic teaching strategies). Also, these projects present a portrait of students that you simply would not get by looking at a series of scores. And perhaps most important, these projects all serve to inform teaching. Michelle Bahr's action research project provides a sense of adolescents' attitudes about reading. Although her findings cannot reasonably be generalized to a larger population, they do help in understanding this population.

This was a powerful educational exercise for me. In doing this action research project I noticed some interesting things related to students' attitudes toward reading. I surveyed 10 students who were friends of my 17-year-old son to get a sense of their attitude toward reading (see Figure A.8). They were in grades 11 and 12 and ages 16 and 17. At least two that I know of have some learning difficulties.

Findings

Reading and Interest Inventory

Under Reading and Interest Inventory only one statement received a unanimous "Yes" by all respondents. That was item 12, "I like to read song lyrics." Also, most of these students borrow and buy books for both pleasure reading and educational reading. All except one student were read to by their parents when they were young. And they definitely did not like reading poetry. From this set of questions I learned that song lyrics seemed to be a hot item for reading. I'm thinking that this might be an excellent source to use to get adolescent students reading.

Five of the teens mentioned a sports-related book as one of their favorite books to read. The Bible was mentioned by five students.

Date: _____   Your age: _____   Grade: _____

READING ATTITUDE SURVEY

Reading and Interest Inventory

(yes or no answers here please)

1. ____ I borrow books from the library or school for educational reading.
2. ____ I borrow books from the library or school for pleasure reading.
3. ____ I buy books for educational reading.
4. ____ I buy books for pleasure reading.
5. ____ My parents used to (or still do) read to me.
6. ____ I read before I go to bed.
7. ____ I read magazines.
8. ____ I read only when I have to.
9. ____ I read for enjoyment.
10. ____ I read the newspaper sometimes.
11. ____ I like to read poetry.
12. ____ I like to read song lyrics.
13. ____ I like to receive books as gifts.
14. ____ I would like to hear my teacher read out loud more.

What are your top three favorite books

1.
2.
3.

Reading Questions

(please fill in the blanks)

1. I think books are ...
2. I think reading ...
3. Reading is hard when ...
4. Reading is easy when ...
5. My favorite magazine is ...
6. I think the newspaper is ...

Information Questions

(please fill in the blanks)

1. School is ...
2. I wish teachers ...
3. When I finish high school ...
4. When I get my report card ...
5. I'd read more if ...
6. I cannot read when ...
7. I like reading about ...
8. I don't like to read about ...
9. When I read out loud ...
10. To me books are ...

I read because ...

I write because ...

Are there any other comments about reading you'd like to share?

FIGURE A.8   Michelle Bahr's Reading Survey

Reading Questions

These kids seemed to like books that are fun. Their definition of fun was "a good book that isn't too hard to read." In response to item 3 under Reading Questions, "Reading is hard when . . .," all said that reading was hard when they didn't like what they were reading. This makes perfect sense. Choice, choice, choice! Even if students don't like a textbook used in school, I will try to supplement their reading with related books that would be defined as "fun." There are many alternatives to using only a textbook in my classes.

Information Questions

The most interesting and important insights came from the Information Questions. School is boring for most of these students. They wish their teachers were not so crabby, peppier, and that they understood them better. They also wished that teachers would make assignments more fun and would take more time in going over lessons and assignments. They seemed to be genuinely frustrated when there wasn't enough time for an assignment or when they didn't understand the assignment and they got a bad grade. These are all things that are relatively easy to fix.

The majority of these students have difficulty reading when there is noise and lots of distractions like people talking or hearing noises from another classroom. A quiet classroom environment when reading seems to be important. The kinds of books they liked reading included biographies and war and murder stories. The kinds of books they didn't like to read included romance, history, and any English textbook.

In response to the prompt, "I read because . . .," most responded, "Because I have to" or "it's something to do when I'm bored." In response to the prompt, "I write because . . .," student responses included "Because it's fun," "it's an easy way to express myself," "I can put my thoughts on paper," and "I can list pros and cons to help me make decisions."

Ideas

The sample size was small in this survey, but still it gave me some important new insights. I will certainly be much more careful about my choice of reading selections for my students. I want to make sure that I find books that students want to read. Also, I will make sure that in regard to selecting reading material, students have choice, choice, and choice!!!

Sample A.9 Kim Schafer, Minnetonka, Minnesota

Kim Schafer was also a student in my graduate literacy methods class. She conducted a reading interest inventory in her second-grade class that she followed up with individual interviews. To extend her research she then compared her results with a reading miscue analysis that she had done previously. At the end of her report she describes how she would like to extend this project to look for change over time.

My second grade classroom includes wide range of abilities, from emergent readers to truly independent readers. Included here are children who receive reading support services, although most students are at the expected second grade level for our school.

Before administering my reading survey to the whole class (Figure A.9), I went over each question to make sure they could read it and understand it. I followed up this survey with individual interviews in order to get a better feel for at-home reading experiences. After analyzing the survey results I compared them to a miscue analysis I had done earlier. I wanted to see if there were any trends or correlations.

Findings

Interestingly, those students who were more able readers (had fewer mistakes in their miscue analyses) thought about reading in a more global sense. For example, many wanted to learn how to read maps or how to read mysteries. They also seemed to have broader reading experiences with magazines and newspapers. These more able readers also said they lost themselves in books or liked reading because they used their imaginations.

Those students who were less able readers (had more mistakes in their miscue analyses) tended to like to read fact books about specific subjects. They did not see reading as a viable entertainment option. Almost every one of these students said he or she wanted to learn to read chapter books—not

Name: _____   Age: ____   Date: _____

1. When I read I feel ...
2. I enjoy reading books that are: facts/stories
3. I like to read about ...
4. I don't like to read about ...
5. At home I am read to. Yes/No
6. At home I read to myself. Yes/No
7. When I read at home I am usually ...
8. When I go to the library I like to get books about ...
9. This year I would like to learn to read ...
10. I read things in the newspaper. Yes/No
Other things you want me to know about your reading

FIGURE A.9 Kim Schafer's Reading Survey

about anything special, just chapter books. Being able to read chapter books is considered a milestone by most second graders, although those who do read them think it is no big deal and will often read picture books.

I would like to redo and extend this survey in February or March and then compare answers. My hope is that all students will begin to take a more global view of reading and see themselves as capable readers. In addition, I am hoping that they will be able to express a greater knowledge of genre and be able to elaborate further when explaining their likes and dislikes in reading.

Sample A. 10 Barbara King, Prairie Elementary School, Worthington, Minnesota

As part of my action research class, Barb King conducted a survey related to the reading habits and preferences of adults. Her survey is included to give you a sense of how survey data might be reported.

ADULT READING PREFERENCES
Purpose

The purpose of this survey was to determine the reading habits and preferences of adults including how much time adults spend reading per week.

Methods

The survey included six questions; one open-ended and five closed response (see Appendix A). The population surveyed included 22 adults ranging in age from 18-71. All adults surveyed were Caucasian and all reside in southwest Minnesota. There were 14 females and 8 males in the survey. Most males were reluctant to participate in the survey which was conducted both by email and in person. No males responded by email. All male responses were in person.

Data collected were organized to see if there were differences in male and female reading habits and preferences. I was also interested in seeing the types of material adults read each day, their preference for fiction or non-fiction, and the types of fiction and non-fiction material read.

Findings

The survey results are presented in Table A.1.

Conclusions

Based on the data collected, the follow observations can be made:

- Women in this survey seemed more enthusiastic about completing surveys than men.

TABLE A.1   Reading Preferences

	FEMALE	MALE	TOTAL
1. What sorts of materials do you read each day?			
• newspaper	10	7	17
• E-mail/Facebook	7	3	10
• magazines	7	2	9
• books	7	0	7
• online news/sports	6	2	8
• professional material (both online and print)	3	4	7
• Bible	2	0	2
• finance	1	2	3
• Craigslist	0	1	1
2. When reading for pleasure do you prefer:			
• fiction	12	5	17
• nonfiction	2	3	5
3. When reading for pleasure which do you prefer?			
• books	12	3	15
• magazines	1	4	5
• online materials	1	1	2
4. What type of fiction do you enjoy?			
• mystery	11	4	15
• drama	9	1	10
• romance	7	0	7
• historical fiction	6	2	8
• comedy/humor	6	1	7
• adventure/action	4	3	7
• horror	1	1	2
• science fiction	0	1	1
• fantasy	0	1	1
5. What types of nonfiction do you prefer?			
• informational	9	3	12
• health	8	1	9
• biographies	6	3	9
• travel	5	2	7
• religious	5	1	6
• instructional (how to)	3	1	4

	FEMALE	MALE	TOTAL
• poetry	3	0	3
• professional	3	0	3
• other	3	0	3
• history	1	2	3
• philosophical	0	0	0

6. How much time would you guess you spend reading (non-required or professional related) per week?

	FEMALE	MALE	TOTAL
• more than 6 hours	6	2	8
• 4–6 hours	6	2	8
• 1–3 hours	2	2	4
• less than 1 hour	0	2	2

- Men seemed to be reluctant to share their reading habits. Several of them commented that they should read more or seemed embarrassed that they don't read much.
- Most of the women in the survey participate in weekly book clubs but none of the men surveyed do so.
- Women in this survey generally read more often than men.
- More women enjoyed reading books than men.
- Most men preferred magazines over books.

Limitations

- Because of the small sample size, generalizations of these results should be limited; however, this survey provides good information for a more in-depth survey.
- One confounding variable is the methods used to complete the survey. Respondents may respond differently to an email survey vs. a survey given in person.
- If I were to do the survey differently some questions would be worded differently. For example question 3 should have had a qualifier behind stating to choose only one answer.

Appendix A
Reading Habits And Preferences Survey

Gender: __male __female

1. What sorts of materials do you read each day including online and print materials? List as many as needed.

2. When reading for pleasure do you prefer:

   __fiction   __nonfiction

3. When reading for pleasure which do you prefer?

   __books   __magazines   __online materials

4. What types of fiction do you enjoy?

   __mystery   __romance   __science fiction
   __drama   __historical fiction   __adventure/action
   __fantasy   __horror   __comedy/humor

5. What types of non-fiction do you prefer?

   __poetry   __philosophical   __religious
   __informational   __health   __professional
   __biographies   __history   __travel
   __instructional   __Other (list below)

6. How much time would you guess you spend reading (nonrequired or profession-related) per week?

   __less than 1 hour   __1–3 hours
   __4–6 hours   __more than 6 hours

Sample A. 11 Annette Tousignant

As part of a postbaccalaureate initial teacher licensure program in special education, I have students conduct e-mail interviews with two special education teachers. I have included Annette's report here. Notice how she planned her interview questions with possible follow-ups. Students find that they get as much information from the follow-up question as they do the original question.

Summer Session 2010

This is the Teacher Interview Project report of Annette Tousignant for SPED 513: Professional Growth and Development. Below are described (a) the conditions, (b) the findings, and (c) specific recommendations.

Conditions

The purpose of this teacher interview project was to gain information about expectations of a first-year special education teacher with regard to time management, differentiated learning experiences for students, methods for staying current with knowledge related to teaching and learning, and recommendations regarding education for future autism spectrum disorder (ASD) teachers. Six initial and three follow-up questions were asked of two interviewees concerning these topics. The interviews were conducted via email.

The first teacher interviewed, Carlyn C., is a female special education teacher at Anytown Middle School in Anytown, Minnesota. She was selected for this interview by recommendation of a general education teacher at HMS. Ms. C. is respected for her work with students who have autism spectrum disorder.

The second individual interviewed, Jane S., is a principal at Sometown Middle School in Sometown, Minnesota. Before working in school administration, Ms. S. was a special education teacher in the Minneapolis School District. Ms. S. was chosen for this project because of her experience and dual perspective as a principal and teacher.

Findings

Time Management

According to these interviews, time management seems to be a constant concern of special education teachers. Teaching, managing caseloads, communicating with general education teachers and parents, assisting individual students, writing individual education programs (IEPs), and engaging in professional development are responsibilities that special educators need to prioritize.

Both individuals interviewed noted special education teachers regularly spend additional time outside of the school day to complete IEPs, other paperwork, and respond to email. Ms. S. reported the timelines mandated by the State of Minnesota for due process paperwork demand special education teachers manage paperwork efficiently. She noted that instructional time, case management time, communication and collaborative planning with general education teachers, and professional development are often compromised because of required legal paperwork. Because of these competing demands, special education teachers often focus on adherence to mandates rather than improved instruction, ultimately compromising long-term instructional growth and competence. Ms. S. added that a well-run, engaging classroom results in fewer discipline issues, which saves a teacher's time. She emphasized that quality development of instructional skills and strategies also gives special educators more credibility when advising general education teachers.

Ms. C. stated she spends time in the summer to organize her students' schedules so students who require similar programming are in the same classes or with the same general education teacher. This ensures her students have similar assignments, resulting in better tracking of their progress and more efficient communication with fewer teachers.

Working with parents proactively is also important to efficient time management. Both interviewees agreed that problems are resolved more quickly when parents trust a teacher is acting as an advocate for their child. Ms. C. recommended frequent phone and email contact with parents to foster good parent/teacher relationships.

Differentiated Learning Experiences

These interviews indicated that learning experiences for special education students are often differentiated. In Ms. S.'s opinion, special education has a reputation for frequently reducing content and expectations for students. She conveyed it is important that differentiated experiences keep students learning and prepare them for a world of high demands as much as their individual disabilities permit.

General education teachers who differentiate learning experiences make assignments achievable for most students. Ms. C. noted, when possible, she chooses general education teachers who regularly differentiate learning for her students. In other situations, special education teachers differentiate learning for students in inclusive classrooms. For example, Ms. C. shared that eliminating or revising abstract or long questions often decreases anxiety for her students with ASD. Vague directions can be clarified. She suggested breaking down tasks step-by-step to allow for completion of complex assignments independently. Allowing more time for assignments or assessments and allowing students to dictate answers are also methods for differentiating learning to accommodate learners, without changing the content of the curriculum.

Ms. S. stated when students are able to understand the material, the content of the curriculum should be maintained when differentiating learning experiences. Students with special needs are entitled to all content provided to general education students. When students are not able to understand content, curriculum may be differentiated to modify the learning experience.

Methods for Staying Current with Teaching and Learning Knowledge

Ms. S. noted she reads educational research to become aware of new findings and methods for teaching and learning. She also belongs to several small professional development groups that promote members learning from each other. Recommendations for reading from Ms. S. include *Education Leadership*, published by the Association for Supervision and Curriculum Development, and additional reading specific to a teacher's license area.

Ms. C. relies on several other ASD specialists who work in her district, and who also instruct at Hamline University in St. Paul, MN, for helpful suggestions and recommendations on workshops. She seeks out and attends workshops directly related to student issues she is experiencing. Ms. C. recommends reading materials written by Kari Dunn Buron, an author and professor who specializes in ASD, as well as information from a website by Jill Kuzma, a speech pathologist who works with students who have ASD. Ms. C. also recommends new special education teachers find a mentor to turn to for advice and support.

Education for Future ASD Teachers

These interviews showed that special education teachers who work with students who have autism spectrum disorder need to be prepared for a rapidly changing field. Ms. S. communicated that special educators need to be familiar with emerging research related to ASD, teaching, and learning. She added the structure of schools sometimes does not suit students with ASD. Special education teachers need behavioral management and consultation skills to help general education teachers feel confident in educating and working with students who have ASD.

Ms. S. shared that having additional licensures makes a future educator more marketable, but also requires that a teacher be willing to be assigned in any licensed area, regardless of the teacher's preference. In her opinion, EBD teachers should consider earning a license in an additional area because many EBD training programs do not offer ample background in academic interventions.

Ms. S. believes it is important to be a life-long learner. When hiring new teachers, she looks for individuals who are growth orientated and seek out learning opportunities for themselves. She also maintains that teachers who can build productive relationships with colleagues in special education and general education will be most successful.

Ms. C. noted some school districts are reducing the number of ASD teachers and putting students with ASD into caseloads and classes with other special needs students. She recommended that future special education teachers get a well-rounded education to ensure they have the skills to work with students, regardless of type of disability.

Recommendations

Future special education teachers will need to be prepared to manage their time and attend to competing responsibilities if they are to be efficient and effective. It is recommended that new special educators prioritize development of instructional skills and strategies to ensure it is not overlooked due to competition for time with other duties. Studying emerging research can aid in continued development of instructional, consultation, and behavior management knowledge.

Other time management strategies recommended include grouping students with similar needs to promote tracking students' progress and efficient contact with general education teachers, and working with parents to achieve trust and resolve issues proactively. In addition, special educators should be prepared to spend additional time outside of the school day to complete professional responsibilities.

Differentiation of learning experiences supports special education students in inclusive classrooms. It is recommended that special education teachers organize their students' schedules to include general education teachers who consistently differentiate learning experiences. It is also recommended that special educators differentiate learning experiences themselves when general education teachers have not provided these opportunities for students in need. Differentiation should include providing accommodations that retain the content of the curriculum. If a student is not able to participate in the experience with accommodations, modifications that change content can be provided.

Professional development for educators might include reading from professional journals, books, and websites, attending educational opportunities, and networking with colleagues to increase knowledge of teaching and learning. Time spent on continued learning will be an investment in an educator's future success. Specific resources to investigate include the following:

- *Education Leadership*, published by the Association for Supervision and Curriculum Development
- Material written by Kari Dunn Buron, ASD author and professor
- A website compiled by Jill Kuzma, speech pathologist who works with students who have ASD (http://jillkuzma.wordpress.com/)

In concluding these interviews, both interviewees agreed that special education is a rapidly changing field. Special education teachers are urged to become astute, lifelong learners. Future teachers need to develop time management, behavior management, and instructional and consultation skills to successfully work with students, general education teachers, and parents. Obtaining a well-rounded educational foundation is fundamental for special educators to help promote all students' learning.

APPENDIX
Teacher Interview Questions

1. What do you find most difficult for a special educator regarding time management?
   - *Follow-up question:* On average, how much time do you spend on work-related items outside of the normal school day?
2. How do you divide your day between teaching and managing your caseload?
3. What are your thoughts on differentiating instruction, assignments, and/or assessments for all students, including special education students?
4. How do you stay current with knowledge related to teaching and learning?
   - *Follow-up question:* What specific resources have you found helpful?
5. What advice do you have regarding training/education/licensure for future special educators specifically interested in working with students who have autism spectrum disorder?
   - *Follow-up question:* Would you advise that future special educators get licensed in more than one area or get ASD certification to be more attractive to future employers?
6. What advice do you have for first-year special education teachers? What do you wish you had known?

A FINAL WORD

The length and complexity of an action research project do not always increase its rigor and insight. Many short action research projects provide important insight and information. The goal of action research is to increase understanding to improve teaching practice. All the reports in this appendix meet this criterion.

GLOSSARY

abstract—this is found at the beginning of a scholarly article, research report, thesis, or dissertation and used to a brief summary of what is to follow.

academic journals—journals that contain articles written by specialists in the field who describe their research, secondary research, novel applications of existing theories, or interesting new ideas set in a theoretical context. Before acceptance, each article is peer-reviewed, which means it is critiqued by a jury of three to six experts in the field to check for accuracy and validity.

academic learning time (ALT)—time spent by a student actively engaged in a task that is directly related to the teacher's desired outcome and during which the student is able to successfully complete the task. Academic learning time is different from engaged time in that students are able to successfully complete the task. It is positively correlated with achievement.

academic writing style—a writing style that uses concise, objective language. This is the style of writing preferred for action research reports. Ideas are presented in a logical, orderly manner so that the reader is able to gain a maximum amount of understanding with a minimum amount of time and effort. This writing style creates a more readable and credible report.

accuracy—a quality in action research in which the data collected creates a fairly true picture of the bit of reality being observed.

action research—a systematic and orderly way for teachers to observe their practice or to explore a problem and a possible course of action.

allotted time—the time allotted during the school day to teach a specific subject.

analysis of variance (ANOVA) —statistical procedure used to compare the difference in mean between or within three or more groups.

anecdotal evidence— when a general conclusion is based on a single incidence or experience.

annotated bibliography—a description and short analysis of individual research reports or scholarly articles related to a particular topic or question.

archival data—data sources that include past grades, test scores, cumulative folders, health records, parental occupation, or attendance records.

attitude scales—a series of statements given to respondents who must then choose from a set of responses for each statement. Their choice for each statement indicates their level of agreement or disagreement.

best practice—informed, thoughtful teaching that is supported by research and research-based theory.

brainstorm and list—a method of generating ideas where, given a problem or a prompt, you list ideas without evaluating them. The nonevaluative aspect of this method is important, as it gets you thinking outside of conventional boundaries.

causal–comparative research—a type of research designed to find the reason for existing differences between two or more groups. It is used when the random assignment of participants for groups necessary for the true experiment cannot be met, which is certainly the case in most classrooms. Like correlational research, it is used to describe an existing situation. It is called causal–comparative research as it compares groups in order to find a cause for differences in measures or scores.

checklist—a list that specifies certain attributes, such as behaviors, traits, assignments, or skills. When that attribute is seen, some method is used to check it off or indicate the number of times it was present.

checklist for collecting data—a checklist used to record which data were collected and when. This ensures that data are collected systematically and that all types of data are equally represented.

chi square—statistical procedure used to compare frequencies of two or more groups.

closed-ended questions (also called **closed response questions**)—questions for which there is a specific answer or response.

conclusion—found at the end of an action research report, the conclusion is a paragraph or two that describes your current state of knowing or a list of things you have come to believe as a result of your study. It should bring together the important data and explain what they mean. The conclusion will be the basis for your recommendation or plan of action.

conference—a data source in which one or more students talk about their work or some aspect of classroom functioning. Prompts may be used to get students talking about a particular topic; however, lists of planned questions are not used. Conferences can be conducted individually or in small groups known as focus groups.

Confounding variables—independent variables that are unknown or have not been controlled and which affect the results or dependent variables. They make it possible for other interpretations of the results.

control group—in an experiment, a group as similar as possible in all characteristics to the treatment group that is not exposed to the particular treatment for the purposes of comparison.

correlational research—a type of research designed to determine whether and to what degree a statistical relationship exists between two or more variables. It is used primarily to describe an existing condition or something that has happened in the past.

correlation coefficient—a numerical value that describes the degree or strength of a relationship between two variables. A positive correlation means that when one variable increases, the other one also increases. A negative correlation means that when one variable increases, the other one decreases. A correlation coefficient of 1.00 would indicate a perfect one-to-one positive correlation. This rarely happens. A correlation coefficient of .0 means that there is absolutely no correlation between to variables. A correlation coefficient of

−1.00 would indicate a perfect negative correlation. This also rarely happens.

creative problem solving (CPS)—a problem-solving strategy in which you define the problem, generate as many ideas as possible, then chose one or two to refine and test.

credibility—a quality in action research that indicates it is trustworthy or capable of being believed. This quality enables you and others to use your data with confidence.

data retrieval charts—visual organizers that are used to help collect and organize information. These can come in a variety of forms.

dependent variable—the particular result or the effect of the treatment or condition. The dependent variable depends on the treatment or independent variable.

descriptive statistics—statistical analyses used to describe an existing set of data. There are three major types of descriptive statistics: measure of central tendency, frequency distribution, and measures of variability.

discussion—the part of a thesis or action research report where you provide an overview of the study and a summary of the findings. It may also include some or all of the following: conclusions, recommendations, and an evaluation of the study.

equivalent time-sample design—a quasi-experimental research design in which the treatment is presented at irregular intervals; however, the measures or observations are made at regular intervals. This allows the researcher to account for and control outside influences.

ERIC—the Educational Resources Information Center, sponsored by the National Library of Education at the U.S. Department of Education, it is a massive database containing information on all imaginable subjects related to education (www. eric.ed.gov).

evaluation of the study—after reporting conclusions and recommendations, this section of a thesis or action research report evaluates the effectiveness of the study, explains particular aspects of it, or describes how it might be done more effectively the next time.

experimental research—a mode of inquiry in which a hypothesis is proposed and tested by examining relationships between independent and dependent variables. In experimental research the researcher creates an artificial environment in order to maintain control over all factors that may affect the result of the experiment. True experimental research uses random sampling of subjects.

field notes—a data source that includes written observations of what you see taking place as you conduct your action research project.

figures—information found in visual form such as lists, graphs, diagrams, or pictures.

focus group—a small-group conference used to gather data. The moderator uses questions as prompts and guides. The goal is to get participants to carry the conversation as much as possible.

frequency distribution—a way of organizing information that tells the scores or numbers that were attained and the frequency, or how many times each score or number was attained.

Hawthorne effect—when participants in a study behave differently because they know they are in a study. Here the difference in effects is not a result of treatment; rather, it is a result of getting special attention and recognition for being part of a study.

hypothesis—a tentative statement that can be supported or rejected depending on the outcome of an experiment.

independent variable—the treatment or factor that the researcher manipulates to determine a particular effect. It is what is done or not done to a group of people, animals, plants, or things in an experiment or other types of research.

inductive analysis—the process of looking at a field or group of data and inducing or creating order by organizing what is observed into groups.

inferential statistics—statistical analyses used to determine how likely a given outcome is for an entire population based on a sample size. These analyses allow the researcher to make inferences to larger populations by collecting data on a small sample size. The most common inferential statistical analyses are the t-test, analysis of variance (ANOVA), and chi square.

instructional time—the time during a class in which you are actually engaged in instruction.

interview—a data source in which students respond to a series of planned questions.

inquiry—using methods of science as a pedagogical strategy.

I-think-isms—when conclusions are drawn or decisions are made based on what one thinks or what seems to make good sense, instead of using data or a body of research.

levels of significance—the level at which we can be reasonably certain that the differences in scores or other measures are due to something other than chance or sampling error. In educational research, two different levels of significance or probability are generally used: $p = .05$ and $p = .01$.

literature review—an examination of journal articles, research, research reports, ERIC documents, books, and other sources related to a particular topic.

mean—the arithmetic average of a set of scores or numbers.

means-end analysis (MEA)—a problem-solving strategy in which you first describe the desired outcome or end state and then list the goals necessary to reach the end stage.

measures of central tendency—a way of describing a set of data with a single number. The three measures of central tendency are the mode, the median, and the mean.

measures of variability—a measure that describes the spread of scores or how close they cluster around the mean. There are three measures of variability: range, variance, and standard deviation.

median—in a set of scores or numbers it is the point at which 50% of the scores are above and 50% are below.

mission statement—a statement that defines the core purpose of a school or district. It often contains some or all of the following: goals, a defining philosophy, a statement of beliefs related to teaching and learning.

mode—in a set of scores or numbers, it is the score or number attained most frequently.

Moses effect—a situation in which researchers hand down research edicts to teachers with the expectation that they will be passive receivers of these edicts.

negative correlation—a relationship between variables in which one variable increases at the same time as the other one decreases.

open-ended checklist—a checklist that contains a list of skills with enough space for students to describe their ability, understanding, or usage of each skill.

open-ended questions—questions for which there are no set answers or responses.

paradigm—a common framework from which to view reality. It includes a set of beliefs or assumptions that (a) establishes boundaries and principles within a particular field, (b) guides perception, and (c) describes a particular view of reality.

plan of action—the plan describing the actions you will take based on the findings of your action research.

positive correlation—a relationship between variables in which one variable increases at the same time as the other one also increases.

pretest–posttest design—a quasi-experimental research design in which a group is given a pretest, a treatment, and a posttest. Pretest and posttest scores are compared.

Product and Performance Assessment Form (PPAF) —a rating checklist that is used to analyze and evaluate any type of product or performance, such as science projects, inventions, dramas, dances, or experiments.

pseudoscience—any inquiry that starts with the answer and looks only for data that supports that answer. Whereas science uses data to determine reality, pseudoscience uses beliefs to determine a perceived reality.

qualitative research—research that uses some type of systematic observation to understand a phenomenon, condition, situation, or environment. Qualitative researchers take the world as they find it instead of trying to manipulate conditions to isolate variables. The research questions are more open ended and less defined, with plenty of room to collect a variety of data through collateral observations.

quantitative research (also called experimental research) —the researcher takes an active role in setting up an observation or experiment to isolate a variable. The goal is to determine the effect (dependent variable) of a particular approach or treatment (independent variable). The strength of effect is determined by measurable (quantifiable) data.

quasi-action research—quasi-experimental research used in an action research setting.

quasi-experimental research—experimental research without random assignment to groups.

range—in a set of scores or numbers, the difference between the highest and lowest score or number.

rating checklist—a checklist that specifies traits you are looking for in a product or performance and allows the observer to assign levels of performance to each trait. This is similar to a rubric; however, whereas a rubric uses a sentence or more to provide a description of each level, a rating checklist uses one-word indicators.

rating scales—a scale used to determine the strength of a response. These are often used to determine how much, how often, or how many times something occurs.

recommendation—found after the conclusions in an action research report, the recommendation section describes what is believed to be an effective action based on the findings. You tell how your findings might be used.

reference page—a list of the books, journal articles, and other sources cited in your thesis action research report. This informs readers what sources were used and allows them to locate these sources if necessary.

reliability—the degree to which a study or experiment can be repeated with similar results.

research—a variety of procedures that are used to view and review the world to understand it. Research is the systematic method used to collect data to answer questions.

research journal (also known as a **log**) —a notebook used to record thoughts and observations related to all parts of your research. A variety of data may be included here such as insights, analyses, interpretations, impressions, ideas, diagrams, sketches, quotes, student comments, scores, questions, or chronology of your research project.

research proposals— a document submitted to get permission or approval to conduct a research project. It usually contains some or all of the following elements: topic, research questions, annotated bibliography, and a description of the methodology.

research question—the purpose of a research study put in the form of a specific question for which the researcher seeks to find an answer.

rubrics—a type of authentic assessment that can also be used for data collection. This identifies the specific traits you are looking for in a product or performance and describes and quantifies various levels of performance for each trait.

science—the processes used to objectively examine and organize the world around us. To engage in the process of science means to look, to seek to understand or know, to guess and test guesses, to create order from chaos, and to develop concepts. True science does not start with an answer.

small-group conference—a focus group used to gather data. The moderator uses questions as prompts and guides. The goal is to get participants to carry the conversation as much as possible.

standard deviation—the square root of the variance. It is the most frequently used index to describe variability or the dispersion of scores. Whereas variance tells you how tightly the scores are clustered, standard deviation tells you how tightly the scores are clustered around the mean in a set of data.

statistical significance—a measure that describes the likelihood that differences in mean between two or more scores or numbers were caused by chance or sampling error.

student checklist—checklists that are completed by students to evaluate their own performance or the performance of the group in which they are working.

students' products or performances—samples of students' work that are used as data sources.

surveys—a data source that enables you to get a variety of information from respondents fairly quickly. Surveys contain a predesigned list of questions that can be either open-ended or closed response.

teacher checklist—checklists designed for use by teachers to indicate exactly what skills have been introduced or mastered and when. Checklists can often be used to indicate the level of student performance for each skill.

theory—an interrelated set of concepts that is used to explain a body of data. A theory is a way to explain a set of facts.

time-on-task—in a class it is the time students are actively engaged in relevant learning tasks.

time series design—a quasi-experimental research design in which a group is examined over time, both before and after the treatment. This is essentially an elaborate pretest–posttest design except that here the researcher collects an extensive amount a data to look for patterns over time.

transition time—the time in a classroom between one class or activity and the next.

treatment group (also called **experimental group**)—the group of subjects, participants, or objects that are exposed to the particular treatment.

triangulation—using different kinds of data to look at something from more than one perspective.

t-test—statistical procedure used to determine whether the difference between two means is statistically significant.

validity—the degree to which a thing measures what it reports to measure.

variable—the thing that is changed or varied in an experiment. In a qualitative study the variable is the category or thing to be examined.

variance—a mathematical procedure that describes the amount of spread among a set of numbers or test scores. If the variance is small, the scores are bunched together. If the variance is large, the scores are spread out.

wait time—the time between asking a question and answering a question. This gives students time to think about and fully process the question. About 7 seconds is usually recommended for most questions; however, higher-level and more complex questions require longer wait time.

REFERENCES

Allington, R. (2002). *Big brother and the National Reading Panel: How ideology trumped evidence.* Portsmouth, NH: Heinemann.

American Psychological Association. (2009). *Publication manual of the American Psychological Association* (6th ed.). Washington, DC: Author.

Armbruster, B. (1993). Science and reading. *The Reading Teacher, 46,* 346–347.

Barone, T., Berliner, D. C., Blanchard, J., Casanova, U., & McGown, T. (1996). A future for teacher education: Developing a strong sense of professionalism. In J. Sikula (Ed.), *Handbook of research on teacher education* (4th ed., pp. 1108–1149). New York: Macmillan Library Reference USA.

Berliner, D. C., & Biddle, B. J. (1996). *The manufactured crisis: Myths, fraud, and the attack on America's public schools* (2nd ed.). Cambridge, MA: Perseus Books.

Birman, B. F., Desimone, L., Porter, A. C., & Garet, M. S. (2000). Designing professional development that works. *Educational Leadership, 57,* 28–33.

Book, C. L. (1996). Professional development schools. In J. Sikula (Ed.), *Handbook of research on teacher education* (4th ed., pp. 194–210). New York: Macmillan Library Reference USA.

Bracey, G. W. (2000). *Bail me out! Handling difficult data and tough questions about public schools.* Thousand Oaks, CA: Corwin Press.

Bracey, G. W. (2006). *Reading educational research: How to avoid getting statistically snookered.* Portsmouth, NH: Heinemann.

Bruer, J. T. (1999). *Schools for thought: A science of learning in the classroom.* Cambridge, MA: MIT Press.

Craik, F. I. M., & Lockhart, R. S. (1972). Levels of processing: A framework for memory research. *Journal of Verbal Learning and Verbal Behavior, 11,* 671–684.

Creswell, J. W. (2004). *Educational research: Planning, conducting, and evaluating quantitative and qualitative research* (2nd ed.). Upper Saddle River, NJ: Pearson/Prentice Hall.

Csikszentmihalyi, M. (1990). *Flow: The psychology of optimal experience.* New York: HarperPerennial.

Danielson, C. (1996). *Enhancing professional practice: A framework for teaching.* Alexandria, VA: ASCD.

Darling-Hammond, L. (1999). *Teacher quality and study achievement: A review of state policy evidence.* Seattle, WA: Center for the Study of Teaching and Policy, University of Washington.

Davis, G. A., & Rimm, S. B. (1998). *Education of the gifted and talented* (4th ed.). Boston: Allyn & Bacon.

Detert, J. R., Louis, K. S., & Schroeder, R. G. (2001). A culture framework for education: Defining quality values and their impact in U.S. high schools. *School Effectiveness and School Improvement, 12,* 183–212.

Dinkelman, T. (1997). The promise of action research for critically reflective teacher education. *The Teacher Educator, 32*(4), 250–257.

Eggen, P., & Kauchak, D. (2010). *Educational psychology: Windows on classrooms* (8th ed.). Upper Saddle River, NJ: Pearson.

Eisenhart, M., & Towne, L. (2003). Contestation and change in national policy on "scientifically based" education research. *Educational Researcher, 32*(7), 31–38.

Eisner, E. (1998). *The enlightened eye: Qualitative inquiry and the enhancement of educational practice.* Upper Saddle River, NJ: Prentice Hall.

Erickson, F. (1986). Qualitative methods in research on teaching. In M. Wittrock (Ed.), *Handbook of research on teaching* (3rd ed., pp. 119–161). New York: Macmillan.

Foshy, A. W. (1998). Action research in the nineties. *The Educational Forum, 62,* 108–112.

Gallagher, J. J., & Gallagher, S. A. (1994). *Teaching the gifted child* (4th ed.). Boston: Allyn & Bacon.

Gardner, H. (1983). *Frames of mind.* New York: HarperCollins.

Gay, L. R., & Airaison, P. (2008). *Educational research: Competencies for analysis and applications* (9th ed.). Upper Saddle River, NJ: Pearson/Prentice Hall.

Gentry, R. J. (1992). *Teaching kids to spell.* Portsmouth, NH: Heinemann.

Gillies, R. M. (2006). Teachers' and students' verbal behaviors during cooperative and small-group learning. *British Journal of Educational Psychology, 76,* 271–287.

Gillies, R. M., & Ashman, A. F. (2000). The effects of cooperative learning on students with learning difficulties in the lower elementary school. *Journal of Special Education, 34*(1), 19–27.

Gillies, R. M., & Boyle, M. (2006). Ten Australian elementary teachers' discourse and reported pedagogical practices during cooperative learning. *The Elementary School Journal, 106*(5), 429–451.

Goodman, K. (1986). *What's whole in whole language?* Portsmouth, NH: Heinemann.

Graves, D. H. (1992). *A fresh look at writing.* Portsmouth, NH: Heinemann.

Harman, W., & Rheingold, H. (1984). *Higher creativity: Liberating the unconscious for breakthrough insights.* Los Angeles: Tarcher.

Hensen, K. T. (1996). Teachers as researchers. In J. Sikula (Ed.), *Handbook of research on teacher education* (2nd ed., pp. 53–66). New York: Macmillan.

Hodson, D. (1988). Toward a philosophically more valid science curriculum. *Science Education, 72,* 19–40.

Hunter, M. (1982). *Mastery teaching.* El Segundo, CA: TIP Publications.

Imag, D. G., & Switzer, T. J. (1996). Changing teacher education programs: Restructuring collegiate-based teacher education. In J. Sikula (Ed.), *Handbook of research on teacher education* (2nd ed., pp. 213–226). New York: Macmillan.

Johnson, A. (2000b). *Up and out: Using creative and critical thinking skills to enhance learning.* Boston: Allyn & Bacon.

Johnson, A. (2003a). *A short guide to academic writing.* Lanham, MD: University Press of America.

Johnson, A. (2009). *Making connections in elementary and middle school social studies* (2nd ed.). Thousand Oaks, CA: Sage Publications Inc.

Johnson, A. (2010). *Field experiences in teacher education: using research and reason.* Unpublished manuscript.

Johnson, A. P. (2008). *Teaching reading and writing: A guidebook for tutoring and remediating students.* Lanham, MD: Rowman and Littlefield.

Kessler, R. (2000). *The soul of education: Helping students find connection, compassion, and character at school.* Alexandria, VA: ASCD.

Knight, S. L., Wiseman, D. L., & Cooner, D. (2000). Using collaborative teacher research to determine the impact of professional development school activities on elementary students' math and writing outcomes. *Journal of Teacher Education, 51,* 26–38.

Leedy, P. D., & Ormrod, J. E. (2001). *Practical research: Planning and design* (7th ed.). Upper Saddle River, NJ: Merrill Prentice Hall.

Leedy, P. D., & Ormrod, J. E. (2010). *Practical research: Planning and design* (9th ed.). Boston: Pearson.

Marks, H. M., & Louis, K. S. (1997). Does teacher empowerment affect the classroom? The implication of teacher empowerment for instruction, practice and student performance. *Educational Evaluation and Policy Analysis, 19,* 245–275.

Marzano, R. J. (2003). *What works in schools: Translating research into action.* Alexandria, VA: ASCD.

Marzano, R. J., Pickering, D. J., & Pollock, J. E. (2001). *Classroom instruction that works: Research-based strategies for increasing student achievement.* Alexandria, VA: ASCD.

McNiff, J., Lomax, P., & Whitehead, J. (1996). *You and your action research project.* New York: Routledge.

McQuillan, J. (1998). *The literacy crisis: False claims, real solutions.* Portsmouth, NH: Heinemann.

McTaggart, R. (1997). Reading the collection. In R. McTaggart (Ed.), *Participatory action research* (pp. 1–12). Albany, NY: SUNY Press.

Miller, J. P. (1996). *The holistic curriculum.* Toronto: OISE Press.

National Center for Educational Statistics. (1998). *NAEP 1996 trends in educational progress: Addendum.* Jessup, MD: U.S. Department of Education.

Patterson, L., & Shannon, P. (1993). Reflection, inquiry, and action. In L. Patterson, C. Santa, K. Short, & K. Smith (Eds.), *Teachers are researchers: Reflection and action* (pp. 7–11). Newark, DE: International Reading Association.

Perkins, D. N. (1987). Thinking frames: An integrative perspective on teaching cognitive skills. In J. B. Baron & R. J. Sternberg (Eds.), *Teaching thinking skills: Theory and practice* (pp. 41–61). New York: W. H. Freeman.

Renzulli, J. S., & Reis, S. M. (1997). The Schoolwide Enrichment Model: New directions for developing high-end learning. In N. Colangelo & G. A. Davis (Ed.), *Handbook of gifted education* (2nd ed., pp. 136–154). Boston: Allyn & Bacon.

Routmann, R. (1996). *Literacy at the crossroads: Crucial talk about reading, writing, and other teaching dilemmas.* Portsmouth, NH: Heinemann.

Schmuck, R. A. (1997). *Practical action research for change.* Arlington Heights, IL: IRI/Skylight Training and Publishing.

Stanovich, K. (1992). *How to think straight about psychology* (3rd ed.). New York: HarperCollins.

Sternberg, R. J., & Williams, W. M. (2002). *Educational psychology.* Boston: Allyn & Bacon.

Sternberg, R. J., & Williams, W. M. (2009). *Educational psychology* (2nd ed.). Boston: Allyn & Bacon.

Sweetland, S. R., & Hoy, W. K. (2002). School characteristics and educational outcomes: Toward an organizational model of student achievement in middle schools. *Educational Administration Quarterly, 36,* 703–729.

Taylor, S. J., & Bogdan, R. (1998). *Introduction to qualitative research methods: A guidebook and resource* (3rd ed.). New York: John Wiley & Sons.

Thelen, J. N. (1984). *Improving reading in science* (2nd ed.). Newark, DE: International Reading Association.

Tomlinson, C. A. (1995). Action research and practical inquiry: An overview and an invitation to teachers of gifted learners. *Journal for the Education of the Gifted, 18*(4), 468–484.

U.S. Census Bureau. (2005). *United States Census 2000.* Available from http://www.census.gov.

Watts, S., & Johnson, A. (1995). Toward reflection in teacher education: The role of dialogue journals. *Journal of Reading Education, 21,* 27–38.

Zemelman, S., Daniels, H., & Hyde, A. (2006). *Best practice: New standards for teaching and learning in America's schools* (3rd ed.). Portsmouth, NH: Heinemann.

INDEX